OXFORD READINGS IN POLITICS
AND GOVERNMENT

COMMUNITARIANISM AND
INDIVIDUALISM

OXFORD READINGS IN POLITICS AND GOVERNMENT

General Editors: Vernon Bogdanor and Geoffrey Marshall

The readings in this series are chosen from a variety of journals and other sources to cover major areas or issues in the study of politics, government, and political theory. Each volume contains an introductory essay by the editor and a select guide to further reading.

OTHER TITLES IN THIS SERIES

Marxist Theory
Edited by Alex Callinicos

Parliamentary versus Presidential Government
Edited by Arend Lijphart

The West European Party System
Edited by Peter Mair

Ministerial Responsibility
Edited by Geoffrey Marshall

Liberty
Edited by David Miller

Legislatures
Edited by Philip Norton

COMMUNITARIANISM AND INDIVIDUALISM

EDITED BY

SHLOMO AVINERI
AND
AVNER DE-SHALIT

OXFORD UNIVERSITY PRESS

1992

Oxford University Press, Walton Street, Oxford OX2 6DP
Oxford New York Toronto
Delhi Bombay Calcutta Madras Karachi
Petaling Jaya Singapore Hong Kong Tokyo
Nairobi Dar es Salaam Cape Town
Melbourne Auckland
and associated companies in
Berlin Ibadan

Oxford is a trade mark of Oxford University Press

Published in the United States
by Oxford University Press, New York

Introduction and compilation © Shlomo Avineri and Avner de-Shalit 1992

British Library Cataloguing in Publication Data
Data available

Library of Congress Cataloging in Publication Data
Communitarianism and individualism / edited by Shlomo Avineri and
Avner de-Shalit.
p. cm. — (Oxford readings in politics and government)
Includes bibliographical references and index.
1. Individualism. 2. Liberalism. 3. Community. I. Avineri,
Shlomo. II. De-Shalit, Avner. III. Series.
JC571.C462 1992 302.5'12—dc20 91-25173
ISBN 0-19-878027-3 ISBN 0-19-878028-1 (Pbk)

Typeset by Colset Pte Ltd, Singapore
Printed and bound in
Great Britain by Biddles Ltd,
Guildford & King's Lynn

CONTENTS

Introduction   1
   Shlomo Avineri and Avner de-Shalit

1. The Procedural Republic and the Unencumbered Self   12
   Michael Sandel

2. Atomism   29
   Charles Taylor

3. Justice as a Virtue: Changing Conceptions   51
   Alasdair MacIntyre

4. Membership   65
   Michael Walzer

5. Community and Citizenship   85
   David Miller

6. Feminism and Modern Friendship: Dislocating the
   Community   101
   Marilyn Friedman

7. Communitarian Critics of Liberalism   120
   Amy Gutmann

8. Distributive Justice   137
   Robert Nozick

9. The Liberal Individual   151
   David Gauthier

10. Liberal Individualism and Liberal Neutrality   165
   Will Kymlicka

11. Justice as Fairness: Political not Metaphysical   186
   John Rawls

12. Liberal Community   205
   Ronald Dworkin

Notes on Contributors   225

Select Bibliography   227

Index   231

INTRODUCTION

SHLOMO AVINERI AND AVNER DE-SHALIT

1

In 1971 John Rawls published *A Theory of Justice*, a book often regarded as the most important text of political thought in the post-war Western world. Rawls's theory was the major catalyst in the revival of political philosophy. He abandoned the then-ruling theory of utilitarianism and erected his own in the tradition of contract theories and Kantian liberalism. Moreover, Rawls's theory bypassed the heretofore heavily discussed questions of political obligation and the state, and raised the issue of distributive justice, as well as—indirectly—the welfare state. It was a theory that put the issue of rights back on the agenda and was constructed in individualist terms.

This gave rise to several challenges, among them attacks from utilitarian philosophers who hurried to defend their stand and libertarians who rejected the egalitarian tones of this new liberal thought. However, at the beginning of the 1980s it became clear that, sooner or later, the most crucial and substantive challenge to the neo-Kantian theories would emerge from the scholars who were called 'communitarians'. And, indeed, the debate between individualists and communitarians has become one of the most important and fascinating issues of political philosophy in the 1980s.

The term 'community' is not new in political thought. In fact it goes back to Greek philosophy, to Aristotle's works, through Cicero and the Roman community of law and common interests, St Augustine's community of emotional ties, Thomas Aquinas's idea of the community as a body politic, Edmund Burke's well-known concept of the community as a partnership 'not only between the living, but between those who are living, those who are dead, and those who are to be born', and the works of Rousseau in France and Hegel in Germany.

The significance and meaning of the concepts of community and communal relations have changed several times from

Aristotle through to today. However, Hegel's works are thought to serve as the inspiration for some contemporary communitarians,[1] especially in Hegel's distinction between *Moralität* and *Sittlichkeit*. The former term refers to the abstract or universal rules of morality, and the latter encompasses the ethical principles that are specific to a certain community. In liberal thought, *Moralität* is a higher level of morality, tying in with the notion of the abstract and universal individual who stands as an entity unto herself, the free and rational person, and the priority of the right over the good, which are discussed below. But Hegel, and the contemporary communitarians who followed him, argue that, on the contrary, *Sittlichkeit* is the higher level of morality, for it is the only way that genuine moral autonomy and freedom can be achieved.

This is one example supporting the claim that the first modern communitarian works were written as a response to the individualist theories advanced by Rawls and others. However, during the 1970s and 1980s a general theory of communitarianism gradually emerged. What, then, is the substance of the debate between contemporary communitarian and individualist political theories?

2

Communitarianism is put forward in two spheres. One is methodological, the communitarians arguing that the premisses of individualism such as the rational individual who chooses freely are wrong or false, and that the only way to understand human behaviour is to refer to individuals in their social, cultural, and historical contexts. That is to say, in order to discuss individuals one must look first at their communities and their communal relationships. The second sphere is the normative one, communitarians asserting that the premisses of individualism give rise to morally unsatisfactory consequences. Among them are the impossibility of achieving a genuine community, the neglect of some ideas of the good life that should be sustained by the state, or others that should be dismissed, or—as

---

[1] See, e.g., C. Taylor, *Hegel* (Cambridge, 1975).

some communitarians argue—an unjust distribution of goods. In other words, the community is a good that people should seek for several reasons and should not be dismissed. Let us start with the methodological challenge and the individualist response to it.

Both communitarian and individualist theories begin with the image of the individual. But the former claims that there are social attachments which determine the self and thus individuals are constituted by the community of which they are a part. In that sense the individualist image of the self is ontologically false. Individualists also fail to see that this community is not necessarily a voluntary one, and that the social attachments which determine the self are not necessarily chosen ones.

Sandel's notion of the individualist 'unencumbered self' serves to advocate this argument.[2] Sandel postulates the image of a person with 'constitutive ends', those ends which constitute who the person is. We must consider people's aims and values if we want to understand who they are. We cannot analyse their behaviour as if they were abstract entities, as if their values existed somewhere in the distance, 'outside', so to speak. This is a critique of the image of the person put forward by the individualists, who tend to distinguish between who one is and the values one has. This distinction is emphasized in Rawls's terms of the original position and the 'veil of ignorance', according to which participants in the original position are supposed to be ignorant of any information about their beliefs, norms, class, status, etc. Thus, while individualists think in terms of the priority of the self over its aims, communitarians regard this distinction and this priority as artificial, even impossible.

A similar argument is put forward by MacIntyre: one understands one's life only by looking at one's actions within a story, a 'narrative'. But one's narrative converges with the narratives of other people, who come to be a part of one's own narrative. Thus an understanding of oneself can be attained only in the context of the community, that sets up the form and shape as well as the circumstances and the background of these narratives.

But MacIntyre's view of the form these communities take is

---

[2] See especially ch. 1.

4   SHLOMO AVINERI AND AVNER DE-SHALIT

limited to the family, the tribe, and the neighbourhood, rather
than to the state, the nation, or the class. Indeed, the state,
according to MacIntyre, exhibits a confusion of values, lacking
even a shared understanding of the content of values. Therefore
the modern state cannot be said to hold any common moral
beliefs; beliefs which are, however, necessary for a community
to be genuine.

Charles Taylor takes a different path to describe what constitutes the self, although he reaches the same conclusions. In
Taylor's interpretation community constitutes a common culture, which is the precondition of moral autonomy, i.e. the
capacity to form independent moral convictions. This includes
a common language, and also has implications for questions of
culture.[3]

A new image of the individual implies a new conception of
community. The 'communitarian' community is more than a
mere association; it is a unity in which the individuals are
members. This membership is neither artificial nor instrumental, but rather has its own intrinsic value. This is in contrast to
the individualist conception of community, which communitarians hold to be superficial, even obnoxious. The free person
conceived of by the individualists, Sandel argues, is someone
who is freed, as it were, from 'the dictates of nature and the sanction of the social roles', but this does not make any sense of our
social life.

Lastly, it has been argued that some of the consequences of
the metaethical premisses of communitarianism may tend
towards moral relativism. Indeed, some communitarians con-
tend that morality cannot be conceived in universal terms.
Universal and absolute justice, for example, is but another illusion of individualism. Since the values that people hold in
general, and the concept of justice in particular, derive from
their communities, there is no way for this concept to be universal or absolute. This is Walzer's argument, but MacIntyre is
even sharper, stating that our notions of justice and morality in
general are confused and that we have been unable to agree
upon either the hierarchy of values or their content. His book,

[3] See ch. 2, and C. Taylor, 'Language and Human Nature', in C. Taylor,
Human Agency and Language Philosophical Papers, i. (Cambridge, 1985).

After Virtue, is an historical examination of the 'grave disorder' in moral terminology.

3

The individualist response to the methodological challenge takes two directions. One is illustrated by Gauthier, who pictures the individualist self as one facet of a 'non-communitarian community', a community based on co-operation for mutual advantage. Gauthier also emphasizes the theoretical and instrumental character of the individualist image of the self. However, he believes that this image is not only plausible, but also morally warranted.[4]

Another direction is taken by John Rawls. In two of his essays he provides an extremely interesting response to the communitarian argument that liberalism, so far as it is individualistic, rests on mistaken metaphysical premisses. Rawls sees this challenge as irrelevant to the discussion of justice, or indeed to the discussion of politics in general. The image of the individualist self as Sandel and others draw it may very well be true; however, this image only serves as a theoretical device to construct a theory likely to gain consensus in a society whose members are deeply divided on conceptions of the good. This aim is now presented by Rawls and others as liberal neutrality between ideas of the good and impartiality.[5]

As for the issue of moral relativism, the individualist argument essentially states that, if one follows moral relativism, one removes the vigour from the moral and political discourse. Once a standpoint of moral relativism is taken, it makes no sense for a Westerner to raise an argument against the caste system in India, or for an American to complain about the abuse of human rights in Iran. The debate becomes fruitless and meaningless. The alternative offered by individualists is that the philosophers practise objectivity and thereby reach universal generalizations. A measure of intellectual withdrawal from one's society and

---

[4] See ch. 9.
[5] See chs. 11 and 10. See also J. Rawls, 'The Priority of Right and Ideas of the Good', *Philosophy and Public Affairs*, 17 (1988).

culture may help the philosopher find answers to moral dilemmas. Moral principles, it is thought, are universal and capable
of being discovered (some say invented) if the philosopher prac-
tises philosophy in a 'detached' way.[6]

4

But the communitarian argument and the individualist
response go beyond the issue of methodology to include the normative discourse. From the ontological argument communitarians conclude that, in order to justify the special obligations
that we hold to members of our communities—families,
nations, and so forth—one must attach some intrinsic (i.e. non-
instrumental) value to the community itself and to our relations
with other members of the community. That these obligations
are not always voluntary does not detract from the fact that they
are taken for granted by most people. On the other hand, communitarians argue, how can an individualist theory justify an
obligation to fight for the state in the case of war? The communitarian contention is that their theory better justifies obligations that are not universal but rather specific and particular,
because these obligations are part of what constitutes the self.
For such a self, which is constituted by its relations to others in
the community and which wishes to sustain the community, it
is only natural to hold these obligations. The individualist self,
on the other hand, is determined by its distance from others or
by instrumental attachments alone. Thus for the individualist,
the communitarians argue, it is more difficult, indeed virtually
impossible, to justify such obligations, with which our lives are
replete.[7]

Indeed, the term 'community' as used in contemporary
political thought is a normative concept, in the sense that it
describes a desired level of human relationships. The community, as a body with some common values, norms, and goals,

[6] For further reading, see A. Montefiore (ed.), *Neutrality and Impartiality,
the University and Political Commitment* (Cambridge, 1975).
[7] For an interesting attempt to explain these obligations in individualistic,
albeit utilitarian terms, see R. E. Goodin, *Protecting the Vulnerable* (Chicago,
1985).

in which each member regards the common goals as her own, is a good in itself. Communitarians argue that it is morally good that the self be constituted by its communal ties.

For instance, communitarians often argue that personal autonomy is better achieved within the community than outside communal life, or that the community gives our lives their moral meaning. Thus Taylor, following Hegel, sees the community as a good because only by virtue of our being members in communities can we find a deep meaning and substance to our moral beliefs. And, since the individual 'can only maintain his identity within a society/culture of a certain kind', she is concerned for this society and interested in having certain activities, institutions, and even some norms in the society flourish.

In general, communitarians regard the community as a need. In that sense the communitarian response is directed to individualists like Gauthier, who explain social behaviour as a process of co-operation in which people seek to find mutual advantage. It may be reasonable to regard society as a contract, Walzer says, but then this contract is valid only if people's needs are met, and among those needs is community.[8] Walzer regards membership in a human community not only as a condition for participation in the process of the state's provision of goods, but also as a distributed good in itself, in fact, as the primary good that we distribute to one another. Walzer has been attacked because *prima facie* his ideas of membership suggest intolerance for immigrants and refugees. But his critics fail to see that Walzer's emphasis on membership and community also implies that every person in a certain territory should hold a single political status, namely, citizenship. 'If the community is so radically divided that a single citizenship is impossible, then its territory must be divided.'

Sandel distinguishes the line between individualism and communitarianism by asserting that liberalism, in so far as it is individualistic, is the politics of rights while communitarianism is the politics of the common good. This suggests that liberalism is about how to limit the sphere of politics while communitarianism is about how to extend it. Furthermore, the communitarians argue that active political participation is another good

[8] Ch. 4, pp. 65–84.

which is devalued by individualists, who at best regard it as an instrumental good. This should suggest that communitarians advance the notion of a political community; but it is not quite so. Not all communitarian philosophers view the community in political terms, although some do: Walzer regards the country as one's community and Miller devotes a long part of his essay to discussing the nation and citizenship as a community.[9] However, this distinction between communitarianism as the politics of the common good and liberalism (in so far as it is individualistic) as the politics of rights, is perhaps not so obvious, because one can still argue that the common good of Western liberal societies is neutrality and basic liberties; hence liberalism does not fall short of the demands of communitarianism.

5

We have thus arrived at the individualist response to the communitarian normative argument. Dworkin has taken the largest step towards accepting some aspects of the communitarian critique of individualism. He rejects the interpretation of community as a need in general, but concedes that it is a need in the sense that 'people need the community in order to identify with it and recognize that the value of their own lives is only a reflection of and is derivative from the value of the life of the community as a whole'.[10]

Other individualists do not go so far; although agreeing that the concept of the community as a good is not alien to individualism or liberalism, this does not necessarily contradict the priority of the right. Kymlicka, for instance, argues that rights can be a means of achieving some of the communitarian goals of community, as well as defending communities of

[9] Rather than appealing to the inherent value of community, Miller argues for community as a consequence of a distributive critique of liberalism. However, this is a rather extreme case of political community among communitarian philosophers. Miller's communitarian theory is part of his works on a socialist theory, whereas most of the communitarians argue with liberals.

[10] See ch. 12.

minorities, and that a policy of neutrality (one of the main
liberal institutions) is not excessively individualistic.

On the other hand, libertarians adamantly reject any attempt
to derogate from the priority of liberties. In the excerpt in this
volume, Nozick claims that rights should not be pushed aside
for the sake of any idea of a general good. The role of government is to ensure basic rights; it is not the business of government to promote or sustain any idea of the good life. Nozick's
argument appears in much libertarian writing: If, for example,
the state taxes its citizens because it believes that equality is good
and should be extended to more and more spheres of life, then
the state is violating its citizens' rights of freedom. These rights
have priority over any general good (e.g. equal distribution),
and therefore this act of taxation is of the same standard as
forced labour: it is immoral.[11]

How then should one regard this debate on the actual policies
of communitarianism and individualism? It is an open question
whether communitarians and individualists will, at the end of
the day, recommend the same policies, based on different moral
grounds—as Sandel sometimes thinks—or whether the two
theories will be able to find any mutual meeting points at all.
Communitarianism seems to be a very broad conception that
includes methodological and normative arguments, moral and
political claims, radical scholars alongside more conservative
ones. What all communitarians hold in common, if and when
they refer to the political sphere, is the advocacy of involvement
in public life, increased participation in small communities,
firms, and clubs. Because of the importance of these mediating
structures, communitarians are less fearful of the emergence of
an oppressive government as a result of the politics of the common good, whereas many individualists argue that the politics
of the common good is likely to result in intolerance and semi-
or fully totalitarian regimes.[12]

Indeed, communitarianism has been accused for being rather
conservative. At least one of the foremost communitarians,

---

[11] See R. Nozick, *Anarchy, State and Utopia* (Oxford, 1974), 169.
[12] Cf. H. Arendt, *The Origins of Totalitarianism* (New York, 1958); K. R.
Popper, *The Open Society and its Enemies* (London, 1945); J. Talmon, *The Origins
of Totalitarian Democracy* (London, 1955).

MacIntyre, has been challenged more than once for advancing a morally conservative theory.[13] In addition, communitarianism has been reproached for being conservative in its implications. If the communitarians are right in saying that we are not free to choose but rather that our values are determined by our community, the individualists say, then there is no reason to criticize the values of one's society.

But such criticism is far too hasty, firstly because many communitarian philosophers are quite radical in their social demands and in the way they would like society to change. Walzer's egalitarianism, Miller's market-socialism, Friedman's feminism, and Gutmann's readiness to renew liberal thought are only four examples. Secondly, communitarians do think in terms of 'reflection', 'critical scrutiny', and 'corrections of beliefs' in communities which are engaged in a process of a public debate and self-criticism.[14] Moreover, communitarians believe that the roots of totalitarianism do not lie in their own premises, but in limiting the political sphere, in alienating people from public debate and public activity. This constitutes their main argument in favour of extending political participation. And, thirdly, the modern conception of community is less deterministic and holistic than is sometimes believed. Contemporary communitarians leave room for non-communitarian relationships in society, the market being the most common example.[15]

Finally, some individualists accuse the communitarians of being too ambiguous, even ambivalent. It is not quite clear, these individualists say, whether the communitarians reject the view that the principles of individual rights are the most fundamental principles in political life, or whether communitarians attack liberalism as a more general conception of man and society; it is also difficult to know whether communitarians reject the very idea of individual rights and offer an alternative

[13] See also Gutmann, p. 121 below.
[14] As we have noted, individualists argue that self-criticism is impossible if one follows the communitarian premises. This debate led to the publication of Walzer's two recent books in which he defends the idea of criticism from within one's society. See *Interpretations and Social Criticism* (Cambridge, Mass., 1987), and *The Company of Critics: Social Criticism and Political Commitment in the Twentieth Century* (London, 1989).
[15] Walzer, p. 65 below, and Miller, ch. 5.

of teleological politics in which the *telos* is the community, or whether they argue that the weight and priority that individualists attach to these rights are exaggerated.[16] Some communitarians are thought to base their argument on the idea of autonomy, but others begin from an alternative concept of the self; and sometimes communitarians would offer the same policies as the individualists, at other times recommending more radical ones.

But individualism itself does not always offer a clearer view. Individualists define liberalism in different ways, rather far-removed from one other. The concept of neutrality serves to advocate the variety in interpretations of liberalism. By some, neutrality is defined as non-intervention; by others, it is taken to imply that 'one of the main goals of government authority . . . is to ensure for all persons an equal ability to pursue in their lives and promote in their societies any ideal of the good of their choosing',[17] i.e. state intervention. Sometimes neutrality is thought to require neutrality in the consequences of policies; sometimes it refers to the manner in which policies are justified.[18] Some argue that liberalism is a theory of the minimal government, others argue that it is the theory of basic individual rights, and yet others, especially Dworkin and Rawls, define liberalism as an egalitarian philosophy, Dworkin arguing that the main idea of liberalism is equality rather than liberty. However, it seems that the communitarian challenge to the individualists is fruitful in that it has made individualists and liberals in general rethink their theory and has helped them to hone their arguments. In that sense Gutmann's wish to see liberal thought renewed according to the communitarian critique has been realized to a certain degree, and political thought in general may have benefited considerably from this debate.

---

[16] Cf. A. Buchanan, 'Assessing the Communitarian Critique of Liberalism', *Ethics*, 99 (1989), 852–82.

[17] J. Raz, *The Morality of Freedom* (Oxford, 1986), 115.

[18] Ibid., ch. 5.

1

THE PROCEDURAL REPUBLIC AND
THE UNENCUMBERED SELF

MICHAEL SANDEL

Political philosophy seems often to reside at a distance from the
world. Principles are one thing, politics another, and even our
best efforts to 'live up' to our ideals typically founder on the gap
between theory and practice.[1]

But if political philosophy is unrealizable in one sense, it is
unavoidable in another. This is the sense in which philosophy
inhabits the world from the start; our practices and institutions
are embodiments of theory. To engage in a political practice is
already to stand in relation to theory.[2] For all our uncertainties
about ultimate questions of political philosophy—of justice and
value and the nature of the good life—the one thing we know
is that we live *some* answer all the time.

In this essay I will try to explore the answer we live now,
in contemporary America. What is the political philosophy
implicit in our practices and institutions? How does it stand, as
philosophy? And how do tensions in the philosophy find expression in our present political condition?

It may be objected that it is a mistake to look for a single

Michael Sandel, from *Political Theory*, 12 (1984), 81–96. Copyright © 1984
by Sage Publications Inc. Used by permission.

[1] An excellent example of this view can be found in S. Huntington,
American Politics: The Promise of Disharmony (Cambridge, Mass., 1981). See
especially his discussion of the 'ideals versus institutions' gap, pp. 10–12,
39–41, 61–84, 221–62.
[2] See, e.g., the conceptions of a 'practice' advanced by A. MacIntyre and
C. Taylor. MacIntyre, *After Virtue* (Notre Dame, Ind., 1973), 175–209.
Taylor, 'Interpretation and the Sciences of Man', *Review of Metaphysics*, 25
(1971), 3–51.

philosophy, that we live no 'answer', only answers. But a plurality of answers is itself a kind of answer. And the political theory that affirms this plurality is the theory I propose to explore.

THE RIGHT AND THE GOOD

We might begin by considering a certain moral and political vision. It is a liberal vision, and like most liberal visions gives pride of place to justice, fairness, and individual rights. Its core thesis is this: a just society seeks not to promote any particular ends, but enables its citizens to pursue their own ends, consistent with a similar liberty for all; it therefore must govern by principles that do not presuppose any particular conception of the good. What justifies these regulative principles above all is not that they maximize the general welfare, or cultivate virtue, or otherwise promote the good, but rather that they conform to the concept of *right*, a moral category given prior to the good, and independent of it.

This liberalism says, in other words, that what makes the just society just is not the *telos* or purpose or end at which it aims, but precisely its refusal to choose in advance among competing purposes and ends. In its constitution and its laws, the just society seeks to provide a framework within which its citizens can pursue their own values and ends, consistent with a similar liberty for others.

The ideal I've described might be summed up in the claim that the right is prior to the good, and in two senses: the priority of the right means, first, that individual rights cannot be sacrificed for the sake of the general good (in this it opposes utilitarianism), and, second, that the principles of justice that specify these rights cannot be premissed on any particular vision of the good life. (In this it opposes teleological conceptions in general.)

This is the liberalism of much contemporary moral and political philosophy, most fully elaborated by Rawls, and indebted to Kant for its philosophical foundations.[3] But I am

---

[3] J. Rawls, *A Theory of Justice* (Oxford, 1971). I. Kant, *Groundwork of the*

14   MICHAEL SANDEL

concerned here less with the lineage of this vision than with what seem to me three striking facts about it.

First, it has a deep and powerful philosophical appeal. Second, despite its philosophical force, the claim for the priority of the right over the good ultimately fails. And, third, despite its philosophical failure, this liberal vision is the one by which we live. For us in late-twentieth-century America, it is our vision, the theory most thoroughly embodied in the practices and institutions most central to our public life. And seeing how it goes wrong as philosophy may help us to diagnose our present political condition. So, first, its philosophical power; second, its philosophical failure; and, third, however briefly, its uneasy embodiment in the world.

But before taking up these three claims, it is worth pointing out a central theme that connects them. And that is a certain conception of the person, of what it is to be a moral agent. Like all political theories, the liberal theory I have described is something more than a set of regulative principles. It is also a view about the way the world is, and the way we move within it. At the heart of this ethic lies a vision of the person that both inspires and undoes it. As I will try to argue now, what makes this ethic so compelling, but also, finally, vulnerable, are the promise and the failure of the unencumbered self.

KANTIAN FOUNDATIONS

The liberal ethic asserts the priority of right, and seeks principles of justice that do not presuppose any particular conception of the good.[4] This is what Kant means by the supremacy of the moral

---

Metaphysics of Morals, trans. H. J. Paton (1785; New York, 1956). Kant, *Critique of Pure Reason*, trans. N. Kemp Smith (1781, 1787; London, 1929). Kant, *Critique of Practical Reason*, trans. L. W. Beck (1788; Indianapolis, 1956). Kant, 'On the Common Saying: "This may be true in theory, but it does not apply in practice",' in H. Reiss (ed.), *Kant's Political Writings* (1793; Cambridge, 1970). Other recent versions of the claim for the priority of the right over good can be found in R. Nozick, *Anarchy, State and Utopia* (New York, 1974); R. Dworkin, *Taking Rights Seriously* (London, 1977); B. Ackerman, *Social Justice in the Liberal State* (New Haven, Conn., 1980).

[4] This section, and the two that follow, summarize arguments developed more fully in M. Sandel, *Liberalism and the Limits of Justice* (Cambridge, 1982).

law, and what Rawls means when he writes that 'justice is the first virtue of social institutions'.[5] Justice is more than just another value. It provides the framework that *regulates* the play of competing values and ends; it must therefore have a sanction independent of those ends. But it is not obvious where such a sanction could be found.

Theories of justice, and, for that matter, ethics, have typically founded their claims on one or another conception of human purposes and ends. Thus Aristotle said the measure of a *polis* is the good at which it aims, and even J. S. Mill, who in the nineteenth century called 'justice the chief part, and incomparably the most binding part of all morality', made justice an instrument of utilitarian ends.[6]

This is the solution Kant's ethic rejects. Different persons typically have different desires and ends, and so any principle derived from them can only be contingent. But the moral law needs a *categorical* foundation, not a contingent one. Even so universal a desire as happiness will not do. People still differ in what happiness consists of, and to install any particular conception as regulative would impose on some the conceptions of others, and so deny at least to some the freedom to choose their *own* conceptions. In any case, to govern ourselves in conformity with desires and inclinations, given as they are by nature or circumstance, is not really to be *self*-governing at all. It is rather a refusal of freedom, a capitulation to determinations given outside us.

According to Kant, the right is 'derived entirely from the concept of freedom in the external relationships of human beings, and has nothing to do with the end which all men have by nature [i.e. the aim of achieving happiness] or with the recognized means of attaining this end'.[7] As such, it must have a basis prior to all empirical ends. Only when I am governed by principles that do not presuppose any particular ends am I free to pursue my own ends consistent with a similar freedom for all.

But this still leaves the question of what the basis of the right

---

[5] Rawls, *A Theory of Justice*, p. 3.

[6] J. S. Mill, *Utilitarianism*, in *The Utilitarians* (1893; New York, 1973), 465. Mill, *On Liberty*, in *The Utilitarians*, p. 485 (originally published 1849).

[7] Kant, 'On the Common Saying', p. 73.

could possibly be. If it must be a basis prior to all purposes and ends, unconditioned even by what Kant calls 'the special circumstances of human nature',[8] where could such a basis conceivably be found? Given the stringent demands of the Kantian ethic, the moral law would seem almost to require a foundation in nothing, for any empirical precondition would undermine its priority. 'Duty!' asks Kant at his most lyrical, 'What origin is there worthy of thee, and where is to be found the root of thy noble descent which proudly rejects all kinship with the inclinations?'[9]

His answer is that the basis of the moral law is to be found in the *subject*, not the object of practical reason, a subject capable of an autonomous will. No empirical end, but rather 'a subject of ends, namely a rational being himself, must be made the ground for all maxims of action'.[10] Nothing other than what Kant calls 'the subject of all possible ends himself' can give rise to the right, for only this subject is also the subject of an autonomous will. Only this subject could be that 'something which elevates man above himself as part of the world of sense' and enables him to participate in an ideal, unconditioned realm wholly independent of our social and psychological inclinations. And only this thoroughgoing independence can afford us the detachment we need if we are ever freely to choose for ourselves, unconditioned by the vagaries of circumstance.[11]

Who or what exactly *is* this subject? It is, in a certain sense, *us*. The moral law, after all, is a law we give *ourselves*; we don't *find* it, we *will* it. That is how it (and we) escape the reign of nature and circumstance and merely empirical ends. But what is important to see is that the 'we' who do the willing are not 'we' *qua* particular persons, you and me, each for ourselves—the moral law is not up to us as individuals—but 'we' *qua* participants in what Kant calls 'pure practical reason', 'we' *qua* participants in a transcendental subject.

Now what is to guarantee that I *am* a subject of this kind, capable of exercising pure practical reason? Well, strictly speak-

[8] Kant, *Groundwork*, p. 92.
[9] Kant, *Critique of Practical Reason*, p. 89.
[10] Kant, *Groundwork*, p. 92.
[11] Kant, *Critique of Practical Reason*, p. 89.

ing, there *is* no guarantee; the transcendental subject is only a possibility. But it is a possibility I must *presuppose* if I am to think of myself as a free moral agent. Were I wholly an empirical being, I would not be capable of freedom, for every exercise of will would be conditioned by the desire for some object. All choice would be heteronomous choice, governed by the pursuit of some end. My will could never be a first cause, only the effect of some prior cause, the instrument of one or another impulse or inclination. 'When we think of ourselves as free,' writes Kant, 'we transfer ourselves into the intelligible world as members and recognize the autonomy of the will'.[12] And so the notion of a subject prior to and independent of experience, such as the Kantian ethic requires, appears not only possible but indispensable, a necessary presupposition of the possibility of freedom.

How does all of this come back to politics? As the subject is prior to its ends, so the right is prior to the good. Society is best arranged when it is governed by principles that do not presuppose any particular conception of the good, for any other arrangement would fail to respect persons as being capable of choice; it would treat them as objects rather than subjects, as means rather than ends in themselves.

We can see in this way how Kant's notion of the subject is bound up with the claim for the priority of right. But for those in the Anglo-American tradition, the transcendental subject will seem a strange foundation for a familiar ethic. Surely, one may think, we can take rights seriously and affirm the primacy of justice without embracing the *Critique of Pure Reason*. This, in any case, is the project of Rawls.

He wants to save the priority of right from the obscurity of the transcendental subject. Kant's idealist metaphysic, for all its moral and political advantage, cedes too much to the transcendent, and wins for justice its primacy only by denying it its human situation. 'To develop a viable Kantian conception of justice,' Rawls writes, 'the force and content of Kant's doctrine must be detached from its background in transcendental idealism' and recast within the 'canons of a reasonable

[12] Kant, *Groundwork*, p. 92.

empiricism'.[13] And so Rawls's project is to preserve Kant's moral and political teaching by replacing Germanic obscurities with a domesticated metaphysic more congenial to the Anglo-American temper. This is the role of the original position.

FROM TRANSCENDENTAL SUBJECT TO UNENCUMBERED SELF

The original position tries to provide what Kant's transcendental argument cannot—a foundation for the right that is prior to the good, but still situated in the world. Sparing all but essentials, the original position works like this: It invites us to imagine the principles we would choose to govern our society if we were to choose them in advance, before we knew the particular persons we would be—whether rich or poor, strong or weak, lucky or unlucky—before we knew even our interests or aims or conceptions of the good. These principles—the ones we would choose in that imaginary situation—are the principles of justice. What is more, if it works, they are principles that do not presuppose any particular ends.

What they *do* presuppose is a certain picture of the person, of the way we must be if we are beings for whom justice is the first virtue. This is the picture of the unencumbered self, a self understood as prior to and independent of purposes and ends.

Now the unencumbered self describes first of all the way we stand towards the things we have, or want, or seek. It means there is always a distinction between the values I *have* and the person I *am*. To identify any characteristics as *my* aims, ambitions, desires, and so on, is always to imply some subject 'me' standing behind them, at a certain distance, and the shape of this 'me' must be given prior to any of the aims or attributes I bear. One consequence of this distance is to put the self *itself* beyond the reach of its experience, to secure its identity once and for all. Or to put the point another way, it rules out the possibility of what we might call *constitutive* ends. No role or commitment could define me so completely that I could not understand

[13] Rawls, 'The Basic Structure as Subject', *American Philosophical Quarterly* (1977), 165.

myself without it. No project could be so essential that turning away from it would call into question the person I am.

For the unencumbered self, what matters above all, what is most essential to our personhood, are not the ends we choose but our capacity to choose them. The original position sums up this central claim about us. 'It is not our aims that primarily reveal our nature,' writes Rawls, 'but rather the principles that we would acknowledge to govern the background conditions under which these aims are to be formed . . . We should therefore reverse the relation between the right and the good proposed by teleological doctrines and view the right as prior'.[14]

Only if the self is prior to its ends can the right be prior to the good. Only if my identity is never tied to the aims and interests I may have at any moment can I think of myself as a free and independent agent, capable of choice.

This notion of independence carries consequences for the kind of community of which we are capable. Understood as unencumbered selves, we are of course free to join in voluntary association with others, and so are capable of community in the co-operative sense. What is denied to the unencumbered self is the possibility of membership in any community bound by moral ties antecedent to choice; he cannot belong to any community where the self *itself* could be at stake. Such a community —call it constitutive as against merely co-operative—would engage the identity as well as the interests of the participants, and so implicate its members in a citizenship more thorough-going than the unencumbered self can know.

For justice to be primary, then, we must be creatures of a certain kind, related to human circumstance in a certain way. We must stand to our circumstance always at a certain distance, whether as transcendental subject in the case of Kant, or as unencumbered selves in the case of Rawls. Only in this way can we view ourselves as subjects as well as objects of experience, as agents and not just instruments of the purposes we pursue.

The unencumbered self and the ethic it inspires, taken together, hold out a liberating vision. Freed from the dictates of nature and the sanction of social roles, the human subject is installed as sovereign, cast as the author of the only moral

[14] Rawls, *A Theory of Justice*, p. 560.

meanings there are. As participants in pure practical reason, or as parties to the original position, we are free to construct principles of justice unconstrained by an order of value antecedently given. And as actual, individual selves, we are free to choose our purposes and ends unbound by such an order, or by custom or tradition or inherited status. So long as they are not unjust, our conceptions of the good carry weight, whatever they are, simply in virtue of our having chosen them. We are, in Rawls's words, 'self-originating sources of valid claims'.[15]

This is an exhilarating promise, and the liberalism it animates is perhaps the fullest expression of the Enlightenment's quest for the self-defining subject. But is it true? Can we make sense of our moral and political life by the light of the self-image it requires? I do not think we can, and I will try to show why not by arguing first within the liberal project, then beyond it.

JUSTICE AND COMMUNITY

We have focused so far on the foundations of the liberal vision, on the way it derives the principles it defends. Let us turn briefly now to the substance of those principles, using Rawls as our example. Sparing all but essentials once again, Rawls's two principles of justice are these: first, equal basic liberties for all, and, second, only those social and economic inequalities that benefit the least-advantaged members of society (the difference principle).

In arguing for these principles, Rawls argues against two familiar alternatives—utilitarianism and libertarianism. He argues against utilitarianism that it fails to take seriously the distinction between persons. In seeking to maximize the general welfare, the utilitarian treats society as a whole as if it were a single person; it conflates our many, diverse desires into a single system of desires, and tries to maximize. It is indifferent to the distribution of satisfactions among persons, except in so far as this may affect the overall sum. But this fails to respect our plurality and distinctness. It uses some as means to the hap-

---

[15] Rawls, 'Kantian Constructivism in Moral Theory: The Dewey Lectures 1980', *Journal of Philosophy*, 77 (1980), 543.

piness of all, and so fails to respect each as an end in himself. While utilitarians may sometimes defend individual rights, their defence must rest on the calculation that respecting those rights will serve utility in the long run. But this calculation is contingent and uncertain. So long as utility is what Mill said it is, 'the ultimate appeal on all ethical questions',[16] individual rights can never be secure. To avoid the danger that their life prospects might one day be sacrificed for the greater good of others, the parties to the original position therefore insist on certain basic liberties for all, and make those liberties prior.

If utilitarians fail to take seriously the distinctness of persons, libertarians go wrong by failing to acknowledge the arbitrariness of fortune. They define as just whatever distribution results from an efficient market economy, and oppose all redistribution on the grounds that people are entitled to whatever they get, so long as they do not cheat or steal or otherwise violate someone's rights in getting it. Rawls opposes this principle on the ground that the distribution of talents and assets and even efforts by which some get more and others get less is arbitrary from a moral point of view, a matter of good luck. To distribute the good things in life on the basis of these differences is not to do justice, but simply to carry over into human arrangements the arbitrariness of social and natural contingency. We deserve, as individuals, neither the talents our good fortune may have brought, nor the benefits that flow from them. We should therefore regard these talents as common assets, and regard one another as common beneficiaries of the rewards they bring. 'Those who have been favored by nature, whoever they are, may gain from their good fortune only on terms that improve the situation of those who have lost out . . . In justice as fairness, men agree to share one another's fate'.[17]

This is the reasoning that leads to the difference principle. Notice how it reveals, in yet another guise, the logic of the unencumbered self. I cannot be said to deserve the benefits that flow from, say, my fine physique and good looks, because they are only accidental, not essential facts about me. They describe attributes I *have*, not the person I *am*, and so cannot give rise to

[16] Mill, *On Liberty*, p. 485.
[17] Rawls, *A Theory of Justice*, pp. 101-2.

a claim of desert. Being an unencumbered self, this is true of *everything* about me. And so I cannot, as an individual, deserve anything at all.

However jarring to our ordinary understandings this argument may be, the picture so far remains intact; the priority of right, the denial of desert, and the unencumbered self all hang impressively together.

But the difference principle requires more, and it is here that the argument comes undone. The difference principle begins with the thought, congenial to the unencumbered self, that the assets I have are only accidentally mine. But it ends by assuming that these assets are therefore *common* assets and that society has a prior claim on the fruits of their exercise. But this assumption is without warrant. Simply because I, as an individual, do not have a privileged claim on the assets accidentally residing 'here', it does not follow that everyone in the world collectively does. For there is no reason to think that their location in society's province, or, for that matter, within the province of humankind, is any *less* arbitrary from a moral point of view. And if their arbitrariness within *me* makes them ineligible to serve *my* ends, there seems no obvious reason why their arbitrariness within any particular society should not make them ineligible to serve that society's ends as well.

To put the point another way, the difference principle, like utilitarianism, is a principle of sharing. As such, it must presuppose some prior moral tie among those whose assets it would deploy and whose efforts it would enlist in a common endeavour. Otherwise, it is simply a formula for using some as means to others' ends, a formula this liberalism is committed to reject.

But on the co-operative vision of community alone, it is unclear what the moral basis for this sharing could be. Short of the constitutive conception, deploying an individual's assets for the sake of the common good would seem an offence against the 'plurality and distinctness' of individuals this liberalism seeks above all to secure.

If those whose fate I am required to share really are, morally speaking, *others*, rather than fellow participants in a way of life with which my identity is bound, the difference principle falls prey to the same objections as utilitarianism. Its claim on me is not the claim of a constitutive community whose attachments I acknowledge, but rather the claim of a concatenated collectivity whose entanglements I confront.

What the difference principle requires, but cannot provide, is some way of identifying those *among* whom the assets I bear are properly regarded as common, some way of seeing ourselves as mutually indebted and morally engaged to begin with. But as we have seen, the constitutive aims and attachments that would save and situate the difference principle are precisely the ones denied to the liberal self; the moral encumbrances and antecedent obligations they imply would undercut the priority of right.

What, then, of those encumbrances? The point so far is that we cannot be persons for whom justice is primary, and also be persons for whom the difference principle is a principle of justice. But which must give way? Can we view ourselves as independent selves, independent in the sense that our identity is never tied to our aims and attachments?[18]

I do not think we can, at least not without cost to those loyalties and convictions whose moral force consists partly in the fact that living by them is inseparable from understanding ourselves as the particular persons we are—as members of this family or community or nation or people, as bearers of that history, as citizens of this republic. Allegiances such as these are more than values I happen to have, and to hold, at a certain distance. They go beyond the obligations I voluntarily incur and the 'natural duties' I owe to human beings as such. They allow that to some I owe more than justice requires or even permits, not by reason of agreements I have made but instead in virtue of those more or less enduring attachments and commitments that, taken together, partly define the person I am.

To imagine a person incapable of constitutive attachments such as these is not to conceive an ideally free and rational agent, but to imagine a person wholly without character, without moral depth. For to have character is to know that I move in a history I neither summon nor command, which carries consequences none the less for my choices and conduct. It draws me closer to

---

[18] The account that follows is a tentative formulation of themes requiring more detailed elaboration and support.

some and more distant from others; it makes some aims more appropriate, others less so. As a self-interpreting being, I am able to reflect on my history and in this sense to distance myself from it, but the distance is always precarious and provisional, the point of reflection never finally secured outside the history itself. But the liberal ethic puts the self beyond the reach of its experience, beyond deliberation and reflection. Denied the expansive self-understandings that could shape a common life, the liberal self is left to lurch between detachment on the one hand, and entanglement on the other. Such is the fate of the unencumbered self, and its liberating promise.

THE PROCEDURAL REPUBLIC

But before my case can be complete, I need to consider one powerful reply. While it comes from a liberal direction, its spirit is more practical than philosophical. It says, in short, that I am asking too much. It is one thing to seek constitutive attachments in our private lives; among families and friends, and certain tightly knit groups, there may be found a common good that makes justice and rights less pressing. But with public life—at least today, and probably always—it is different. So long as the nation-state is the primary form of political association, talk of constitutive community too easily suggests a darker politics rather than a brighter one; amid echoes of the moral majority, the priority of right, for all its philosophical faults, still seems the safer hope.

This is a challenging rejoinder, and no account of political community in the twentieth century can fail to take it seriously. It is challenging not least because it calls into question the status of political philosophy and its relation to the world. For if my argument is correct, if the liberal vision we have considered is not morally self-sufficient but parasitic on a notion of community it officially rejects, then we should expect to find that the political practice that embodies this vision is not *practically* self-sufficient either—that it must draw on a sense of community it cannot supply and may even undermine. But is that so far from the circumstance we face today? Could it be that through the original position darkly, on the far side of the veil of ignorance, we may glimpse an intimation of our predicament, a refracted vision of ourselves?

How does the liberal vision—and its failure—help us make sense of our public life and its predicament? Consider, to begin, the following paradox in the citizen's relation to the modern welfare state. In many ways, we in the 1980s stand near the completion of a liberal project that has run its course from the New Deal through the Great Society and into the present. But notwithstanding the extension of the franchise and the expansion on individual rights and entitlements in recent decades, there is a widespread sense that, individually and collectively, our control over the forces that govern our lives is receding rather than increasing. This sense is deepened by what appear simultaneously as the power and the powerlessness of the nation-state. On the one hand, increasing numbers of citizens view the state as an overly intrusive presence, more likely to frustrate their purposes than advance them. And yet, despite its unprecedented role in the economy and society, the modern state seems itself disempowered, unable effectively to control the domestic economy, to respond to persisting social ills, or to work America's will in the world.

This is a paradox that has fed the appeals of recent politicians (including Carter and Reagan), even as it has frustrated their attempts to govern. To sort it out, we need to identify the public philosophy implicit in our political practice, and to reconstruct its arrival. We need to trace the advent of the procedural republic, by which I mean a public life animated by the liberal vision and self-image we've considered.

The story of the procedural republic goes back in some ways to the founding of the republic, but its central drama begins to unfold around the turn of the century. As national markets and large-scale enterprise displaced a decentralized economy, the decentralized political forms of the early republic became outmoded as well. If democracy was to survive, the concentration of economic power would have to be met by a similar concentration of political power. But the Progressives understood, or some of them did, that the success of democracy required more than the centralization of government; it also required the nationalization of politics. The primary form of political community had to be a recast on a national scale. For Herbert Croly, writing in 1909, the 'nationalizing of American political, economic, and social life' was 'an essentially formative and enlightening political transformation'. We would become more of a democracy only as we became 'more of a nation . . . in ideas, in institutions, and in spirit'.[19]

This nationalizing project would be consummated in the New Deal, but, for the democratic tradition in America, the embrace of the nation was a decisive departure. From Jefferson to the populists, the party of democracy in American political debate had been, roughly speaking, the party of the provinces, of decentralized power, of small-town and small-scale America. And against them had stood the party of the nation—first Federalists, then Whigs, then the Republicans of Lincoln—a party that spoke for the consolidation of the union. It was thus the historic achievement of the New Deal to unite, in a single party and political programme, what Samuel Beer has called 'liberalism and the national idea'.[20]

What matters for our purpose is that, in the twentieth century, liberalism made its peace with concentrated power. But it was understood at the start that the terms of this peace required a strong sense of national community, morally and politically to underwrite the extended involvements of a modern industrial order. If a virtuous republic of small-scale, democratic communities was no longer a possibility, a national republic seemed democracy's next best hope. This was still, in principle at least, a politics of the common good. It looked to the nation, not as a neutral framework for the play of competing interests, but rather as a formative community, concerned to shape a common life suited to the scale of modern social and economic forms.

But this project failed. By the mid- or late twentieth century the national republic had run its course. Except for extraordinary moments, such as war, the nation proved too vast a scale across which to cultivate the shared self-understandings necessary to community in the formative, or constitutive sense. And so the gradual shift, in our practices and institutions, from a public philosophy of common purposes to one of fair proce-

[19] H. Croly, *The Promise of American Life* (Indianapolis, 1965), 270–3.
[20] S. Beer, 'Liberalism and the National Idea', *The Public Interest*, Fall (1966), 70–82.

dures, from a politics of good to a politics of right, from the national republic to the procedural republic.

OUR PRESENT PREDICAMENT

A full account of this transition would take a detailed look at the changing shape of political institutions, constitutional interpretation, and the terms of political discourse in the broadest sense. But I suspect we would find in the *practice* of the procedural republic two broad tendencies foreshadowed by its philosophy: first, a tendency to crowd out democratic possibilities; second, a tendency to undercut the kind of community on which it none the less depends.

Where liberty in the early republic was understood as a function of democratic institutions and dispersed power,[21] liberty in the procedural republic is defined, in opposition to democracy, as an individual's guarantee against what the majority might will. I am free in so far as I am the bearer of rights, where rights are trumps.[22] Unlike the liberty of the early republic, the modern version permits—in fact even requires—concentrated power. This has to do with the universalizing logic of rights. In so far as I have a right, whether to free speech or a minimum income, its provision cannot be left to the vagaries of local preferences but must be assured at the most comprehensive level of political association. It cannot be one thing in New York and another in Alabama. As rights and entitlements expand, politics is therefore displaced from smaller forms of association and relocated at the most universal form—in our case, the nation. And even as politics flows to the nation, power shifts away from democratic institutions (such as legislatures and political parties) and towards institutions designed to be insulated from democratic pressures, and hence better equipped to dispense and defend individual rights (notably the judiciary and bureaucracy).

---

[21] See, e.g., L. Tribe, *American Constitutional Law* (Mincola, NY, 1978), 2-3.
[22] See R. Dworkin, 'Liberalism', in S. Hampshire (ed.), *Public and Private Morality* (Cambridge, 1978), 136.

These institutional developments may begin to account for the sense of powerlessness that the welfare state fails to address and in some ways doubtless deepens. But it seems to me a further clue to our condition recalls even more directly the predicament of the unencumbered self—lurching, as we left it, between detachment on the one hand, the entanglement on the other. For it is a striking feature of the welfare state that it offers a powerful promise of individual rights, and also demands of its citizens a high measure of mutual engagement. But the self-image that attends the rights cannot sustain the engagement.

As bearers of rights, where rights are trumps, we think of ourselves as freely choosing, individual selves, unbound by obligations antecedent to rights, or to the agreements we make. And yet, as citizens of the procedural republic that secures these rights, we find ourselves implicated willy-nilly in a formidable array of dependencies and expectations we did not choose and increasingly reject.

In our public life, we are more entangled, but less attached, than ever before. It is as though the unencumbered self presupposed by the liberal ethic had begun to come true—less liberated than disempowered, entangled in a network of obligations and involvements unassociated with any act of will, and yet unmediated by those common identifications or expansive self-definitions that would make them tolerable. As the scale of social and political organization has become more comprehensive, the terms of our collective identity have become more fragmented, and the forms of political life have outrun the common purpose needed to sustain them.

Something like this, it seems to me, has been unfolding in America for the past half-century or so. I hope I have said at least enough to suggest the shape a fuller story might take. And I hope in any case to have conveyed a certain view about politics and philosophy and the relation between them—that our practices and institutions are themselves embodiments of theory, and to unravel their predicament is, at least in part, to seek after the self-image of the age.

2

ATOMISM

CHARLES TAYLOR

I would like to examine the issue of political atomism, or at least to try to clarify what this issue is. I want to say what I think atomist doctrines consist in, and to examine how the issue can be joined around them—this is, how they might be proved or disproved, or at least cogently argued for or against, and what in turn they may be used to prove.

The term 'atomism' is used loosely to characterize the doctrines of social-contract theory which arose in the seventeenth century and also successor doctrines which may not have made use of the notion of social contract but which inherited a vision of society as in some sense constituted by individuals for the fulfilment of ends which were primarily individual. Certain forms of utilitarianism are successor doctrines in this sense. The term is also applied to contemporary doctrines which hark back to social-contract theory, or which try to defend in some sense the priority of the individual and his rights over society, or which present a purely instrumental view of society.

Of course, any term loosely used in political discourse can be defined in a host of ways. And perhaps one should even leave out of philosophical discourse altogether those terms which tend to be branded as epithets of condemnation in the battle between different views. One might well argue that 'atomism' is one such, because it seems to be used almost exclusively by its enemies. Even extreme individualists like Nozick don't seem to warm to this term, but tend to prefer others, like 'individualism'.

Perhaps I am dealing with the wrong term. But there is a

Charles Taylor, excerpts from *Philosophy and the Human Sciences: Philosophical Papers*, ii (1985), 187–210 © Charles Taylor 1979. First published in Alkis Kontos, *Powers, Possessions and Freedom*, 39–61 (University of Toronto Press, 1979).

central issue in political theory which is eminently worth getting at under some description. And perhaps the best way of getting at it is this: what I am calling atomist doctrines underlie the seventeenth-century revolution in the terms of normative discourse, which we associate with the names of Hobbes and Locke.

These writers, and others who presented social-contract views, have left us a legacy of political thinking in which the notion of rights plays a central part in the justification of political structures and action. The central doctrine of this tradition is an affirmation of what we could call the primacy of rights.

Theories which assert the primacy of rights are those which take as the fundamental, or at least a fundamental, principle of their political theory the ascription of certain rights to individuals and which deny the same status to a principle of belonging or obligation, that is a principle which states our obligation as men to belong to or sustain society, or a society of a certain type, or to obey authority or an authority of a certain type. Primacy-of-right theories in other words accept a principle ascribing rights to men as binding unconditionally,[1] binding, that is, on men as such. But they do not accept as similarly unconditional a principle of belonging or obligation. Rather our obligation to belong to or sustain a society, or to obey its authorities, is seen as derivative, as laid on us conditionally, through our consent, or through its being to our advantage. The obligation to belong

---

[1] The words 'conditional/unconditional' may mislead, because there are certain theories of belonging, to use this term for them, which hold that our obligation to obey, or to belong to a particular society, may in certain circumstances be inoperative. For instance, medieval theories which justified tyrannicide still portrayed man as a social animal and were thus theories of belonging in the sense used here. But they allowed that in certain circumstances our obligation to obey that authority by which our society cohered was abrogated, and that when the ruler was a tyrant he might be killed. In this sense we could say that the obligation to obey was 'conditional'. But this is not the same as a theory of the primacy of right. For in theories of belonging it is clear that men *qua* men have an obligation to belong to and sustain society. There may be a restriction on what kind of society would fulfil the underlying goal, and from this a licence to break with perverted forms; but the obligation to belong itself was fundamental and unconditional; it held 'by nature'. In primacy-of-right theories the notion is that simply by nature we are under no obligation to belong whatever; we have first to contract such an obligation.

is derived in certain conditions from the more fundamental principle which ascribes rights.[2]

The paradigm of primacy-of-right theories is plainly that of Locke. But there are contemporary theories of this kind, one of the best known in recent years being that of Robert Nozick.[3] Nozick too makes the assertion of rights to individuals fundamental and then proceeds to discuss whether and in what conditions we can legitimately demand obedience to a state.

Primacy-of-right theories have been one of the formative influences on modern political consciousness. Thus arguments like that of Nozick have at least a surface plausibility for our contemporaries and sometimes considerably more. At the very least, opponents are brought up short, and have to ponder how to meet the claims of an argument which reaches conclusions about political obedience which lie far outside the common sense of our society; and this because the starting-point in individual rights has an undeniable *prima facie* force for us.

This is striking because it would not always have been so. In an earlier phase of Western civilization, of course, not to speak of other civilizations, these arguments would have seemed wildly eccentric and implausible. The very idea of starting an argument whose foundation was the rights of the individual would have been strange and puzzling—about as puzzling as if I were to start with the premiss that the Queen rules by divine right. You might not dismiss what I said out of hand, but you would expect that I should at least have the sense to start with some less contentious premiss and argue up to divine right, not take it as my starting-point.

Why do we even begin to find it reasonable to start a political theory with an assertion of individual rights and to give these primacy? I want to argue that the answer to this question lies in the hold on us of what I have called atomism. Atomism

---

[2] This may not be true of all doctrines which found a political theory on an affirmation of natural right. For the new doctrine of human rights which Professor Macpherson envisages in, for example, *Democratic Theory: Essays in Retrieval* (Oxford, 1973), 236, and which would free itself of 'the postulate of the inherent and permanent contentiousness of men', would seem to involve an affirmation of individual rights which presuppose society, rather than merely setting the boundary conditions of its possible legitimacy.

[3] R. Nozick, *Anarchy, State and Utopia* (Cambridge, Mass., 1974).

represents a view about human nature and the human condition which (among other things) makes a doctrine of the primacy of rights plausible; or, to put it negatively, it is a view in the absence of which this doctrine is suspect to the point of being virtually untenable.

How can we formulate this view? Perhaps the best way is to borrow the terms of the opposed thesis—the view that man is a social animal. One of the most influential formulations of this view is Aristotle's. He puts the point in terms of the notion of self-sufficiency (*autarkeia*). Man is a social animal, indeed a political animal, because he is not self-sufficient alone, and in an important sense is not self-sufficient outside a *polis*. Borrowing this term then, we could say that atomism affirms the self-sufficiency of man alone or, if you prefer, of the individual.

That the primacy-of-rights doctrine needs a background of this kind may appear evident to some; but it needs to be argued because it is vigorously denied by others. And generally proponents of the doctrine are among the most vigorous deniers. They will not generally admit that the assertion of rights is dependent on any particular view about the nature of man, especially one as difficult to formulate and make clear as this. And to make their political theory dependent on a thesis formulated in just this way seems to be adding insult to injury. For if atomism means that man is self-sufficient alone, then surely it is a very questionable thesis. [. . .]

The claim I am trying to make could be summed up in this way. (1) To ascribe the natural (not just legal) right of X to agent A is to affirm that A commands our respect, such that we are normally bound not to interfere with A's doing or enjoying of X. This means that to ascribe the right is far more than simply to issue the injunction: don't interfere with A's doing or enjoying X. The injunction can be issued, to self or others, without grounds, should we so choose. But to affirm the right is to say that a creature such as A lays a moral claim on us not to interfere. It thus also asserts something about A: A is such that this injunction is somehow inescapable.

(2) We may probe further and try to define what it is about A which makes the injunction inescapable. We can call this, whatever it is, A's essential property or properties, E. Then it is E (in our case, the essentially human capacities) which defines

not only who are the bearers of rights but what they have rights to. A has a natural right to X, if doing or enjoying X is essentially part of manifesting E (e.g. if E is being a rational life-form, then A's have a natural right to life and also to the unimpeded development of rationality); or if X is a causally necessary condition of manifesting E (e.g. the ownership of property, which has been widely believed to be a necessary safeguard of life or freedom, or a living wage).

(3) The assertion of a natural right, while it lays on us the injunction to respect A in his doing or enjoying of X, cannot but have other moral consequences as well. For if A is such that this injunction is inescapable and he is such in virtue of E, then E is of great moral worth and ought to be fostered and developed in a host of appropriate ways, and not just not interfered with.

Hence asserting a right is more than issuing an injunction. It has an essential conceptual background, in some notion of the moral worth of certain properties or capacities, without which it would not make sense. Thus, for example, our position would be incomprehensible and incoherent if we ascribed rights to human beings in respect of the specifically human capacities (such as the right to one's own convictions or to the free choice of one's life-style or profession) while at the same time denying that these capacities ought to be developed, or if we thought it a matter of indifference whether they were realized or stifled in ourselves or others.

From this we can see that the answer to [the] question [. . .] why do we ascribe these rights to men and not to animals, rocks, or trees [. . .] is quite straightforward. It is because men and women are the beings who exhibit certain capacities which are worthy of respect. The fact that we ascribe rights to idiots, people in a coma, bad men who have irretrievably turned their back on the proper development of these capacities, and so on, does not show that the capacities are irrelevant. It shows only that we have a powerful sense that the status of being a creature defined by its potential for these capacities cannot be lost. This sense has been given a rational account in certain ways, such as, for instance, by the belief in an immortal soul. But it is interestingly enough shared even by those who have rejected all such traditional rationales. We sense that in the incurable psychotic there runs a current of human life, where the definition of 'human'

may be uncertain but relates to the specifically human capacities; we sense that he has feelings that only a human being, a
language-using animal, can have, that his dreams and fantasies
are those which only a human can have. Pushed however deep,
and however distorted, his humanity cannot be eradicated.

If we look at another extreme case, that of persons in a ter-
minal but long-lasting coma, it would seem that the sense that
many have that the life-support machines should be discon-
nected is based partly on the feeling that the patients themselves,
should they *per impossible* be able to choose, would not want to
continue, precisely because the range of human life has been
shrunk here to zero.

How does the notion then arise that we can assert rights outside
of a context of affirming the worth of certain capacities? The
answer to this question will take us deep into the issue central
to modern thought of the nature of the subject. We can give but
a partial account here. There clearly are a wide number of
different conceptions of the characteristically human capacities
and thus differences too in what are recognized as rights. I will
come back to this in another connection later.

But what is relevant for our purposes here is that there are
some views of the properly human which give absolutely central
importance to the freedom to choose one's own mode of life.
Those who hold this ultra-liberal view are chary about allowing
that the assertion of right involves any affirmation about realizing certain potentialities; for they fear that the affirming of any
obligations will offer a pretext for the restriction of freedom. To
say that we have a right to be free to choose our life-form must
be to say that any choice is equally compatible with this principle of freedom and that no choices can be judged morally better or worse by this principle—although, of course, we might
want to discriminate between them on the basis of other
principles.

Thus if I have a right to do what I want with my property,
then any disposition I choose is equally justifiable from the point
of view of this principle: I may be judged uncharitable if I hoard
it to myself and won't help those in need, or uncreative if I bury
it in the ground and don't engage in interesting enterprises with
it. But these latter criticisms arise from our accepting other

moral standards, quite independent from the view that we have a right to do what we want with our own.

But this independence from a moral obligation of self-realization cannot be made good all around. All choices are equally valid; but they must be *choices*. The view that makes freedom of choice this absolute is one that exalts choice as a human capacity. It carries with it the demand that we become beings capable of choice, that we rise to the level of self-consciousness and autonomy where we can exercise choice, that we not remain enmired through fear, sloth, ignorance, or superstition in some code imposed by tradition, society, or fate which tells us how we should dispose of what belongs to us. Ultra-liberalism can only appear unconnected with any affirmation of worth and hence obligation of self-fulfilment, where people have come to accept the utterly facile moral psychology of traditional empiricism, according to which human agents possess the full capacity of choice as a given rather than as a potential which has to be developed.

If all this is valid, then the doctrine of the primacy of rights is not as independent as its proponents want to claim from considerations about human nature and the human social condition. For the doctrine could be undermined by arguments which succeeded in showing that men were not self-sufficient in the sense of the above argument—that is, that they could not develop their characteristically human potentialities outside of society or outside of certain kinds of society. The doctrine would in this sense be dependent on an atomist thesis, which affirms this kind of self-sufficiency.

The connection I want to establish here can be made following the earlier discussion of the background of rights. If we cannot ascribe natural rights without affirming the worth of certain human capacities, and if this affirmation has other normative consequences (i.e. that we should foster and nurture these capacities in ourselves and others), then any proof that these capacities can only develop in society or in a society of a certain kind is a proof that we ought to belong to or sustain society or this kind of society. But then, provided a social (i.e. an anti-atomist) thesis of the right kind can be true, an assertion of the primacy of rights is impossible; for to assert the rights in question is to affirm the capacities, and, granted the social thesis is true concerning these capacities, this commits us to an obligation to belong. This will be as fundamental as the assertion of rights, because it will be inseparable from it. So it would be incoherent to try to assert the rights, while denying the obligation or giving it the status of optional extra which we may or may not contract; this assertion is what the primacy doctrine makes.

The normative incoherence becomes evident if we see what it would be to assert the primacy of rights in the face of such a social thesis. Let us accept, for the sake of this argument, the view that men cannot develop the fullness of moral autonomy— that is, the capacity to form independent moral convictions— outside a political culture sustained by institutions of political participation and guarantees of personal independence. In fact, I do not think this thesis is true as it stands, although I do believe that a much more complicated view, formed from this one by adding a number of significant reservations, is tenable. But, for the sake of simplicity, let us accept this thesis in order to see the logic of the arguments.

Now if we assert the right to one's own independent moral convictions, we cannot in the face of this social thesis go on to assert the primacy of rights, that is, claim that we are not under obligation 'by nature' to belong to and sustain a society of the relevant type. We could not, for instance, unreservedly assert our right in the face of, or at the expense of, such a society; in the event of conflict we should have to acknowledge that we were legitimately pulled both ways. For in undermining such a society we should be making the activity defended by the right assertion impossible of realization. But if we are justified in asserting the right, we cannot be justified in our undermining; for the same considerations which justify the first condemn the second.

In whatever way the conflict might arise it poses a moral dilemma for us. It may be that we have already been formed in this culture and that the demise of this mode of society will not deprive us of this capacity. But in asserting our rights to the point of destroying the society, we should be depriving all those who follow after us of the exercise of the same capacity. To believe that there is a right to independent moral convictions must be to believe that the exercise of the relevant capacity is a human good. But then it cannot be right, if no over-riding considerations intervene, to act so as to make this good less available to others, even though in so doing I could not be said to be depriving them of their rights.

The incoherence of asserting primacy of rights is even clearer if we imagine another way in which the conflict could arise: that, in destroying the society, I would be undermining my own future ability to realize this capacity. For then, in defending my right, I should be condemning myself to what I should have to acknowledge as a truncated mode of life, in virtue of the same considerations that make me affirm the right. And this would be a paradoxical thing to defend as an affirmation of my rights—in the same way as it would be paradoxical for me to offer to defend you against those who menace your freedom by hiding you in my deep freeze. I would have to have misunderstood what freedom is all about; and similarly, in the above case, I should have lost my grasp of what affirming a right is.

We could put the point in another way. The affirmation of certain rights involves us in affirming the worth of certain capacities and thus in accepting certain standards by which a life may be judged full or truncated. We cannot then sensibly claim the morality of a truncated form of life for people on the ground of defending their rights. Would I be respecting your right to life if I agreed to leave you alive in a hospital bed, in an irreversible coma, hooked up to life-support machines? Or suppose I offered to use my new machine to erase totally your personality and memories and give you quite different ones? These questions are inescapably rhetorical. We cannot take them seriously as genuine questions because of the whole set of intuitions which surround our affirmation of the right to life. We assert this right because human life has a certain worth; but exactly wherein it has worth is negated by the appalling conditions I am offering you. That is why the offer is a sick joke, the lines of the mad scientist in a B movie.

It is the mad scientist's question, and not the question whether the person in the coma still enjoys rights, which should be decisive for the issue of whether asserting rights involves affirming the worth of certain capacities. For the latter question just probes the conditions of a right being valid; whereas the former shows us what it is to respect a right and hence what is really being asserted in a rights claim. It enables us to see what else we are committed to in asserting a right.

How would it do for the scientist to say, 'Well, I have respected his right to *life*, it is other rights (free movement, exercise of his profession, etc.) which I have violated'? For the separation in this context is absurd. True, we do sometimes enumerate these and other rights. But the right to life could never have been understood as excluding all these activities, as a right just to biological non-death in a coma. It is incomprehensible how anyone could assert a right to life meaning just this. 'Who calls that living?' would be the standard reaction. We could understand such an exiguous definition of life in the context of forensic medicine, for instance, but not in the affirmation of a right to life. And this is because the right-assertion is also an affirmation of worth, and this would be incomprehensible on behalf of this shadow of life.

If these arguments are valid, then the terms of the arguments are very different from what they are seen to be by most believers in the primacy of rights. Nozick, for instance, seems to feel that he can start from our intuitions that people have certain rights to dispose, say, of what they own so long as they harm no one else in doing so; and that we can build up (or fail to build up) a case for legitimate allegiance to certain forms of society and/or authority from this basis, by showing how they do not violate the rights. But he does not recognize that asserting rights itself involves acknowledging an obligation to belong. If the above considerations are valid, one cannot just baldly start with such an assertion of primacy. We would have to show that the relevant potentially mediating social theses are not valid; or, in other terms, we would have to defend a thesis of social atomism, that men are self-sufficient outside of society. We would have to establish the validity of arguing from the primacy of right.

But we can still try to resist this conclusion, in two ways. We can resist it first of all in asserting a certain schedule of rights. Suppose I make the basic right I assert that to life, on the grounds of sentience. This I understand in the broad sense that includes also other animals. Now sentience, as was said above, is not a capacity which can be realized or remain undeveloped; living things have it, and in dying they fail to have it; and there

is an end to it. This is not to say that there are not conditions
of severe impairment which constitute an infringement on sentient life, short of death. And clearly a right to life based on sentience would rule out accepting the mad scientist's offer just as
much as any other conception of this right. But sentient life,
while it can be impaired, is not a potential which we must
develop and frequently fail to develop, as is the capacity to
be a morally autonomous agent, or the capacity for self-
determining freedom, or the capacity for the full realization of
our talents.

But if we are not dealing with a capacity which can be
underdeveloped in this sense, then there is no room for a thesis
about the conditions of its development, whether social or otherwise. No social thesis is relevant. We are sentient beings
whatever the social organization (or lack of it) of our existence;
and if our basic right is to life, and the grounds of this right concern sentience (being capable of self-feeling, of desire and its
satisfaction/frustration, of experiencing pain and pleasure),
then surely we are beings of this kind in any society or none. In
this regard we are surely self-sufficient.

I am not sure that even this is true—that is, that we really are
self-sufficient even in regard to sentience. But it certainly is
widely thought likely that we are. And therefore it is not surprising that the turn to theories of the primacy of rights goes along
with an accentuation of the right to life which stresses life as
sentience. For Hobbes our attachment to life is our desire to go
on being agents of desire. The connection is not hard to understand. Social theories require a conception of the properly
human life which is such that we are not assured it by simply
being alive, but it must be developed and it can fail to be
developed; on this basis they can argue that society or a certain
form of society is the essential condition of this development.
But Hobbesian nominalism involves rejecting utterly all such
talk of forms or qualities of life which are properly human. Man
is a being with desires, all of them on the same level. 'What-
soever is the object of any man's desire . . . that is it which he
for his part calleth good.'[4] At one stroke there is no further

<hr />

[4] T. Hobbes, *Leviathan*, pt. 1, ch. 6.

room for a social thesis; and at the same time the right to life is interpreted in terms of desire. To be alive now in the meaning of the act is to be an agent of desires.

So we can escape the whole argument about self-sufficiency, it would seem, by making our schedule of rights sparse enough. Primacy-of-rights talk tends to go with a tough-mindedness which dismisses discussion of the properly human life-form as empty and metaphysical. From within its philosophical position, it is impregnable; but this does not mean that it is not still open to objection.

For the impregnability is purchased at a high price. To affirm a right for man merely *qua* desiring being, or a being feeling pleasure and pain, is to restrict his rights to those of life, desire-fulfilment, and freedom and pain. Other widely claimed rights, like freedom, enter only as means to these basic ones. If one is a monster of (at least attempted) consistency, like Hobbes, then one will be willing to stick to this exiguous conception of rights regardless of the consequences. But even then the question will arise of what on this view is the value of human as against animal life; and of whether it really is not a violation of people's rights if we transform them, unknown to themselves, into child-like lotus-eaters, say, by injecting them with some drug.

In fact, most of those who want to affirm the primacy of rights are more interested in asserting the right of freedom, and moreover, in a sense which can only be attributed to humans, freedom to choose life plans, to dispose of possessions, to form one's own convictions and within reason act on them, and so on. But then we are dealing with capacities which do not simply belong to us in virtue of being alive—capacities which at least in some cases can fail to be properly developed; thus, the question of the proper conditions for their development arises.

We might query whether this is so with one of the freedoms mentioned above—that to dispose of one's own possessions. This is the right to property which has figured prominently with the right to life in the schedules put forward by defenders of primacy. Surely this right, while not something we can attribute to an animal, does not presuppose a capacity which could fail to be developed, at least for normal adults! We all are capable of possessing things, of knowing what we possess, and of deciding what we want to do with these possessions. This right does not seem to presuppose a capacity needing development, as does the right to profess independent convictions, for instance.

But those who assert this right almost always are affirming a capacity which we can fail to develop. And this becomes evident when we probe the reason for asserting this right. The standard answer, which comes to us from Locke, is that we need the right to property as an essential underpinning of life. But this is patently not true. Men have survived very well in communal societies all the way from paleolithic hunting clans through the Inca empire to contemporary China. And if one protests that the issue is not under what conditions one would not starve to death, but rather under what conditions one is independent enough of society not to be at its mercy for one's life, then the answer is that, if the whole point is being secure in my life, then I would be at less risk of death from agents of my own society in the contemporary Chinese commune than I would be in contemporary Chile. The property regime is hardly the only relevant variable.

But the real point is this: supposing a proponent of the right to property were to admit that the above was true—that the right to property does not as such secure life—would he change his mind? And the answer is, in the vast majority of cases, no. For what is at stake for him is not just life, but life in freedom. My life is safe in a Chinese commune, he might agree, but that is so only for so long as I keep quiet and do not profess heterodox opinions; otherwise the risks are very great. Private property is seen as essential, because it is thought to be an essential part of a life of genuine independence. But realizing a life of this form involves developing the capacity to act and choose in a genuinely independent way. And here the issue of whether a relevant social thesis is not valid can arise.

Hence this way of resisting the necessity of arguing for self-sufficiency (by scaling down one's schedules of rights to mere sentience or desire) is hardly likely to appeal to most proponents of primacy—once they understand the price they pay. For it involves sacrificing the central good of freedom, which it is their principal motive to safeguard.

There remains another way of avoiding the issue. A proponent of primacy could admit that the question arises of the conditions for the development of the relevant capacities; he could even agree that a human being entirely alone could not possibly develop them (this is pretty hard to contest: wolf-boys are not candidates for properly human freedoms), and yet argue that society in the relevant sense was not necessary.

Certainly humans need others in order to develop as full human beings, he would agree. We must all be nurtured by others as children. We can only flourish as adults in relationship with friends, mates, children, and so on. But all this has nothing to do with any obligations to belong to political society. The argument about the state of nature should never have been taken as applying to human beings alone in the wilderness. This is a Rousseauian gloss, but is clearly not the conception of the state of nature with Locke, for instance. Rather it is clear that men must live in families (however families are constituted); that they need families even to grow up human; and that they continue to need them to express an important part of their humanity.

But what obligations to belong does this put on them? It gives us obligations in regard to our parents. But these are obligations of gratitude, and are of a different kind; for when we are ready to discharge these obligations our parents are no longer essential conditions of our human development. The corresponding obligations are to our children, to give them what we have been given; and for the rest we owe a debt to those with whom we are linked in marriage, friendship, association, and the like. But all this is perfectly acceptable to a proponent of the primacy of rights. For all obligations to other adults are freely taken on in contracting marriage, friendships, and the like; there is no natural obligation to belong. The only involuntary associations are those between generations: our obligations to our parents and those to our children (if we can think of these as involuntary associations, since no one picks his children in the process of natural generation). But these are obligations to specific people and do not necessarily involve continuing associations; and they are neither of them cases where the obligation arises in the way it does in the social thesis, that is that we must maintain the association as a condition of our continued development.

Hence we can accommodate whatever is valid in the social thesis without any danger to the primacy of rights. Family obligations and obligations of friendship can be kept separate from any obligations to belong.

I do not think that this argument will hold. But I cannot really undertake to refute it here, not just on the usual cowardly grounds of lack of space, but because we enter here precisely on the central issue of the human condition which divides atomism from social theories. And this issue concerning as it does the human condition cannot be settled in a knockdown argument. My aim in this paper was just to show that it is an issue, and therefore has to be addressed by proponents of primacy. For this purpose I would like to lay out some considerations to which I subscribe, but of which I can do more than sketch an outline in these pages.

The kind of freedom valued by the protagonists of the primacy of rights, and indeed by many others of us as well, is a freedom by which men are capable of conceiving alternatives and arriving at a definition of what they really want, as well as discerning what commands their adherence or their allegiance. This kind of freedom is unavailable to one whose sympathies and horizons are so narrow that he can conceive only one way of life, for whom indeed the very notion of a way of life which is *his* as against everyone's has no sense. Nor is it available to one who is riveted by fear of the unknown to one familiar lifeform, or who has been so formed in suspicion and hate of outsiders that he can never put himself in their place. Moreover, this capacity to conceive alternatives must not only be available for the less important choices of one's life. The greatest bigot or the narrowest xenophobe can ponder whether to have Dover sole or Wiener schnitzel for dinner. What is truly important is that one be able to exercise autonomy in the basic issues of life, in one's most important commitments.

Now, it is very dubious whether the developed capacity for this kind of autonomy can arise simply within the family. Of course, men may learn, and perhaps in part must learn, this from those close to them. But my question is whether this kind of capacity can develop within the compass of a single family. Surely it is something which only develops within an entire civilization. Think of the developments of art, philosophy, theology, science, of the evolving practices of politics and social organization, which have contributed to the historic birth of this aspiration to freedom, to making this ideal of autonomy a comprehensible goal men can aim at—something which is in their universe of potential aspiration (and it is not yet so for all men, and may never be).

But this civilization was not only necessary for the genesis of freedom. How could successive generations discover what it is to be an autonomous agent, to have one's own way of feeling, of acting, of expression, which cannot be simply derived from authoritative models? This is an identity, a way of understanding themselves, which men are not born with. They have to acquire it. And they do not in every society; nor do they all successfully come to terms with it in ours. But how can they acquire it unless it is implicit in at least some of their common practices, in the ways that they recognize and treat each other in their common life (for instance, in the acknowledgement of certain rights), or in the manner in which they deliberate with or address each other, or engage in economic exchange, or in some mode of public recognition of individuality and the worth of autonomy?

Thus we live in a world in which there is such a thing as public debate about moral and political questions and other basic issues. We constantly forget how remarkable that is, how it did not have to be so, and may one day no longer be so. What would happen to our capacity to be free agents if this debate should die away, or if the more specialized debate among intellectuals who attempt to define and clarify the alternatives facing us should also cease, or if the attempts to bring the culture of the past to life again as well as the drives to cultural innovation were to fall off? What would there be left to choose between? And if the atrophy went beyond a certain point, could we speak of choice at all? How long would we go on understanding what autonomous choice was? Again, what would happen if our legal culture were not constantly sustained by a contact with our traditions of the rule of law and a confrontation with our contemporary moral institutions? Would we have as sure a grasp of what the rule of law and the defence of rights required?

In other words, the free individual or autonomous moral agent can only achieve and maintain his identity in a certain type of culture, some of whose facets and activities I have briefly referred to. But these and others of the same significance do not come into existence spontaneously each successive instant. They are carried on in institutions and associations which require stability and continuity and frequently also support from society as a whole—almost always the moral support of being commonly recognized as important, but frequently also considerable material support. These bearers of our culture include museums, symphony orchestras, universities, laboratories, political parties, law courts, representative assemblies, newspapers, publishing houses, television stations, and so on. And I have to mention also the mundane elements of infrastructure without which we could not carry on these higher activities: buildings, railroads, sewage plants, power grids, and so on. Thus requirement of a living and varied culture is also the requirement of a complex and integrated society, which is willing and able to support all these institutions.[5]

I am arguing that the free individual of the West is only what he is by virtue of the whole society and civilization which brought him to be and which nourishes him; that our families can only form us up to this capacity and these aspirations because they are set in this civilization; and that a family alone outside of this context—the real old patriarchal family—was a quite different animal which never tended these horizons. And I want to claim finally that all this creates a significant obligation to belong for whoever would affirm the value of this freedom;

[5] This is what makes so paradoxical the position of someone like Robert Nozick. He presents (*Anarchy, State and Utopia*, particularly ch. 10) the model of an ideal society where within the framework of the minimal state individuals form or join only those associations which they desire and which will admit them. There is no requirement laid down concerning the overall pattern that will result from this. But can we really do without this? The aim of Nozick's utopian framework is to enable people to give expression to their real diversity. But what if the essential cultural activities which make a great diversity conceivable to people begin to falter? Or are we somehow guaranteed against this? Nozick does not discuss this; it is as though the conditions of a creative, diversifying freedom were given by nature. In this respect the standard utopian literature, which as Nozick says is concerned with the character of the ideal community and not just with a framework for any community, is more realistic. For it faces the question of what kind of community we need in order to be free men, and then goes on to assume that this is given non-coercively.

this includes all those who want to assert rights either to this freedom or for its sake.

One could answer this by saying that the role of my civilization in forming me is a thing of the past; that, once adult, I have the capacity to be an autonomous being; and that I have no further obligation arising out of the exigencies of my development to sustain this civilization. I doubt whether this is in fact true; I doubt whether we could maintain our sense of ourselves as autonomous beings or whether even only a heroic few of us would succeed in doing so, if this liberal civilization of ours were to be thoroughly destroyed. I hope never to have to make the experiment. But even if we could, the considerations advanced a few pages back would be sufficient here: future generations will need this civilization to reach these aspirations; and if we affirm their worth, we have an obligation to make them available to others. This obligation is only increased if we ourselves have benefited from this civilization and have been enabled to become free agents ourselves.

But then the proponent of primacy could answer by questioning what all this has to do with political authority, with the obligation to belong to a polity or to abide by the rules of a political society. Certainly, we could accept that we are only what we are in virtue of living in a civilization and hence in a large society, since a family or clan could not sustain this. But this does not mean that we must accept allegiance to a polity.

To this there are two responses. First, there is something persuasive about this objection in that it seems to hold out the alternative of an anarchist civilization—one where we have all the benefits of wide association and none of the pains of politics. And indeed, some libertarians come close to espousing an anarchist position and express sympathy for anarchism, as does Nozick. Now it is perfectly true that there is nothing in principle which excludes anarchism in the reflection that we owe our identity as free men to our civilization. But the point is that the commitment we recognize in affirming the worth of this freedom is a commitment to this civilization whatever are the conditions of its survival. If these can be assured in conditions of anarchy, that is very fortunate. But if they can only be assured under some form of representative government to which we all would have to give allegiance, then this is the society we ought to try to create and sustain and belong to. For this is by hypothesis the condition of what we have identified as a crucial human good, by the very fact of affirming this right. (I have, of course, taken as evident that this civilization could not be assured by some tyrannical form of government, because the civilization I am talking about is that which is the essential milieu for free agency.)

The crucial point here is this: since the free individual can only maintain his identity within a society/culture of a certain kind, he has to be concerned about the shape of this society/culture as a whole. He cannot, following the libertarian anarchist model that Nozick sketched,[6] be concerned purely with his individual choices and the associations formed from such choices to the neglect of the matrix in which such choices can be open or closed, rich or meagre. It is important to him that certain activities and institutions flourish in society. It is even of importance to him what the moral tone of the whole society is—shocking as it may be to libertarians to raise this issue— because freedom and individual diversity can only flourish in a society where there is a general recognition of their worth. They are threatened by the spread of bigotry, but also by other conceptions of life—for example, those which look on originality, innovation, and diversity as luxuries which society can ill afford given the need for efficiency, productivity, or growth, or those which in a host of other ways depreciate freedom.

Now, it is possible that a society and culture propitious for freedom might arise from the spontaneous association of anarchist communes. But it seems much more likely from the historical record that we need rather some species of political society. And if this is so then we must acknowledge an obligation to belong to this kind of society in affirming freedom. But there is more. If realizing our freedom partly depends on the society and culture in which we live, then we exercise a fuller freedom if we can help determine the shape of this society and culture. And this we can only do through instruments of common decision. This means that the political institutions in which we live may themselves be a crucial part of what is necessary to realize our identity as free beings.

This is the second answer to the last objection. In fact, men's

---

[6] Ibid., ch. 10.

deliberating together about what will be binding on all of them is an essential part of the exercise of freedom. It is only in this way that they can come to grips with certain basic issues in a way which will actually have an effect in their lives. Those issues, which can only be effectively decided by society as a whole and which often set the boundary and framework for our lives, can indeed be discussed freely by politically irresponsible indivi- duals wherever they have licence to do so. But they can only be truly *deliberated* about politically. A society in which such deliberation was public and involved everyone would realize a freedom not available anywhere else or in any other mode.

Thus, always granted that an anarchist society is not an available option, it is hard to see how one can affirm the worth of freedom in this sense of the exercise of autonomous delibera- tion and at the same time recognize no obligation to bring about and sustain a political order of this kind.

The argument has gone far enough to show how difficult it is to conclude here. This is because we are on a terrain in which our conception of freedom touches on the issue of the nature of the human subject, and the degree and manner in which this subject is a social one. To open this up is to open the issue of atomism, which is all I hoped to do in this paper. I wanted to show that there is an issue in the 'self-sufficiency' or not of man outside political society and that this issue cannot be side- stepped by those who argue from natural rights. This issue, as we can see, leads us very deep, and perhaps we can see some of the motivation of those who have waited to side-step it. It seems much easier and clearer to remain on the level of our intuitions about rights.

For we can now see more clearly what the issue about atomism is, and how uncommonly difficult it is. It concerns self-suffi- ciency, but not in the sense of the ability to survive north of Great Slave Lake. That is a question whether we can fulfil certain causal conditions for our continued existence. But the alleged social conditions for the full development of our human capacities are not causal in the same sense. They open another set of issues altogether: whether the condition for the full devel- opment of our capacities is not that we achieve a certain identity, which requires a certain conception of ourselves; and more fundamentally whether this identity is ever something we can attain on our own, or whether the crucial modes of self-understanding are not always created and sustained by the common expression and recognition they receive in the life of the society.

Thus the thesis just sketched about the social conditions of freedom is based on the notion, first, that developed freedom requires a certain understanding of self, one in which the aspirations to autonomy and self-direction become conceivable; and, second, that this self-understanding is not something we can sustain on our own, but that our identity is always partly defined in conversation with others or through the common understanding which underlies the practices of our society. The thesis is that the identity of the autonomous, self-determining individual requires a social matrix, one, for instance, which through a series of practices recognizes the right to autonomous decision and which calls for the individual having a voice in deliberation about public action.

The issue between the atomists and their opponents therefore goes deep; it touches the nature of freedom, and beyond this what it is to be a human subject; what is human identity, and how it is defined and sustained. It is not surprising therefore that the two sides talk past each other. For atomists the talk about identity and its conditions in social practice seems impossibly abstruse and speculative. They would rather found themselves on the clear and distinct intuition which we all share (all of us in this society, that is) about human rights.

For non-atomists, however, this very confidence in their starting-point is a kind of blindness, a delusion of self-sufficiency which prevents them from seeing that the free individual, the bearer of rights, can only assume this identity thanks to his relationship to a developed liberal civilization; that there is an absurdity in placing this subject in a state of nature where he could never attain this identity and hence never create by contract a society which respects it. Rather, the free individual who affirms himself as such *already* has an obligation to complete, restore, or sustain the society within which this identity is possible.

It is clear that we can only join this issue by opening up questions about the nature of man. But it is also clear that the two sides are not on the same footing in relationship to these questions. Atomists are more comfortable standing with the intuitions of common sense about the rights of individuals and are not at all keen to open these wider issues. And in this they derive support in those philosophical traditions which come to us from the seventeenth century and which started with the postulation of an extensionless subject, epistemologically a *tabula rasa* and politically a presuppositionless bearer of rights. It is not an accident that these epistemological and political doctrines are often found in the writings of the same founding figures.

But if this starting-point no longer appears to us self-evident, then we have to open up questions about the nature of the subject and the conditions of human agency. Among these is the issue about atomism. This is important for any theory of rights, but also for a great deal else besides. For the issue about atomism also underlies many of our discussions about obligation and the nature of freedom, as can already be sensed from the above. That is why it is useful to put it again on our agenda.

3

JUSTICE AS A VIRTUE: CHANGING CONCEPTIONS

ALASDAIR MACINTYRE

When Aristotle praised justice as the first virtue of political life, he did so in such a way as to suggest that a community which lacks practical agreement on a conception of justice must also lack the necessary basis for political community. But the lack of such a basis must therefore threaten our own society. For the outcome of that history [. . .] has not only been an inability to agree upon a catalogue of the virtues and an even more fundamental inability to agree upon the relative importance of the virtue concepts within a moral scheme in which notions of rights and of utility also have a key place. It has also been an inability to agree upon the content and character of particular virtues. For, since a virtue is now generally understood as a disposition or sentiment which will produce in us obedience to certain rules, agreement on what the relevant rules are to be is always a prerequisite for agreement upon the nature and content of a particular virtue. But this prior agreement in rules is [. . .] something which our individualist culture is unable to secure. Nowhere is this more marked and nowhere are the consequences more threatening than in the case of justice. Everyday life is pervaded by them and basic controversies cannot therefore be rationally resolved. Consider one such controversy, endemic in the politics of the United States today—I present it in the form of a debate between two ideal-typical characters unimaginatively named *A* and *B*.

A, who may own a store or be a police officer or a construction worker, has struggled to save enough from his earnings to buy a small house, to send his children to the local college, to pay

Alasdair MacIntyre, excerpts from *After Virtue*, 244–55. Reprinted by permission of Gerald Duckworth & Co. Ltd.

for some special type of medical care for his parents. He now finds all of his projects threatened by rising taxes. He regards this threat to his projects as *unjust*; he claims to have a right to what he has earned and that nobody else has a right to take away what he acquired legitimately and to which he has a just title. He intends to vote for candidates for political office who will defend his property, his projects, *and* his conception of justice.

B, who may be a member of one of the liberal professions, or a social worker, or someone with inherited wealth, is impressed with the arbitrariness of the inequalities in the distribution of wealth, income, and opportunity. He is, if anything, even more impressed with the inability of the poor and the deprived to do very much about their own condition as a result of inequalities in the distribution of power. He regards both these types of inequality as *unjust* and as constantly engendering further injustice. He believes more generally that all inequality stands in need of justification and that the only possible justification for inequality is to improve the condition of the poor and the deprived—by, for example, fostering economic growth. He draws the conclusion that in present circumstances redistributive taxation which will finance welfare and the social services is what justice demands. He intends to vote for candidates for political office who will defend redistributive taxation *and* his conception of justice.

It is clear that in the actual circumstances of our social and political order *A* and *B* are going to disagree about policies and politicians. But *must* they so disagree? The answer seems to be that under certain types of economic condition their disagreement need not manifest itself at the level of political conflict. If *A* and *B* belong to a society where economic resources are such, or are at least believed to be such, that *B*'s public redistributive projects can be carried through at least to a certain point without threatening *A*'s private life-plan projects, *A* and *B* might for some time vote for the same politicians and policies. Indeed they might on occasion be one and the same person. But if it is, or comes to be, the case that economic circumstances are such that either *A*'s projects must be sacrificed to *B*'s or vice versa, it at once becomes clear that *A* and *B* have views of justice which are not only logically incompatible with each other but which [. . .]

invoke considerations which are incommensurable with those advanced by the adversary party.

The logical incompatibility is not difficult to identify. A holds that principles of just acquisition and entitlement set limits to redistributive possibilities. If the outcome of the application of the principles of just acquisition and entitlement is gross inequality, the toleration of such inequality is a price that has to be paid for justice. B holds that principles of just distribution set limits to legitimate acquisition and entitlement. If the outcome of the application of the principles of just distribution is interference—by means of taxation or such devices as eminent domain—with what has up till now been regarded in this social order as legitimate acquisition and entitlement, the toleration of such interference is a price that has to be paid for justice. We may note in passing—it will not be unimportant later—that in the case of both A's principle and B's principle the price for one person or group of persons receiving justice is always paid by someone else. Thus different identifiable social groups have an interest in the acceptance of one of the principles and the rejection of the other. Neither principle is socially or politically neutral.

Moreover it is not simply that A and B advance principles which produce incompatible practical conclusions. The type of concept in terms of which each frames his claim is so different from that of the other that the question of how and whether the dispute between them may be rationally settled begins to pose difficulties. For A aspires to ground the notion of justice in some account of what and how a given person is entitled to in virtue of what he has acquired and earned; B aspires to ground the notion of justice in some account of the equality of the claims of each person in respect of basic needs and of the means to meet such needs. Confronted by a given piece of property or resource, A will be apt to claim that it is justly his because he owns it—he acquired it legitimately, he earned it; B will be apt to claim that it justly ought to be someone else's, because they need it much more, and if they do not have it, their basic needs will not be met. But our pluralist culture possesses no method of weighing, no rational criterion for deciding between claims based on legitimate entitlement against claims based on need. Thus these two types of claim are indeed, as I suggested, incommensurable, and the metaphor of 'weighing' moral claims is not just inappropriate but misleading.

It is at this point that recent analytical moral philosophy makes important claims. For it aspires to provide rational principles to which appeal may be made by contending parties with conflicting interests. And the two most distinguished recent attempts to carry through this project have a special relevance for the argument between A and B. For Robert Nozick's account of justice is at least to some large degree a rational articulation of key elements in A's position, while John Rawls's account is in the same way a rational articulation of key elements in B's position.[1] Thus, if the philosophical considerations which either Rawls or Nozick urge upon us turn out to be rationally compelling, the argument between A and B will have been rationally settled one way or another and my own characterization of the dispute will in consequence turn out to be quite false.

I begin with Rawls's account. Rawls argues that the principles of justice are those which would be chosen by a rational agent 'situated behind a veil of ignorance'[2] such that he does not know what place in society he will occupy—that is, what his class or status will be, what talents and ability he will possess, what his conception of the good or his aims in life will be, what his temperament will be or what kind of economic, political, cultural, or social order he will inhabit. Rawls argues that any rational agent so situated will define a just distribution of goods in *any* social order in terms of two principles and a rule for allocating priorities when the two principles conflict.

The first principle is: 'Each person is to have an equal right to the most extensive total system of equal basic liberties compatible with a similar system of liberty for all.' The second principle is: 'Social and economic inequalities are to be arranged so that they are both (a) to the greatest benefit of the least advantaged, consistent with the joint savings principle [the joint savings principle provides for fair investment in the interests of future generations], and (b) attached to offices and parties open

[1] R. Nozick, *Anarchy, State and Utopia* (Cambridge, Mass., 1974); J. Rawls, *A Theory of Justice* (Cambridge, Mass., 1971).
[2] Rawls, *A Theory of Justice*, p. 136.

to all under conditions of fair equality of opportunity.'[3] The first principle has priority over the second; liberty is to be restricted only for the sake of liberty. And justice generally has priority over efficiency. So Rawls arrives at his general conception: 'All social primary goods—liberty and opportunity, income and wealth, and the bases of self-respect—are to be distributed equally unless an unequal distribution of any or all of these goods is to the advantage of the least favored.'[4]

Many critics of Rawls have focused their attention on the ways in which Rawls derives his principles of justice from his statement of the initial position of the rational agent 'situated behind a veil of ignorance'. Such critics have made a number of telling points, but I do not intend to dwell on them, if only because I take it not only that a rational agent in *some such* situation as that of the veil of ignorance would indeed choose *some such* principles of justice as Rawls claims, but also that it is *only* a rational agent in such a situation who would choose such principles. Later in my argument this point will become important. For the moment however I shall put it on one side in order to turn to a characterization of Nozick's view.

Nozick claims that 'if the world were wholly just'[5] the only people entitled to hold anything, that is to appropriate it for use as they and they alone wished, would be those who had justly acquired what they held by some just act of original acquisition and those who had justly acquired what they held by some just act of transfer from someone else who had either acquired it by some just act of original acquisition or by some just transfer . . . and so on. In other words, the justifiable answer to the question 'Why are you entitled to use that seashell as you wish?' will either be 'I picked it up on the seashore, where it belonged to no one and where there were plenty left for everyone else' (a just act of original acquisition), *or* 'Someone else picked it up at the seashore and freely sold or gave it to someone . . . to someone . . . who freely sold or gave it to me' (a series of just acts of transfer). It follows from Nozick's view as he himself immediately notes that: 'The complete principle of distributive justice

---

[3] Ibid. 302.
[4] Ibid. 303.
[5] Nozick, *Anarchy, State and Utopia*, 151.

would say simply that a distribution is just if everyone is entitled to the holdings that they possess under the distribution.'[6]

Nozick derives these conclusions from premises about the inalienable rights of each individual, premises for which he does not himself offer arguments. As in the case of Rawls, I do not want to quarrel with Nozick's derivation of his principles from his premises; once again I shall want to stress instead that it is *only* from some such premises that such principles could be rationally derived. That is to say, in the case of both Nozick's account of justice and Rawls's account of justice the problems that I want to raise do not concern the coherence of the internal structure of their arguments. Indeed my own argument requires that their accounts do not lack such coherence.

What I want to argue is threefold: first, that the incompatibility of Rawls's and Nozick's accounts does up to a point genuinely mirror the incompatibility of A's position with B's, and that to this extent at least Rawls and Nozick successfully articulate at the level of moral philosophy the disagreement between such ordinary non-philosophical citizens as A and B; but that Rawls and Nozick also reproduce the very same type of incompatibility and incommensurability at the level of philosophical argument that made A's and B's debate unsettlable at the level of social conflict; and, secondly, that there is none the less an element in the position of both A and B which neither Rawls's account nor Nozick's captures, an element which survives from that older classical tradition in which the virtues were central. When we reflect on both these points, a third emerges: namely, that in their conjunction we have an important clue to the social presuppositions which Rawls and Nozick to some degree share.

Rawls makes primary what is in effect a principle of equality with respect to needs. His conception of 'the worst off' sector of the community is a conception of those whose needs are gravest in respect of income, wealth, and other goods. Nozick makes primary what is a principle of equality with respect to entitlement. For Rawls how those who are now in grave need come to be in grave need is irrelevant; justice is made into a matter of present patterns of distribution to which the past is irrelevant.

[6] Ibid. 153.

For Nozick only evidence about what has been legitimately acquired in the past is relevant; present patterns of distribution in themselves must be irrelevant to *justice* (although not perhaps to kindness or generosity). To say even this much makes it clear how close Rawls is to B and how close Nozick is to A. For A appealed against distributive canons to a justice of entitlement, and B appealed against canons of entitlement to a justice which regards needs. Yet it is also at once clear not only that Rawls's priorities are incompatible with Nozick's in a way parallel to that in which B's position is incompatible with A's, but also that Rawls's position is incommensurable with Nozick's in a way similarly parallel to that in which B's is incommensurable with A's. For how can a claim that gives priority to equality of needs be rationally weighed against one which gives priority to entitlements? If Rawls were to argue that anyone *behind the veil of ignorance*, who knew neither whether and how his needs would be met nor what his entitlements would be, ought rationally to prefer a principle which respects needs to one which respects entitlements, invoking perhaps principles of rational decision theory to do so, the immediate answer must be not only that *we* are *never* behind such a veil of ignorance, but also that this leaves unimpugned Nozick's premiss about inalienable rights. And if Nozick were to argue that any distributive principle, if enforced, could violate a freedom to which every one of us is entitled—as he does indeed argue—the immediate answer must be that in so interpreting the inviolability of basic rights he begs the question in favour of his own argument and leaves unimpugned Rawls's premisses.

None the less there is something important, if negative, which Rawls's account shares with Nozick's. Neither of them make any reference to *desert* in their account of justice, nor could they consistently do so. And yet both A and B did make such a reference—and it is imperative here to notice that 'A' and 'B' are not the names of mere arbitrary constructions of my own; their arguments faithfully reproduce, for example, a good deal of what was actually said in recent fiscal debates in California, New Jersey, and elsewhere. What A complains of on his own behalf is not merely that he is entitled to what he has earned, but that he *deserves* it in virtue of his life of hard work; what B complains of on behalf of the poor and deprived is that their poverty and deprivation is *undeserved* and therefore unwarranted. And it seems clear that in the case of the real-life counterparts of *A* and *B* it is the reference to desert which makes them feel strongly that what they are complaining about is injustice, rather than some other kind of wrong or harm.

Neither Rawls's account nor Nozick's allows this central place, or indeed any kind of place, for desert in claims about justice and injustice. Rawls allows that common-sense views of justice connect it with desert,[7] but argues, first, that we do not know what anyone deserves until we have already formulated the rules of justice (and hence we cannot base our understanding of justice upon desert), and, secondly, that when we have formulated the rules of justice it turns out that it is not desert that is in question anyway, but only legitimate expectations. He also argues that to attempt to apply notions of desert would be impracticable—the ghost of Hume walks in his pages at this point.

Nozick is less explicit, but his scheme of justice being based exclusively on entitlements can allow no place for desert. He does at one point discuss the possibility of a principle for the rectification of injustice, but what he writes on that point is so tentative and cryptic that it affords no guidance for amending his general viewpoint. It is in any case clear that for both Nozick and Rawls a society is composed of individuals, each with his or her own interest, who then have to come together and formulate common rules of life. In Nozick's case there is the additional negative constraint of a set of basic rights. In Rawls's case the only constraints are those that a prudent rationality would impose. Individuals are thus in both accounts primary and society secondary, and the identification of individual interests is prior to, and independent of, the construction of any moral or social bonds between them. But we have already seen that the notion of desert is at home only in the context of a community whose primary bond is a shared understanding both of the good for man and of the good of that community and where individuals identify their primary interests with reference to those goods. Rawls explicitly makes it a presupposition of his view that we must expect to disagree with others about what the good life

---

[7] Rawls, *A Theory of Justice*, 310.

for man is and must therefore exclude any understanding of it that we may have from our formulation of the principles of justice. Only those goods in which everyone, whatever their view of the good life, takes an interest are to be admitted to consideration. In Nozick's argument, too, the concept of community required for the notion of desert to have application is simply absent. To understand this is to clarify two further points.

The first concerns the shared social presuppositions of Rawls and Nozick. It is, from both standpoints, as though we had been shipwrecked on an uninhabited island with a group of other individuals, each of whom is a stranger to me and to all the others. What have to be worked out are rules which will safeguard each one of us maximally in such a situation. Nozick's premiss concerning rights introduces a strong set of constraints; we do know that certain types of interference with each other are absolutely prohibited. But there is a limit to the bonds between us, a limit set by our private and competing interests. This individualistic view has of course, as I noticed earlier, a distinguished ancestry: Hobbes, Locke (whose views Nozick treats with great respect), Machiavelli, and others. And it contains within itself a certain note of realism about modern society; modern society is indeed often, at least in surface appearance, nothing but a collection of strangers, each pursuing his or her own interests under minimal constraints. We still of course, even in modern society, find it difficult to think of families, colleges, and other genuine communities in this way; but even our thinking about those is now invaded to an increasing degree by individualist conceptions, especially in the law courts. Thus Rawls and Nozick articulate with great power a shared view which envisages entry into social life as—at least ideally—the voluntary act of at least potentially rational individuals with prior interests who have to ask the question 'What kind of social contract with others is it reasonable for me to enter into?' Not surprisingly it is a consequence of this that their views exclude any account of human community in which the notion of desert in relation to contributions to the common tasks of that community in pursuing shared goods could provide the basis for judgements about virtue and injustice.

Desert is ruled out too in another way. I have remarked upon

60   ALASDAIR MACINTYRE

how Rawls's distributive principles exclude reference to the past
and so to claims to desert based on past actions and sufferings.
Nozick too excludes that of the past on which such claims might
be based, by making a concern for the legitimacy of entitlements
the sole ground for taking an interest in the past in connection
with justice. What makes this important is that Nozick's account
serves the interest of a particular mythology about the past
precisely by what it excludes from view. For central to Nozick's
account is the thesis that all legitimate entitlements can be traced
to legitimate acts of original acquisition. But, if that is so, there
are in fact very few, and in some large areas of the world *no*,
legitimate entitlements. The property-owners of the modern
world are not the legitimate heirs of Lockean individuals who
performed quasi-Lockean ('quasi' to allow for Nozick's emen-
dations of Locke) acts of original acquisition; they are the
inheritors of those who, for example, stole, and used violence
to steal, the common lands of England from the common people,
vast tracts of North America from the American Indian, much
of Ireland from the Irish, and Prussia from the original non-
German Prussians. This is the historical reality ideologically
concealed behind any Lockean thesis. The lack of any principle
of rectification is thus not a small side issue for a thesis such as
Nozick's; it tends to vitiate the theory as a whole—even if we
were to suppress the overwhelming objections to any belief in
inalienable human rights.

A and *B* differ from Rawls and Nozick at the price of inconsistency. Each of them in conjoining either Rawls's principles
or Nozick's with an appeal to desert exhibits an adherence to an
older, more traditional, more Aristotelian and Christian view of
justice. This inconsistency is thus a tribute to the residual power
and influence of the tradition, a power and influence with two
distinct sources. In the conceptual *melange* of moral thought and
practice today fragments from the tradition—virtue concepts
for the most part—are still found alongside characteristically
modern and individualist concepts such as those of rights or
utility. But the tradition also survives in a much less fragmented,
much less distorted form in the lives of certain communities
whose historical ties with their past remain strong. So the older
moral tradition is discernible in the United States and elsewhere
among, for example, some Catholic Irish, some Orthodox

Greeks, and some Jews of an Orthodox persuasion, all of them communities that inherit their moral tradition not only through their religion, but also from the structure of the peasant villages and households which their immediate ancestors inhabited on the margins of modern Europe. Moreover it would be wrong to conclude from the stress that I have laid on the medieval background that Protestantism did not in some areas become the bearer of this very same moral tradition; in Scotland, for example, Aristotle's *Nicomachean Ethics* and *Politics* were the secular moral texts in the universities, coexisting happily with a Calvinist theology which was often elsewhere hostile to them until 1690 and after. And there are today both black and white Protestant communities in the United States, especially perhaps those in or from the South, who will recognize in the tradition of the virtues a key part of their own cultural inheritance.

Even, however, in such communities the need to enter into public debate enforces participation in the cultural *melange* in the search for a common stock of concepts and norms which all may employ and to which all may appeal. Consequently the allegiance of such marginal communities to the tradition is constantly in danger of being eroded, and this in search of what, if my argument is correct, is a chimera. For what analysis of A's and B's position reveals once again is that we have all too many disparate and rival moral concepts, in this case rival and disparate concepts of justice, and that the moral resources of the culture allow us no way of settling the issue between them rationally. Moral philosophy, as it is dominantly understood, reflects the debates and disagreements of the culture so faithfully that its controversies turn out to be unsettlable in just the way that the political and moral debates themselves are.

It follows that our society cannot hope to achieve moral consensus. For quite non-Marxist reasons Marx was in the right when he argued against the English trade unionists of the 1860s that appeals to justice were pointless, since there are rival conceptions of justice formed by and informing the life of rival groups. Marx was of course mistaken in supposing that such disagreements over justice are merely secondary phenomena, that they merely reflect the interests of rival economic classes. Conceptions of justice and allegiance to such conceptions are partly constitutive of the lives of social groups, and economic interests are often partially defined in terms of such conceptions and not vice versa. None the less Marx was fundamentally right in seeing conflict and not consensus at the heart of modern social structure. It is not just that we live too much by a variety and multiplicity of fragmented concepts; it is that these are used at one and the same time to express rival and incompatible social ideals and policies *and* to furnish us with a pluralist political rhetoric whose function is to conceal the depth of our conflicts.

Important conclusions follow for constitutional theory. Liberal writers such as Ronald Dworkin invite us to see the Supreme Court's function as that of invoking a set of consistent principles, most and perhaps all of them of moral import, in the light of which particular laws and particular decisions are to be evaluated. Those who hold such a view are bound to consider certain decisions of the Supreme Court inadequate in the light of these supposed principles. The type of decision which I have in mind is exemplified by the Bakke case, where two, at first sight strongly incompatible, views were held by members of the court, and Mr Justice Powell, who wrote the decision, was the one justice to hold both views. But, if my argument is correct, one function of the Supreme Court must be to keep the peace between rival social groups adhering to rival and incompatible principles of justice by displaying a fairness which consists in even-handedness in its adjudications. So the Supreme Court in *Bakke* both forbade precise ethnic quotas for admission to colleges and universities, but allowed discrimination in favour of previously deprived minority groups. Try to conjure up a set of consistent principles behind such a decision and ingenuity may or may not allow you to find the court not guilty of formal inconsistency. But even to make such an attempt is to miss the point. The Supreme Court in *Bakke*, as on occasion in other cases, played the role of a peacemaking or truce-keeping body by negotiating its way through an impasse of conflict, not by invoking our shared moral first principles. For our society as a whole has none.

What this brings out is that modern politics cannot be a matter of genuine moral consensus. And it is not. Modern politics is civil war carried on by other means, and *Bakke* was an engagement whose antecedents were at Gettysburg and Shiloh. The truth on this matter was set out by Adam Ferguson: 'We are not to expect that the laws of any country are to be framed as so many lessons of morality. . . . Laws, whether civil or political, are expedients of policy to adjust the pretensions of parties, and to secure the peace of society. The expedient is accommodated to special circumstances . . .' (*Principles of Moral and Political Science*, ii. 144). The nature of any society, therefore, is not to be deciphered from its laws alone, but from those understood as an index of its conflicts. What our laws show is the extent and degree to which conflict has to be suppressed.

Yet, if this is so, another virtue too has been displaced. Patriotism cannot be what it was because we lack in the fullest sense a *patria*. The point that I am making must not be confused with the commonplace liberal rejection of patriotism. Liberals have often—not always—taken a negative or even hostile attitude towards patriotism, partly because their allegiance is to values which they take to be universal and not local and particular, and partly because of a well-justified suspicion that in the modern world patriotism is often a façade behind which chauvinism and imperialism are fostered. But my present point is not that patriotism is good or bad as a sentiment, but that the practice of patriotism as a virtue is in advanced societies no longer possible in the way that it once was. In any society where government does not express or represent the moral community of the citizens, but is instead a set of institutional arrangements for imposing a bureaucratized unity on a society which lacks genuine moral consensus, the nature of political obligation becomes systematically unclear. Patriotism is or was a virtue founded on attachment primarily to a political and moral community and only secondarily to the government of that community; but it is characteristically exercised in discharging responsibility to and in such government. When, however, the relationship of government to the moral community is put in question both by the changed nature of government and the lack of moral consensus in the society, it becomes difficult any longer to have any clear, simple, and teachable conception of patriotism. Loyalty to my country, to my community—which remains unalterably a central virtue—becomes detached from obedience to the government which happens to rule me.

Just as this understanding of the displacement of patriotism must not be confused with the liberal critique of moral

particularity, so this necessary distancing of the moral self from
the governments of modern states must not be confused with any
anarchist critique of the state. Nothing in my argument suggests, let alone implies, any good grounds for rejecting certain
forms of government as necessary and legitimate; what the argument does entail is that the modern state is not such a form of
government. It must have been clear from earlier parts of my
argument that the tradition of the virtues is at variance with central features of the modern economic order and more especially
its individualism, its acquisitiveness, and its elevation of the
values of the market to a central social place. It now becomes
clear that it also involves a rejection of the modern political
order. This does not mean that there are not many tasks only
to be performed in and through government which still require
performing: the rule of law, so far as it is possible in a modern
state, has to be vindicated, injustice and unwarranted suffering
have to be dealt with, generosity has to be exercised, and liberty
has to be defended, in ways that are sometimes only possible
through the use of governmental institutions. But each particular task, each particular responsibility, has to be evaluated
on its own merits. Modern systematic politics, whether liberal,
conservative, radical, or socialist, simply has to be rejected from
a standpoint that owes genuine allegiance to the tradition of the
virtues; for modern politics itself expresses in its institutional
forms a systematic rejection of that tradition.

4

MEMBERSHIP

MICHAEL WALZER

MEMBERS AND STRANGERS

The idea of distributive justice presupposes a bounded world within which distributions take place: a group of people committed to dividing, exchanging, and sharing social goods, first of all among themselves. That world [. . .] is the political community, whose members distribute power to one another and avoid, if they possibly can, sharing it with anyone else. When we think about distributive justice, we think about independent cities or countries capable of arranging their own patterns of division and exchange, justly or unjustly. We assume an established group and a fixed population, and so we miss the first and most important distributive question: How is that group constituted?

I don't mean, How *was* it constituted? I am concerned here, not with the historical origins of the different groups, but with the decisions they make in the present about their present and future populations. The primary good that we distribute to one another is membership in some human community. And what we do with regard to membership structures all our other distributive choices: it determines with whom we make those choices, from whom we require obedience and collect taxes, to whom we allocate goods and services.

Men and women without membership anywhere are stateless persons. That condition doesn't preclude every sort of distributive relation: markets, for example, are commonly open to all comers. But non-members are vulnerable and unprotected in the market-place. Although they participate freely in the exchange of goods, they have no part in those goods that are shared. They are cut off from the communal provision of security and welfare. Even those aspects of security and welfare that are, like public health, collectively distributed are not guaranteed to non-members: for they have no guaranteed place in the collectivity and are always liable to expulsion. Statelessness is a condition of infinite danger.

But membership and non-membership are not the only—or, for our purposes, the most important—set of possibilities. It is also possible to be a member of a poor or a rich country, to live in a densely crowded or a largely empty country, to be the subject of an authoritarian regime, or the citizen of a democracy. Since human beings are highly mobile, large numbers of men and women regularly attempt to change their residence and their membership, moving from unfavoured to favoured environments. Affluent and free countries are, like élite universities, besieged by applicants. They have to decide on their own size and character. More precisely, as citizens of such a country, we have to decide: Whom should we admit? Ought we to have open admissions? Can we choose among applicants? What are the appropriate criteria for distributing membership?

The plural pronouns that I have used in asking these questions suggest the conventional answer to them: we who are already members do the choosing, in accordance with our own understanding of what membership means in our community and of what sort of a community we want to have. Membership as a social good is constituted by our understanding; its value is fixed by our work and conversation; and then we are in charge (who else could be in charge?) of its distribution. But we don't distribute it among ourselves; it is already ours. We give it out to strangers. Hence the choice is also governed by our relationships with strangers—not only by our understanding of those relationships but also by the actual contacts, connections, alliances we have established and the effects we have had beyond our borders. But I shall focus first on strangers in the literal sense, men and women whom we meet, so to speak, for the first time. We don't know who they are or what they think, yet we recognize them as men and women. Like us but not of us: when we decide on membership, we have to consider them as well as ourselves.

I won't try to recount here the history of Western ideas about strangers. In a number of ancient languages, Latin among them, strangers and enemies were named by a single word. We have come only slowly, through a long process of trial and error, to distinguish the two and to acknowledge that, in certain circumstances, strangers (but not enemies) might be entitled to our hospitality, assistance, and good will. This acknowledgement can be formalized as the principle of mutual aid, which suggests the duties that we owe, as John Rawls has written, 'not only to definite individuals, say to those cooperating together in some social arrangement, but to persons generally'.[1] Mutual aid extends across political (and also cultural, religious, and linguistic) frontiers. The philosophical grounds of the principle are hard to specify (its history provides its practical ground). I doubt that Rawls is right to argue that we can establish it simply by imagining 'what a society would be like if this duty were rejected'[2]—for rejection is not an issue within any particular society; the issue arises only among people who don't share, or don't know themselves to share, a common life. People who do share a common life have much stronger duties.

It is the absence of any co-operative arrangements that sets the context for mutual aid: two strangers meet at sea or in the desert or, as in the Good Samaritan story, by the side of the road. What precisely they owe one another is by no means clear, but we commonly say of such cases that positive assistance is required if (1) it is needed or urgently needed by one of the parties; and (2) if the risks and costs of giving it are relatively low for the other party. Given these conditions, I ought to stop and help the injured stranger, wherever I meet him, whatever his membership or my own. This is our morality; conceivably his, too. It is, moreover, an obligation that can be read out in roughly the same form at the collective level. Groups of people

---

[1] J. Rawls, *A Theory of Justice* (Cambridge, Mass., 1971), 115. For a useful discussion of mutual aid as a possible right, see T. M. Benditt, *Rights* (Totowa, NJ, 1982), ch. 5.

[2] Rawls, *Theory of Justice*, p. 339.

ought to help necessitous strangers whom they somehow discover in their midst or on their path. But the limit on risks and costs in these cases is sharply drawn. I need not take the injured stranger into my home, except briefly, and I certainly need not care for him or even associate with him for the rest of my life. My life cannot be shaped and determined by such chance encounters. Governor John Winthrop, arguing against free immigration to the new Puritan commonwealth of Massachusetts, insisted that this right of refusal applies also to collective mutual aid: 'As for hospitality, that rule does not bind further than for some present occasion, not for continual residence.'[3] Whether Winthrop's view can be defended is a question that I shall come to only gradually. Here I only want to point to mutual aid as a (possible) external principle for the distribution of membership, a principle that doesn't depend upon the prevailing view of membership within a particular society. The force of the principle is uncertain, in part because of its own vagueness, in part because it sometimes comes up against the internal force of social meanings. And these meanings can be specified, and are specified, through the decision-making processes of the political community.

We might opt for a world without particular meanings and without political communities: where no one was a member or where everyone 'belonged' to a single global state. These are the two forms of simple equality with regard to membership. If all human beings were strangers to one another, if all our meetings were like meetings at sea or in the desert or by the side of the road, then there would be no membership to distribute. Admissions policy would never be an issue. Where and how we lived, and with whom we lived, would depend upon our individual desires and then upon our partnerships and affairs. Justice would be nothing more than non-coercion, good faith, and Good Samaritanism—a matter entirely of external principles. If, by contrast, all human beings were members of a global state, membership would already have been distributed, equally; and there would be nothing more to do. The first of these arrangements suggests a kind of global libertarianism; the

---

[3] J. Winthrop, in *Puritan Political Ideas: 1558-1794*, ed. E. S. Morgan (Indianapolis, 1965), 146.

second, a kind of global socialism. These are the two conditions under which the distribution of membership would never arise. Either there would be no such status to distribute, or it would simply come (to everyone) with birth. But neither of these arrangements is likely to be realized in the foreseeable future; and there are impressive arguments, which I will come to later, against both of them. In any case, so long as members and strangers are, as they are at present, two distinct groups, admissions decisions have to be made, men and women taken in or refused. Given the indeterminate requirements of mutual aid, these decisions are not constrained by any widely accepted standard. That's why the admissions policies of countries are rarely criticized, except in terms suggesting that the only relevant criteria are those of charity, not justice. It is certainly possible that a deeper criticism would lead one to deny the member/stranger distinction. But I shall try, nevertheless, to defend that distinction and then to describe the internal and the external principles that govern the distribution of membership.

The argument will require a careful review of both immigration and naturalization policy. But it is worth noting first, briefly, that there are certain similarities between strangers in political space (immigrants) and descendants in time (children). People enter a country by being born to parents already there, as well as, and more often than, by crossing the frontier. Both these processes can be controlled. In the first case, however, unless we practise a selective infanticide, we will be dealing with unborn and hence unknown individuals. Subsidies for large families and programmes of birth control determine only the size of the population, not the characteristics of its inhabitants. We might, of course, award the right to give birth differentially to different groups of parents, establishing ethnic quotas (like country-of-origin quotas in immigration policy), or class or intelligence quotas, or allowing right-to-give-birth certificates to be traded on the market. These are ways of regulating who has children and of shaping the character of the future population. They are, however, indirect and inefficient ways, even with regard to ethnicity, unless the state also regulates intermarriage and assimilation. Even well short of that, the policy would require very high, and surely unacceptable, levels of coercion: the dominance of political power over kinship and love. So the

major public policy issue is the size of the population only—
its growth, stability, or decline. To how many people do we
distribute membership? The larger and philosophically more
interesting questions—To what sorts of people? and To what
particular people?—are most clearly confronted when we turn
to the problems involved in admitting or excluding strangers.

ANALOGIES: NEIGHBOURHOODS, CLUBS, AND FAMILIES

Admissions policies are shaped partly by arguments about
economic and political conditions in the host country, partly by
arguments about the character and 'destiny' of the host country,
and partly by arguments about the character of countries
(political communities) in general. The last of these is the most
important, in theory at least; for our understanding of countries
in general will determine whether particular countries have the
right they conventionally claim: to distribute membership for
(their own) particular reasons. But few of us have any direct
experience of what a country is or of what it means to be a
member. We often have strong feelings about our country, but
we have only dim perceptions of it. As a political community
(rather than a place) it is, after all, invisible; we actually see only
its symbols, offices, and representatives. I suspect that we
understand it best when we compare it to other, smaller associations whose compass we can more easily grasp. For we are all
members of formal and informal groups of many different sorts;
we know their workings intimately. And all these groups have,
and necessarily have, admissions policies. Even if we have never
served as state officials, even if we have never emigrated from
one country to another, we have all had the experience of
accepting or rejecting strangers, and we have all had the
experience of being accepted or rejected. I want to draw upon
this experience. My argument will be worked through a series
of rough comparisons, in the course of which the special meaning of political membership will, I think, become increasingly
apparent.

Consider, then, three possible analogues for the political community: we can think of countries as neighbourhoods, clubs, or

families. The list is obviously not exhaustive, but it will serve to illuminate certain key features of admission and exclusion. Schools, bureaucracies, and companies, though they have some of the characteristics of clubs, distribute social and economic status as well as membership; I will take them up separately. Many domestic associations are parasitic for their member-ships, relying on the procedures of other associations: unions depend upon the hiring policies of companies; parent–teacher organizations depend upon the openness of neighbourhoods or upon the selectiveness of private schools. Political parties are generally like clubs; religious congregations are often designed to resemble families. What should countries be like?

The neighbourhood is an enormously complex human asso-ciation, but we have a certain understanding of what it is like —an understanding at least partially reflected (though also increasingly challenged) in contemporary American law. It is an association without an organized or legally enforceable admis-sions policy. Strangers can be welcomed or not welcomed; they cannot be admitted or excluded. Of course, being welcomed or not welcomed is sometimes effectively the same thing as being admitted or excluded, but the distinction is theoretically impor-tant. In principle, individuals and families move into a neigh-bourhood for reasons of their own; they choose but are not chosen. Or, rather, in the absence of legal controls, the market controls their movements. Whether they move is determined not only by their own choice but also by their ability to find a job and a place to live (or, in a society different from our own, to find a factory commune or a co-operative apartment house ready to take them in). Ideally, the market works independently of the existing composition of the neighbourhood. The state upholds this independence by refusing to enforce restrictive covenants and by acting to prevent or minimize discrimination in employment. There are no institutional arrangements capable of maintaining 'ethnic purity'—though zoning laws sometimes maintain class segregation.[4] With reference to any

---

[1] On zoning, see R. H. Nelson, *Zoning and Property Rights: An Analysis of the American System of Land Use Regulation* (Cambridge, Mass., 1977), 120–1. The use of zoning laws to bar from neighbourhoods (boroughs, villages, towns) certain sorts of people—namely, those who don't live in conventional

formal criteria, the neighbourhood is a random association, 'not a selection, but rather a specimen of life as a whole. . . . By the very indifference of space,' as Bernard Bosanquet has written, 'we are liable to the direct impact of all possible factors.'[5]

It was a common argument in classical political economy that national territory should be as 'indifferent' as local space. The same writers who defended free trade in the nineteenth century also defended unrestricted immigration. They argued for perfect freedom of contract, without any political restraint. International society, they thought, should take shape as a world of neighbourhoods, with individuals moving freely about, seeking private advancement. In their view, as Henry Sidgwick reported it in the 1890s, the only business of state officials is 'to maintain order over [a] particular territory . . . but not in any way to determine who is to inhabit this territory, or to restrict the enjoyment of its natural advantages to any particular portion of the human race'.[6] Natural advantages (like markets) are open to all comers, within the limits of private property rights; and if they are used up or devalued by overcrowding, people presumably will move on, into the jurisdiction of new sets of officials.

Sidgwick thought that this is possibly the 'ideal of the future', but he offered three arguments against a world of neighbourhoods in the present. First of all, such a world would not allow for patriotic sentiment, and so the 'casual aggregates' that would probably result from the free movement of individuals would 'lack internal cohesion'. Neighbours would be strangers to one another. Second, free movement might interfere with efforts 'to raise the standard of living among the poorer classes' of a particular country, since such efforts could not be undertaken with equal energy and success everywhere in the world. And, third, the promotion of moral and intellectual culture and the efficient working of political institutions might be 'defeated'

---

families—is a new feature of our political history, and I shall not try to comment on it here. See the US Supreme Court's decision in *Village of Belle Terre* v. *Boraas* (October term, 1973).

[5] B. Bosanquet, *The Philosophical Theory of the State* (London, 1958), 286.

[6] H. Sidgwick, *Elements of Politics* (London, 1881), 295–6.

by the continual creation of heterogeneous populations.[7] Sidgwick presented these three arguments as a series of utilitarian considerations that weigh against the benefits of labour mobility and contractual freedom. But they seem to me to have a rather different character. The last two arguments draw their force from the first, but only if the first is conceived in non-utilitarian terms. It is only if patriotic sentiment has some moral basis, only if communal cohesion makes for obligations and shared meanings, only if there are members as well as strangers, that state officials would have any reason to worry especially about the welfare of their own people (and of *all* their own people) and the success of their own culture and politics. For it is at least dubious that the average standard of living of the poorer classes throughout the world would decline under conditions of perfect labour mobility. Nor is there firm evidence that culture cannot thrive in cosmopolitan environments, nor that it is impossible to govern casual aggregations of people. As for the last of these, political theorists long ago discovered that certain sorts of regimes—namely, authoritarian regimes—thrive in the absence of communal cohesion. That perfect mobility makes for authoritarianism might suggest a utilitarian argument against mobility; but such an argument would work only if individual men and women, free to come and go, expressed a desire for some other form of government. And that they might not do.

Perfect labour mobility, however, is probably a mirage, for it is almost certain to be resisted at the local level. Human beings, as I have said, move about a great deal, but not because they love to move. They are, most of them, inclined to stay where they are unless their life is very difficult there. They experience a tension between love of place and the discomforts of a particular place. While some of them leave their homes and become foreigners in new lands, others stay where they are and resent the foreigners in their own land. Hence, if states ever become large neighbourhoods, it is likely that neighbourhoods will become little states. Their members will organize to defend the local politics and culture against strangers. Historically, neighbourhoods have turned into closed or parochial communities (leaving aside cases of legal coercion) whenever the

state was open: in the cosmopolitan cities of multinational
empires, for example, where state officials don't foster any
particular identity but permit different groups to build their
own institutional structures (as in ancient Alexandria), or in
the receiving centres of mass immigration movements (early
twentieth-century New York) where the country is an open but
also an alien world—or, alternatively, a world full of aliens. The
case is similar where the state doesn't exist at all or in areas
where it doesn't function. Where welfare moneys are raised and
spent locally, for example, as in a seventeenth-century English
parish, the local people will seek to exclude newcomers who are
likely welfare recipients. It is only the nationalization of welfare
(or the nationalization of culture and politics) that opens the
neighbourhood communities to whoever chooses to come in.

Neighbourhoods can be open only if countries are at least
potentially closed. Only if the state makes a selection among
would-be members and guarantees the loyalty, security, and
welfare of the individuals it selects, can local communities take
shape as 'indifferent' associations, determined solely by personal preference and market capacity. Since individual choice
is most dependent upon local mobility, this would seem to be
the preferred arrangement in a society like our own. The politics
and the culture of a modern democracy probably require the
kind of largeness, and also the kind of boundedness, that states
provide. I don't mean to deny the value of sectional cultures and
ethnic communities; I mean only to suggest the rigidities that
would be forced upon both in the absence of inclusive and protective states. To tear down the walls of the state is not, as
Sidgwick worriedly suggested, to create a world without walls,
but rather to create a thousand petty fortresses.

The fortresses, too, could be torn down: all that is necessary
is a global state sufficiently powerful to overwhelm the local
communities. Then the result would be the world of the political
economists, as Sidgwick described it—a world of radically
deracinated men and women. Neighbourhoods might maintain
some cohesive culture for a generation or two on a voluntary
basis, but people would move in, people would move out; soon
the cohesion would be gone. The distinctiveness of cultures and
groups depends upon closure and, without it, cannot be conceived as a stable feature of human life. If this distinctiveness

is a value, as most people (though some of them are global pluralists, and others only local loyalists) seem to believe, then closure must be permitted somewhere. At some level of political organization, something like the sovereign state must take shape and claim the authority to make its own admissions policy, to control and sometimes restrain the flow of immigrants.

But this right to control immigration does not include or entail the right to control emigration. The political community can shape its own population in the one way, not in the other; this is a distinction that gets reiterated in different forms throughout the account of membership. The restraint of entry serves to defend the liberty and welfare, the politics and culture of a group of people committed to one another and to their common life. But the restraint of exit replaces commitment with coercion. So far as the coerced members are concerned, there is no longer a community worth defending. A state can, perhaps, banish individual citizens or expel aliens living within its borders (if there is some place ready to receive them). Except in times of national emergency, when everyone is bound to work for the survival of the community, states cannot prevent such people from getting up and leaving. The fact that individuals can rightly leave their own country, however, doesn't generate a right to enter another (any other). Immigration and emigration are morally asymmetrical.[8] Here the appropriate analogy is with the club, for it is a feature of clubs in domestic society—as I have just suggested it is of states in international society—that they can regulate admissions but cannot bar withdrawals.

Like clubs, countries have admissions committees. In the United States, Congress functions as such a committee, though it rarely makes individual selections. Instead, it establishes general qualifications, categories for admission and exclusion, and numerical quotas (limits). Then admissible individuals are taken in, with varying degrees of administrative discretion, mostly on a first-come, first-served basis. This procedure seems eminently defensible, though that does not mean that any particular set of qualifications and categories ought to be defended. To say that states have a right to act in certain areas is not to

---

[8] Cf. M. Cranston, on the common understanding of the right to move, in *What Are Human Rights?* (New York, 1973), 32.

say that anything they do in those areas is right. One can argue about particular admissions standards by appealing, for example, to the condition and character of the host country and to the shared understandings of those who are already members. Such arguments have to be judged morally and politically as well as factually. The claim of American advocates of restricted immigration (in 1920, say) that they were defending a homogeneous white and Protestant country can plausibly be called unjust as well as inaccurate: as if non-white and non-Protestant citizens were invisible men and women, who didn't have to be counted in the national census![9] Earlier Americans, seeking the benefits of economic and geographic expansion, had created a pluralist society; and the moral realities of that society ought to have guided the legislators of the 1920s. If we follow the logic of the club analogy, however, we have to say that the earlier decision might have been different, and the United States might have taken shape as a homogeneous community, an Anglo-Saxon nation-state (assuming what happened in any case: the virtual extermination of the Indians who, understanding correctly the dangers of invasion, struggled as best they could to keep foreigners out of their native lands). Decisions of this sort are subject to constraint, but what the constraints are I am not yet ready to say. It is important first to insist that the distribution of membership in American society, and in any ongoing society, is a matter of political decision. The labour market may be given free rein, as it was for many decades in the United States, but that does not happen by an act of nature or of God; it depends upon choices that are ultimately political. What kind of community do the citizens want to create? With what other men and women do they want to share and exchange social goods?

These are exactly the questions that club members answer when they make membership decisions, though usually with reference to a less extensive community and to a more limited range of social goods. In clubs, only the founders choose themselves (or one another); all other members have been chosen by those who were members before them. Individuals may be able to give good reasons why they should be selected,

---

[9] See J. Higham's account of these debates, *Strangers in the Land* (New York, 1968).

but no one on the outside has a right to be inside. The members decide freely on their future associates, and the decisions they make are authoritative and final. Only when clubs split into factions and fight over property can the state intervene and make its own decision about who the members are. When states split, however, no legal appeal is possible; there is no superior body. Hence, we might imagine states as perfect clubs, with sovereign power over their own selection processes.[10]

But if this description is accurate in regard to the law, it is not an accurate account of the moral life of contemporary political communities. Clearly, citizens often believe themselves morally bound to open the doors of their country—not to anyone who wants to come in, perhaps, but to a particular group of outsiders, recognized as national or ethnic 'relatives'. In this sense, states are like families rather than clubs, for it is a feature of families that their members are morally connected to people they have not chosen, who live outside the household. In time of trouble, the household is also a refuge. Sometimes, under the auspices of the state, we take in fellow citizens to whom we are not related, as English country families took in London children during the blitz; but our more spontaneous beneficence is directed at our own kith and kin. The state recognizes what we can call the 'kinship principle' when it gives priority in immigration to the relatives of citizens. That is current policy in the United States, and it seems especially appropriate in a political community largely formed by the admission of immigrants. It is a way of acknowledging that labour mobility has a social price: since labourers are men and women with families, one cannot admit them for the sake of their labour without accepting some commitment to their aged parents, say, or to their sickly brothers and sisters.

In communities differently formed, where the state represents a nation largely in place, another sort of commitment commonly develops, along lines determined by the principle of nationality. In time of trouble, the state is a refuge for members of the

---

[10] Winthrop made the point clearly: 'If we here be a corporation established by free consent, if the place of our habitation be our own, then no man hath right to come into us . . . without our consent' (*Puritan Political Ideas*, p. 145). [. . .]

nation, whether or not they are residents and citizens. Perhaps the border of the political community was drawn years ago so as to leave their villages and towns on the wrong side; perhaps they are the children or grandchildren of emigrants. They have no legal membership rights, but if they are persecuted in the land where they live, they look to their homeland not only with hope but also with expectation. I am inclined to say that such expectations are legitimate. Greeks driven from Turkey, Turks from Greece, after the wars and revolutions of the early twentieth century, had to be taken in by the states that bore their collective names. What else are such states for? They don't only preside over a piece of territory and a random collection of inhabitants; they are also the political expression of a common life and (most often) of a national 'family' that is never entirely enclosed within their legal boundaries. After the Second World War, millions of Germans, expelled by Poland and Czechoslovakia, were received and cared for by the two Germanies. Even if these states had been free of all responsibility in the expulsions, they would still have had a special obligation to the refugees. Most states recognize obligations of this sort in practice; some do so in law.

TERRITORY

We might, then, think of countries as national clubs or families. But countries are also territorial states. Although clubs and families own property, they neither require nor (except in feudal systems) possess jurisdiction over territory. Leaving children aside, they do not control the physical location of their members. The state does control physical location—if only for the sake of clubs and families and the individual men and women who make them up; and with this control there come certain obligations. We can best examine these if we consider once again the asymmetry of immigration and emigration.

The nationality principle has one significant limit, commonly accepted in theory, if not always in practice. Though the recognition of national affinity is a reason for permitting immigration, nonrecognition is not a reason for expulsion. This is a major issue in the modern world, for many newly independent states find themselves in control of territory into which alien groups have been admitted under the auspices of the old imperial regime. Sometimes these people are forced to leave, the victims of a popular hostility that the new government cannot restrain. More often the government itself fosters such hostility, and takes positive action to drive out the 'alien elements', invoking when it does so some version of the club or the family analogy. Here, however, neither analogy applies: for though no 'alien' has a right to be a member of a club or a family, it is possible, I think, to describe a kind of territorial or locational right.

Hobbes made the argument in classical form when he listed those rights that are given up and those that are retained when the social contract is signed. The retained rights include self-defence and then 'the use of fire, water, free air, *and place to live in*, and . . . all things necessary for life'.[11] The right is not, indeed, to a particular place, but it is enforceable against the state, which exists to protect it; the state's claim to territorial jurisdiction derives ultimately from this individual right to place. Hence the right has a collective as well as an individual form, and these two can come into conflict. But it can't be said that the first always or necessarily supercedes the second, for the first came into existence for the sake of the second. The state owes something to its inhabitants simply, without reference to their collective or national identity. And the first place to which the inhabitants are entitled is surely the place where they and their families have lived and made a life. The attachments and expectations they have formed argue against a forced transfer to another country. If they can't have this particular piece of land (or house or apartment), then some other must be found for them within the same general 'place'. Initially, at least, the sphere of membership is given: the men and women who determine what membership means, and who shape the admissions policies of the political community, are simply the men and women who are already there. New states and governments must make their peace with the old inhabitants of the land they rule. And countries are likely to take shape as closed territories dominated, perhaps, by particular nations (clubs or families),

[11] T. Hobbes, *The Elements of Law*, ed. F. Tönnies (2nd edn., New York, 1969), 88 (pt. I, ch. 17, para. 2) (emphasis added).

but always including aliens of one sort or another—whose expulsion would be unjust.

This common arrangement raises one important possibility: that many of the inhabitants of a particular country won't be allowed full membership (citizenship) because of their nationality. I will consider that possibility, and argue for its rejection, when I turn to the specific problems of naturalization. But one might avoid such problems entirely, at least at the level of the state, by opting for a radically different arrangement. Consider once again the neighbourhood analogy: perhaps we should deny to national states, as we deny to churches and political parties, the collective right of territorial jurisdiction. Perhaps we should insist upon open countries and permit closure only in non-territorial groups. Open neighbourhoods together with closed clubs and families: that is the structure of domestic society. Why can't it, why shouldn't it, be extended to the global society?

An extension of this sort was actually proposed by the Austrian socialist writer Otto Bauer, with reference to the old multinational empires of Central and Eastern Europe. Bauer would have organized nations into autonomous corporations permitted to tax their members for educational and cultural purposes, but denied any territorial dominion. Individuals would be free to move about in political space, within the empire, carrying their national memberships with them, much as individuals move about today in liberal and secular states, carrying their religious memberships and partisan affiliations. Like churches and parties, the corporations could admit or reject new members in accordance with whatever standards their old members thought appropriate.[12]

The major difficulty here is that all the national communities that Bauer wanted to preserve came into existence, and were sustained over the centuries, on the basis of geographical coexistence. It isn't any misunderstanding of their histories that leads nations newly freed from imperial rule to seek a firm territorial status. Nations look for countries because in some deep

---

[12] Bauer made his argument in *Die Nationalitätenfrage und die Sozialdemokratie* (1907); parts of it are excerpted in *Austro-Marxism*, ed. T. Bottomore and P. Goode (Oxford, 1978), 102–25.

sense they already have countries: the link between people and land is a crucial feature of national identity. Their leaders understand, moreover, that because so many critical issues (including issues of distributive justice, such as welfare, education, and so on) can best be resolved within geographical units, the focus of political life can never be established elsewhere. 'Autonomous' corporations will always be adjuncts, and probably parasitic adjuncts, of territorial states; and to give up the state is to give up any effective self-determination. That's why borders, and the movements of individuals and groups across borders, are bitterly disputed as soon as imperial rule recedes and nations begin the process of 'liberation'. And, once again, to reverse this process or to repress its effects would require massive coercion on a global scale. There is no easy way to avoid the country (and the proliferation of countries) as we currently know it. Hence the theory of justice must allow for the territorial state, specifying the rights of its inhabitants and recognizing the collective right of admission and refusal.

The argument cannot stop here, however, for the control of territory opens the state to the claim of necessity. Territory is a social good in a double sense. It is living space, earth and water, mineral resources and potential wealth, a resource for the destitute and the hungry. And it is protected living space, with borders and police, a resource for the persecuted and the stateless. These two resources are different, and we might conclude differently with regard to the kinds of claim that can be made on each. But the issue at stake should first be put in general terms. Can a political community exclude destitute and hungry, persecuted and stateless—in a word, necessitous—men and women simply because they are foreigners? Are citizens bound to take in strangers? Let us assume that the citizens have no formal obligations; they are bound by nothing more stringent than the principle of mutual aid. The principle must be applied, however, not to individuals directly but to the citizens as a group, for immigration is a matter of political decision. Individuals participate in the decision-making, if the state is democratic; but they decide not for themselves but for the community generally. And this fact has moral implications. It replaces immediacy with distance and the personal expense of time and energy with impersonal bureaucratic costs. Despite John

Winthrop's claim, mutual aid is more coercive for political communities than it is for individuals, because a wide range of benevolent actions is open to the community which will only marginally affect its present members considered as a body or even, with possible exceptions, one by one or family by family or club by club. (But benevolence will, perhaps, affect the children or grandchildren or great-grandchildren of the present members—in ways not easy to measure or even to make out. I'm not sure to what extent considerations of this sort can be used to narrow the range of required actions.) These actions probably include the admission of strangers, for admission to a country does not entail the kinds of intimacy that could hardly be avoided in the case of clubs and families. Might not admission, then, be morally imperative, at least for *these* strangers, who have no other place to go?

Some such argument, turning mutual aid into a more stringent charge on communities than it can ever be on individuals, probably underlies the common claim that exclusion rights depend upon the territorial extent and the population density of particular countries. Thus, Sidgwick wrote that he 'cannot concede to a state possessing large tracts of unoccupied land an absolute right of excluding alien elements'.[13] Perhaps, in his view, the citizens can make some selection among necessitous strangers, but they cannot refuse entirely to take strangers in so long as their state has (a great deal of) available space. A much stronger argument might be made from the other side, so to speak, if we consider the necessitous strangers not as objects of beneficent action but as desperate men and women, capable of acting on their own behalf. In *Leviathan*, Hobbes argued that such people, if they cannot earn a living in their own countries, have a right to move into 'countries not sufficiently inhabited: where nevertheless they are not to exterminate those they find there, but constrain them to inhabit closer together and not range a great deal of ground to snatch what they find'.[14]

---

[13] Sidgwick, *Elements of Politics*, p. 295. Cf. J. S. Mill's letter to Henry George on Chinese immigration to America, quoted in A. Saxton, *The Indispensable Enemy: Labor and the Anti-Chinese Movement in California* (Berkeley, Calif., 1971), 103.

[14] T. Hobbes, *Leviathan*, pt. II, ch. 30.

Here the 'Samaritans' are not themselves active but acted upon and (as we shall see in a moment) charged only with nonresistance. [. . .]

MEMBERSHIP AND JUSTICE

The distribution of membership is not pervasively subject to the constraints of justice. Across a considerable range of the decisions that are made, states are simply free to take in strangers (or not)—much as they are free, leaving aside the claims of the needy, to share their wealth with foreign friends, to honour the achievements of foreign artists, scholars, and scientists, to choose their trading partners, and to enter into collective security arrangements with foreign states. But the right to choose an admissions policy is more basic than any of these, for it is not merely a matter of acting in the world, exercising sovereignty, and pursuing national interests. At stake here is the shape of the community that acts in the world, exercises sovereignty, and so on. Admission and exclusion are at the core of communal independence. They suggest the deepest meaning of self-determination. Without them, there could not be *communities of character*, historically stable, ongoing associations of men and women with some special commitment to one another and some special sense of their common life.[15]

But self-determination in the sphere of membership is not absolute. It is a right exercised, most often, by national clubs or families, but it is held in principle by territorial states. Hence it is subject both to internal decisions by the members themselves (*all* the members, including those who hold membership simply by right of place) and to the external principle of mutual aid. Immigration, then, is both a matter of political choice and moral constraint. Naturalization, by contrast, is entirely constrained: every new immigrant, every refugee taken in, every resident and worker must be offered the opportunities of citizenship. If the community is so radically divided that a single citizenship is impossible, then its territory must be divided, too,

---

[15] I have taken the term 'communities of character' from O. Bauer (see *Austro-Marxism*, p. 107).

before the rights of admission and exclusion can be exercised. For these rights are to be exercised only by the community as a whole (even if, in practice, some national majority dominates the decision-making) and only with regard to foreigners, not by some members with regard to others. No community can be half-metic, half-citizen, and claim that its admissions policies are acts of self-determination or that its politics is democratic.

The determination of aliens and guests by an exclusive band of citizens (or of slaves by masters, or women by men, or blacks by whites, or conquered peoples by their conquerors) is not communal freedom but oppression. The citizens are free, of course, to set up a club, make membership as exclusive as they like, write a constitution, and govern one another. But they can't claim territorial jurisdiction and rule over the people with whom they share the territory. To do this is to act outside their sphere, beyond their rights. It is a form of tyranny. Indeed, the rule of citizens over non-citizens, of members over strangers, is probably the most common form of tyranny in human history. I won't say much more than this about the special problems of non-citizens and strangers: henceforth, whether I am talking about the distribution of security and welfare or about hard work or power itself, I shall assume that all the eligible men and women hold a single political status. This assumption doesn't exclude other sorts of inequality further down the road, but it does exclude the piling up of inequalities that is characteristic of divided societies. The denial of membership is always the first of a long train of abuses. There is no way to break the train, so we must deny the rightfulness of the denial. The theory of distributive justice begins, then, with an account of membership rights. It must vindicate at one and the same time the (limited) right of closure, without which there could be no communities at all, and the political inclusiveness of the existing communities. For it is only as members somewhere that men and women can hope to share in all the other social goods—security, wealth, honour, office, and power—that communal life makes possible.

5

COMMUNITY AND CITIZENSHIP

DAVID MILLER

1

[. . .] It is often said that proposals for market socialism effectively abandon the traditional socialist commitment to community.[1] Socialism cannot be understood simply in terms of
policy outcomes—the distribution of consumption goods and so
forth. It is also fundamentally concerned with the quality of
human relationships in so far as these are affected by social
institutions. I [have] argued [. . .] that the apparently anti-
communitarian character of market relations might be offset if
the market were made the subject of deliberate political choice.
This argument does not take us the whole way. It shows that
where community exists, and finds political expression, the
presence of markets need not destroy it, but we have still to show
how community is possible in the first place in modern, econo-
mically developed societies. Markets alone cannot provide it,
even if they can be contained within it.

At the same time, we need to probe the commitment to
community itself. What does it mean for relationships to be
communitarian, and why should their being so be valued? How,
in particular, does a socialist view of community differ from
conservative and liberal views?[2] We must allow the possibility
that some forms of community are in fact antithetical to
other equally important, socialist ideals, so that socialist

David Miller, excerpts from *Market, State, and Community*, 227–51. Reprinted
by permission of Oxford University Press.

[1] See, e.g., A. Buchanan, *Ethics, Efficiency, and the Market* (Oxford, 1985),
106–9.
[2] For the contested character of the concept of community, see R. Plant,
'Community: Concept, Conception and Ideology', *Politics and Society*, 8

communitarianism must be discriminating. We must even consider whether socialists should abandon communitarian commitments altogether. These questions answered, we can return to the practical issue of how community can be realized, and what, in particular, it implies for the politics of socialism. [. . .]

2

The promise of overall community, then, is that it allows people to regard themselves as active subjects shaping the world according to their will; and that it undergirds the distributive arrangements to which socialists (especially) are committed. But now we must begin to ask how, if at all, this promise can be fulfilled in the advanced industrial societies on which our discussion is focused.

The collective identities that people currently possess are predominantly national identities. Here, if anywhere, it seems, the promise of overall community must be redeemed.[3] But the socialist tradition has been overwhelmingly hostile to nationality as a source of identity, usually regarding it merely as an artificially created impediment to the brotherhood of man. And, of course, the historial conjunct 'national socialism' is rightly regarded with the utmost abhorrence.

Despite the weight of this tradition, I believe we need to mount a rescue operation on behalf of nationality if we are to have any hope of providing a socialist theory of community that respects the limits already identified. This operation will have

---

(1978), 79–107. For the breadth of its appeal, see R. Nisbet, *The Quest for Community* (New York, 1953). For an assessment of the recent revival of communitarian thought from a socialist perspective, see my 'In what sense must socialism be communitarian?', *Social Philosophy and Policy* 6(1989), 57–74.

[3] Socialists need not take a stand on the question whether it is ultimately preferable for there to be a plurality of national communities or a single global community. The point is that a feasible form of socialism must begin from the communal identities people actually have, not those which it might be abstractly desirable for them to have. There is presently no sign that national identities are on the wane. In so far as there is any movement, it appears to be in the direction of smaller, more intense forms of nationality rather than towards cosmopolitanism.

two phases. First, I separate the idea of nationality itself from various accretions that have given nationalism a bad name, on the left especially. Second, I try to defuse the charge that nationality is an essentially irrational phenomenon, and therefore an inadmissible basis on which to found a socialist project that aspires to be rational.

What does it mean for people to have a common national identity, to share their nationality? It is essentially not a matter of the objective characteristics that they possess, but of their shared beliefs:[4] a belief that each belongs together with the rest; that this association is neither transitory nor merely instrumental, but stems from a long history of living together which (it is hoped and expected) will continue into the future; that the community is marked off from other communities by its members' distinctive characteristics; that each member recognizes a loyalty to the community, expressed in a willingness to sacrifice personal goals to advance its interests; and that the community should enjoy a measure of political autonomy, normally (but not I think necessarily) in the form of a sovereign state.[5] Where these beliefs are widely held throughout the population in question, we have sufficient grounds for saying that a nation exists.

What needs underlining is how little this definition includes. It contains no assumption that nations are, as it were, natural kinds marked off from one another by physical characteristics. It can easily accommodate the historical fluidity of national identities, and recognize the extent to which nations are brought into being by extraneous circumstances such as conflicts between states. Nor is there any assumption that people who share a nationality will share objective characteristics such as race or language.[6] It is indeed possible that people's *beliefs* about these characteristics may form part of particular national

---

[4] See B. Barry, 'Self-Government Revisited', in D. Miller and L. Siedentop (eds.), *The Nature of Political Theory* (Oxford, 1983).

[5] I hope there is no need to labour the conceptual distinction between a state (a political institution) and a nation (a group of people with shared beliefs of the appropriate kind), nor to dwell on the reasons why most nationalities aspire to form their own sovereign states.

[6] For the sake of argument I assume that race *is* an objective characteristic, though clearly this might be disputed.

identities—for instance, that it is part of (French) people's understanding of what it is to be French that one should speak the French language—but this is quite a different matter. Moreover, the salient characteristics may vary from case to case: one nation may define itself by race, another by religion, a third by nothing more than common history. (In fact these examples are too simple. If we think about existing national identities, we quickly realize that they are almost without exception made up of an array of characteristics, none of which is regarded as strictly necessary to being Italian, Japanese, etc.)

The definition is minimal in another respect too. It embodies no assumptions about how nations ought to behave towards one another. In particular, it does not include the idea that nations are ethically unrestricted, so that powerful nations may justifiably impose themselves on the weak. All that nationality, as such, includes is the idea that one owes a special loyalty to one's compatriots. Now it is certainly true that acknowledging a loyalty of this kind means favouring the interests of members of the group at the expense of outsiders in certain circumstances. That is what loyalty means: talk of impersonal loyalty, or loyalty to the human race as a whole, is meaningless, except in science fiction cases. But to acknowledge loyalty to a group need not imply being ethically indifferent to outsiders, much less being willing to trample on their interests in the name of the group.

Most socialists see the value in attachments to primary groups.[7] They see that owing a special loyalty to your workmates or your neighbours does not exclude caring about and supporting wider constituencies. (Indeed, as I argued earlier, they have often taken such a rosy view of this relationship that they have ignored the structural problems of inter-group relations.) Why, then, should national loyalties be looked on with disfavour? Perhaps it is the fact that national groupings are normally co-extensive with states, so that the group has the organized power to inflict damage on outside groups, if it so wishes. But this, it seems to me, is simply an unavoidable corollary of the feature which should make nationality *attractive*

---

[7] Most, but not all. Godwin was the best-known exponent of the view that one must be rigorously impartial in one's treatment of fellow human beings. But Godwin was in any case an odd sort of socialist, if indeed one at all.

to socialists as a form of community. It is precisely the conjunction of nation and state that makes it possible for national
communities to approach the ideals of self-determination and
distributive justice sketched in the previous section. Only a
politically organized community can aspire to shape its own
future and to distribute resources throughout its membership
according to need.[8] Unfortunately, the power which enables
it to do this will also, if misused, allow it to damage other
communities in ways that are too familiar to need rehearsing.

My strategy so far has been to separate nationality, as the idea
that socialists should hold on to and favour, from nationalism—
a rather inchoate notion, often thought to encompass (a) the idea
that nations are distinct, immutable chunks of humanity, and/or
(b) the idea that national allegiances are to be fostered at the
expense of all other commitments, whether wider or narrower,
and/or (c) the idea that nations may aggress against each other
as forcefully as they are able. These latter ideas may all lead to
repugnant conclusions, but their connection with nationality as
such is no stronger than, say, the connection between football
violence and loyalty to one's chosen team. All particularist
loyalties create at least the *potential* for objectionable behaviour
towards outsiders, but to conclude that we should never pledge
ourselves to anything less than humanity as a whole is to overlook everything that is valuable in these special commitments.[9]

There is, however, a further issue that we must consider
before allowing nationality to stand as our idea of overall

[8] Obviously nation-states are constrained to a varying extent by the international economic and political environment in which they have to act. I do
not mean to imply that any nation can be fully self-determining in the sense
of facing no external impediments at all. Nor would I deny that some nations
are constrained to an extent that makes their nominal self-determination fairly
meaningless. I would simply reiterate that nationality, where it works, holds
out a promise that socialists should find very attractive, in a world that falls
far short of utopia.

[9] For explorations of the value of such commitments, see A. Oldenquist,
'Loyalties', *Journal of Philosophy*, 74 (1982), 173–93; J. Cottingham, 'Par-
tiality, Favouritism and Morality', *Philosophical Quarterly*, 36 (1986), 357–73;
P. Pettit, 'Social Holism and Moral Theory', *Proceedings of the Aristotelean
Society*, 86 (1985–6), 173–97. I have looked more fully at the ethical issues
raised by national allegiances in 'The Ethical Significance of Nationality',
Ethics, 98 (1987–8), 647–62.

community. A socialist view of community, unlike certain conservative views, must embody a condition of rationality. Members of the community must be able to subject their relationship
to critical scrutiny without destroying it. This follows from
socialist egalitarianism—there is no privileged caste holding the
rest of society in intellectual thrall—together with the idea that
the community is an active agent reshaping the world in accordance with its purposes. Now it is often suggested that national
'communities' are in one important sense fictitious, for it is characteristic of nations that their identities are not formed through
spontaneous processes of self-definition, but primarily according to the exigencies of power—the demands of states seeking
to assure themselves of the loyalty of their subjects. Nationality
is to a greater or lesser degree a manufactured item. This is
brought out in Anthony Smith's recent study of the formation
of nations out of older ethnic communities.[10] Smith distinguishes broadly between two cases. In the first, the nation is
based on a single dominant ethnic group, and the culture of that
group is imposed more or less successfully on ethnic minorities
falling within the territorial boundaries of the emergent nation.
In the second, a dominant culture is lacking, and has to be
forged in order to create a nation out of a series of disparate
ethnic groups. In both cases, but especially the second, nation-
building is a work of invention, in particular the invention of a
common national past. As Smith puts it:

If the nation is to become a 'political community' on the Western
territorial and civic model, it must, paradoxically, seek to create those
myths of descent, those historical memories and that common culture
which form the missing elements of their ethnic make-up, along with
a mutual solidarity. It must differentiate itself from its closest neighbours, distinguish its culture from theirs, and emphasize the historic
kinship of its constituent *ethnie* and their common ties of ideological
affinity. This is done by creating or elaborating an 'ideological' myth
of origins and descent.[11]

Let us take it, then, that nations require histories which are
to a greater or lesser degree 'mythical' (as judged by the standards of impartial scholarship); and that those stories are not

[10] A. D. Smith, *The Ethnic Origins of Nations* (Oxford, 1986).
[11] Ibid. 147.

only needed at the time during which a national identity is first being created, but pass into that identity itself—so that, in order to understand what it means to be French or Greek, one has to accept (some version of)[12] the common story. Do these facts imply that national loyalties cannot withstand rational reflection?

To answer this question, we need to make a distinction between beliefs that are constitutive of social relationships, and background beliefs which support those constitutive beliefs. To illustrate the former, consider the example of friendship. For A and B to be friends, it must minimally be true that each is willing to put himself out for the other. Suppose that A believes this of B, but in fact the belief is false. B is merely a fair-weather friend: should an occasion arise on which he is called on to sacrifice something for A's sake, he will certainly renege. A's loyalties to B are then drained of their value, since the reciprocal attitudes that constitute friendship are not in place. An indicator of this is that A, if he is rational, must want to be informed if indeed it is the case that his 'friendship' is not being reciprocated.[13]

But now consider a different case. Suppose there is a family, call them the Smiths, who exemplify all the best features of that relationship: there is love, mutual support, and a wide range of activities performed in common. If asked what it was that made these attitudes to one another appropriate, the Smiths would point, among other things, to the fact that members of the family were biologically related. Suppose now that, owing to some dreadful mix-up at the hospital, one of the Smith children is in fact not a Smith. We can then say that the family relationship is backed up by a false belief: the love and concern they feel for one another is supported by a supposed genetic connection which in one case fails to obtain. But a falsity of this kind doesn't mean that the attachment of each member to the family is itself

---

[12] Very often political disputes within a nation will surface as disputes about the precise character of the national past—e.g. the intense competition between 'Whig' and 'Tory' accounts of English history in eighteenth-century Britain. But the competing accounts will recognizably be different versions of the same general story, with many basic facts not in dispute.

[13] If A resists the passing on of this information, then the emotion he feels for B is not friendship but love, which (proverbially) is blind.

valueless. The *constitutive* beliefs are all in order; each does genuinely identify with the family unit, and his beliefs about the others' attitudes are correct. In contrast to the first case, it would not be rational in these circumstances to want to have the false belief brought to light.[14]

If we apply this distinction to the case of nations, the imagined national past, which as we have seen appears to be an essential element in the process of nation-building, must count as a background (rather than constitutive) belief. It does of course matter (given my definition on pp. 87–8) that nations should see their identities as extending over time, but the constitutive belief is only that there should be some national past. The particular story which a nation tells itself about its past is a background belief. It is important that the story should be generally believed—or, to put the point more precisely, that there should be substantial convergence in the versions of the story that are believed[15]—but not that it should be historically accurate.[16] Indeed, since the story is told for purpose of self-definition, and since the nation's self-definition bears on the goals that its members will try to pursue in the future, we should expect a dynamic nation, actively engaged in critical debate on its common purposes, regularly to reinterpret the past as well.

But there may be doubts whether the distinction I have invoked can do all the work that it is needed to do. For even if we can successfully interpret the national past as a background belief, we may not be able to do the same with the national present. Nations need a common view about what they now are; a view about what distinguishes membership of this nation from

[14] Some may think that it is always rational to divest yourself of irrational beliefs, but this is a superficial view. Here we are on Jon Elster territory; see, e.g., the discussion of 'decisions to believe' in his *Ulysses and the Sirens* (Cambridge, 1979), sect. ii. 3. The essential point is that there may be beliefs which it is valuable for a person to have in the light of his underlying goals, in which case it is rational for him to set up mechanisms which ensure that he has them (and if necessary protect the beliefs from later rational scrutiny).

[15] See n. 12.

[16] Not important from the point of view of constituting the nation. In a wider perspective, it may make a good deal of difference how far removed the national myths are from historical truth. If the distance is great, this may have serious repercussions for scholarly research and intellectual toleration generally.

membership of others. To use an old-fashioned phrase, they need some conception of 'national character'. But, it might be urged, these beliefs are also to a large extent mythical, in the sense that they attribute a spurious homogeneity to a set of people who, if looked at objectively, vary enormously in values, life-styles, cultural attributes, and so on. And this observation destroys a *constitutive* belief, because it is constitutive of national identity that members of a nation should have characteristics in common which make it appropriate for them to be lumped together politically, rather than parcelled out in some other way. Take away 'national character' and all we are left with is *de facto* boundaries between states.

To meet this objection, we need to be able to draw a distinction between a public culture that is shared by all who belong to a particular nation and the various private cultures that may flourish inside it. Since we have rejected objective definitions of nationality, 'national character' must be interpreted in cultural terms—in terms of beliefs and attitudes, ritual observances, and so forth. But given the cultural variety that we observe in most modern nations, it is also clear that the common culture we are looking for must be of a relatively thin kind—it cannot embrace all the rich cultural attributes that particular sections of the society may possess. This raises the issue of how such a public/private distinction can be drawn. Is it possible to have a viable sense of nationality without trespassing in the realm of private culture, or will there be areas in which we have to choose between maintaining national identity and encouraging cultural pluralism? [. . .] Here I have tried to sketch in a minimalist view of nationality which on the one hand is substantial enough to serve as an idea of community, but on the other hand is sufficiently free of irrationalist elements to allow socialists to consider stomaching it.

3

Nations are the only possible form in which overall community can be realized in modern societies. But a nation needs the right kind of political organization if it is to satisfy socialist ideals. I shall describe this organization in terms of citizenship.

Nationality and citizenship complement one another. Without a common national identity, there is nothing to hold citizens together, no reason for extending the role just to these people and not to others. Without citizenship, nationality cannot fulfil the activist idea of a community of people determining its own future; it is at risk of becoming a merely traditional form of association in which received ways of doing things are continued without critical scrutiny. Nationality gives people the common identity that makes it possible for them to conceive of shaping their world together. Citizenship gives them the practical means of doing so.

Citizenship here must mean something more than merely being subject to the laws of a state, which is often how the term is now understood. It must be a social role which is partly, but not wholly, defined in terms of rights.[17] Let us take the rights first. It is conventional to distinguish analytically between three kinds of rights that citizens enjoy. First, there are protective rights, rights safeguarding the private freedom and security of each citizen against invasion by others. Second, there are political rights, rights to take part in decision-making in whatever political arenas the society in question provides. Third, there are welfare rights, rights guaranteeing a level of provision of goods and services that admits the citizen to full membership of his community.[18]

The distinction here is analytical only, because the whole thrust of the citizenship idea is that the different kinds of rights support each other. Protective and welfare rights provide a secure basis upon which the citizen can launch into his political role. The sense of common membership that the exercise of political rights (together with nationality) fosters underpins the obligation to provide for the welfare of fellow citizens. Taken together, the rights confer an equality of status upon

[17] I assume for the time being that this is an appropriate way of understanding citizenship. [. . .]

[18] The best-known analysis of citizenship as a status linking the three kinds of rights is T. H. Marshall, 'Citizenship and Social Class', in *Sociology at the Crossroads and Other Essays* (London, 1963). The implications of citizenship for social policy are drawn out in J. Parker, *Social Policy and Citizenship* (London, 1975). The best critical analysis of the tradition as a whole is D. Harris, *Justifying State Welfare* (Oxford, 1987).

citizens which, it is claimed, bolsters their self-respect. Although inequalities of other kinds may persist, each can draw comfort from the fact that, in the basic political arrangements of his society, he is treated as an equal.[19] Testimony to the force of this idea is provided by the popularity, even in present-day political debate, of the phrase 'second-class citizen'. To say that someone is a second-class citizen is to say that, although nominally holding citizen status, he is deprived in some way that robs him of self-respect—hence he is not, in the full sense, a citizen of this society. It is an argument for adding a new right to the definition of citizenship, or for ensuring that an existing right is properly protected.

This observation may also, however, create anxieties about the whole idea. Isn't the notion of citizenship so amorphous that it can be appealed to in order to resolve any and every issue of social policy? Recall that we are trying to translate the idea of community into a form that leaves room for a sphere of 'civil society' in which private associations and market relations hold sway. How can we be sure that the contents of this sphere will not have to be determined politically in the name of citizenship?

Certainly some forms of private association seem incompatible with the citizenship idea. The most obvious case is slavery. The subservient position held by the slave excludes him from citizenship, as the Greeks understood. A more pertinent case for us is that of people subject to wide-ranging paternalism, such as the inhabitants of Pullman, Illinois, under the hegemony of George Pullman. Michael Walzer concludes that Pullman's well-meaning domination of the lives of the workers who lived in his town ('his' because all the property and the services were owned by Pullman) was incompatible with democratic citizenship. 'George Pullman hired himself a metic population in a political community where self-respect was closely tied to citizenship and where decisions about destinations and risks, even (or especially) local destinations and risks, were supposed to be shared.'[20] Citizenship requires independent citizens who

[19] This argument is found in J. Rawls, *A Theory of Justice* (Cambridge, Mass., 1971), 544–5, though Rawls resists extending its scope beyond civil and political rights to welfare rights.

[20] M. Walzer, *Spheres of Justice* (Oxford, 1983), 297.

are not continually forced to conform their wills to other people's outside the political realm, but have sufficient autonomy in their private lives to gain experience in exercising judgement.[21] It has, therefore, social preconditions.[22] But it does not follow that every aspect of civil society must be geared to the production of citizens, or that there is no space left for market relationships. Under normal circumstances, the independence of action that people enjoy in market contexts is compatible with the requirements of citizenship.[23]

Citizenship, however, is not just a matter of possessing rights, even if these are broadly interpreted. It is also a matter of belief and behaviour. The citizen has to see himself as playing an active role in determining his society's future, and as taking responsibility for the collective decisions that are made. He must be politically active, both in the sense of informing himself about the issues currently under discussion and in the sense of participating in decision-making itself. Moreover, he cannot regard politics merely as an arena in which to pursue his private interests. He must act *as* a citizen, that is as a member of a collectivity who is committed to advancing its common good. We have said that, for the socialist, the sought-after common identity must be an activist one. This has now to be cashed out as a specific way of engaging in politics.

[. . . Later] I [shall] look more closely at the form of politics

---

[21] The argument here can, of course, be run in either direction. I am assuming the value of universal citizenship and inferring that social life ought to be ordered in such a way that everyone develops the capacities of a citizen. An earlier generation of liberals took social relations as given, and argued for the restriction of citizenship to those who were competent to exercise it. See my 'Democracy and Social Justice', *British Journal of Political Science*, 8 (1978), 1–19, repr. in P. Birnbaum, J. Lively, and G. Parry (eds.), *Democracy, Consensus and Social Contract* (London, 1978).

[22] These are explored in D. S. King and J. Waldron, 'Citizenship, Social Citizenship and the Defence of Welfare Provision', *British Journal of Political Science*, 18 (1988), 415–43.

[23] The structure of enterprises will be of considerable significance here. If workers are directly involved in the making of economic decisions, as they are under market socialist arrangements, they are more likely to be active in politics, and hence better prepared for citizenship. For empirical confirmation of this, see E. S. Greenberg, 'Industrial Democracy and the Democratic Citizen', *Journal of Politics*, 43 (1981), 964–81.

which is demanded by the citizenship ideal, and ask whether it is a realistic possibility. At this point, we need only consider the feasibility of the ideal in general terms. Note first that, although the rights of citizenship must be distributed equally to everyone, it isn't necessary that each person should display the same level of political activity. Citizenship requires *some* level of political involvement (and equal opportunities beforehand), but it can allow for differences in taste. Michael Walzer has reminded us that there are ineradicable variations in people's desire for participation, and it would be intolerable to try to iron these out by making a high level of involvement compulsory.[24] There is no need to do so. Citizens can regard themselves as equals, and regard their common status as important, even though they are active to different degrees, just as members of a club can attach equal weight to membership even though they make varying use of the facilities provided.

But can citizenship be an important status in the first place? Scepticism about this claim extends from Marx's somewhat abstract argument that, so long as the division between civil society and state remains in existence, man's membership of the political community must be illusory—'man is the imaginary member of an imaginary sovereignty, divested of his real, individual life, and infused with an unreal universality'[25]—down to Robert Lane's empirical critique of the Rawlsian assertion that the possession and exercise of political rights is an important source of self-esteem.[26] What unites Marx and Lane, unlikely bedfellows in other respects, is the conviction that what really matters to people is the world of work and immediate personal relationship. For Marx, genuine communal relationships must be rooted in the sphere of production; for Lane, it is work, leisure, and family life that provide the major sources of self-esteem. The realm of politics is too distant and intangible for participation in it to be personally meaningful.[27]

[24] M. Walzer, 'A Day in the Life of a Socialist Citizen', in *Obligations* (Cambridge, Mass., 1970).

[25] K. Marx, 'On the Jewish Question', in *Karl Marx: Early Writings*, ed. T. B. Bottomore (London, 1963), 13–14.

[26] R. E. Lane, 'Government and Self-Esteem', *Political Theory*, 10 (1982), 5–31.

[27] Lane's claim is that as a matter of psychological fact political life is

It is tempting to write off these criticisms (and others like them) as merely a response to the limited form of citizenship available in capitalist societies—intuitive in Marx's case, empirically grounded in Lane's. Certainly we need to envisage very different institutions of citizenship—in particular, many more arenas of participation—if the ideal I have been sketching is to become a reality. But one essential contrast between private (including economic) life and political life would still remain. Broadly speaking, in the former realm we experience the results of our activity personally and directly—we see the object we have made, we bear the costs of our own decisions—whereas in the latter realm our voice is always one among many, and our collective decisions normally have quite a remote impact on our lives. Isn't it this almost truistic observation that finally justifies Marx's and Lane's scepticism?

In fact, although the observation is truistic, to infer from it that politics must always play a peripheral role in people's lives is to make a contestable assumption about human nature. The assumption is that material activity, activity which has immediate and tangible results, always counts for more than expressive and symbolic activity. This tenet has only to be spelt out for its frailty to be evident. If it were true, many things would be difficult to explain—the pre-eminent role of religion in many societies, for instance, or the motivating power of nationalism as an ideology capable of stimulating enormous self-sacrifice on behalf of the fatherland. That we find such experiences alien (and usually alarming) is a fact about the public culture of liberal societies, not the reflection of a truth about human nature. In liberal culture the person who is deeply engaged in politics is regarded with suspicion—either he is a fanatic, the victim of irrational impulses, or he is an opportunist, cloaking his ambition in idealist rhetoric. In ancient Greece, by contrast, this pre-

---

of marginal importance to citizens. Marx, writing in a somewhat different context, insists rather on the unreal quality of citizenship (the analogy with religion is used throughout). That is, political life may seem important to the citizen, but in believing this he is somehow deceived. (Marx doesn't explain why the belief is illusory; perhaps he is anticipating his later view that the state appears to act independently, but is in reality subordinate to the needs of civil society.)

sumption was reversed: the person who *withdrew* from normal political life was seen as deficient, as 'idiotic'.[28]

None of this addresses the practical difficulties involved in revivifying the role of citizen for the inhabitants of large, modern societies. To do so requires the exercise of some imagination.[29] The effort will be worthwhile only if the case made above for valuing citizenship is accepted. If so, we should not be deterred by current, disparaging attitudes towards political life. We should take a broader view.

4

How does this vision of community, combining nationality with citizenship, fare when tested against our original touchstone, the radical communitarian vision of Morris and Co.? We have abandoned the idea that communal relationships must be unitary. Instead people are related to one another in a number of different ways—as friends, as competitors in the market, as citizens, and so forth. This introduces an element of artifice into the relationship. We have to decide whether, on a particular occasion, our interaction should be governed by the norms of economic competition, say, or political loyalty. We will need markers to separate the various realms of existence from each other.[30] The transparency and simplicity of human intercourse in the radical vision is replaced by something more familiar, but not, I believe, less attractive. There is in the end something rather flat and insipid about life in the communist utopia, where all dealings between people are informed by the same sentiments of universal good will. Perhaps the idea of role-playing, and of coping with the dilemmas that arise when role-requirements arc

---

[28] See C. Berry, 'Idiotic Politics', *Political Studies*, 27 (1979), 550–63, and more generally H. Arendt, *The Human Condition* (Chicago, 1958), ch. 2.

[29] [. . .] For fuller discussions, see B. Barber, *Strong Democracy* (Berkeley, Calif., 1984), ch. 10, and P. Green, *Retrieving Democracy* (London, 1985), ch. 9.

[30] Bob Goodin's discussion of how the moral realm is kept free from contamination by more mundane motives illustrates this idea. See R. Goodin, 'Making Moral Incentives Pay', *Policy Sciences*, 12 (1980), 131–45.

felt to conflict, will seem on reflection to be integral to our idea of a mature human being.

Also abandoned is the idea of fraternity as an emotional bond linking members of the community, at least if that is understood literally, on the model of brotherhood. The new version still makes room for loyalty and emotional attachments, but the object of attachment is more abstract—a nation, the embodiment of a public culture. I may feel strongly attached to Britain, but it is absurd to suppose that I could feel fraternally towards every individual Briton. Size alone would ensure this, even if complexity of relationship did not. Reasoned conviction is also given a larger role to play in generating ties. I am committed to my compatriots partly because I am committed to the principles and policies that we have worked out together politically. [. . .]

Some elements in the radical vision are preserved. We have held on to the claim that a person's identity should be constituted, in part, by his membership of a collectivity, and shown how nationality and citizenship together can meet this demand. We have also seen how citizenship embodies an equality of status, and to that extent meets the radical ideal of egalitarian community. Finally, citizenship provides a moral underpinning for distribution according to need, and at the same time the practical means for realizing this ideal on a society-wide basis.

Whether the form of socialism I have sketched should be described as 'communitarian' is in the end a matter of definition and taste. To the extent that 'community' conjures up a 'natural' form of association, based on physical proximity and traditional ties—Tönnies's idea of *Gemeinschaft*[31]—some other term is preferable. Again, if community is thought to imply unitary relationships in the sense explained earlier, our proposals do not embody it. If, however, we follow recent debates in assuming that community has centrally to do with the constitutive role of social relationships in personal identity, then we have gone some way towards showing that market socialism can indeed be communitarian. [. . .]

---

[31] See F. Tönnies, *Gemeinschaft und Gesellschaft*, trans. as *Community and Association* (London, 1955).

6

FEMINISM AND MODERN FRIENDSHIP: DISLOCATING THE COMMUNITY

MARILYN FRIEDMAN

A predominant theme in much recent feminist thought has been the critique of the abstract individualism which underlies some important versions of liberal political theory.[1] Abstract individualism considers individual human beings as social atoms, abstracted from their social contexts, and disregards the role of social relationships and human community in constituting the very identity and nature of individual human beings. Sometimes the individuals of abstract individualism are posited as rationally self-interested utility maximizers.[2] Sometimes, also, they are theorized to form communities based fundamentally on competition and conflict among persons vying for scarce resources, communities which represent no deeper social

Marilyn Friedman, excerpted from *Ethics*, 99 (1989), 275–90. Copyright © The University of Chicago Press 1989. Used by permission.

[1] Cf. C. Pateman, *The Problem of Political Obligation: A Critique of Liberal Theory* (Berkeley, Calif., 1979); Z. Eisenstein, *The Radical Future of Liberal Feminism* (New York, 1981); N. C. M. Hartsock, *Money, Sex, and Power* (Boston, 1983); A. M. Jaggar, *Feminist Politics and Human Nature* (Totowa, NJ, 1983); N. Scheman, 'Individualism and the Objects of Psychology', in S. Harding and M. B. Hintikka (eds.), *Discovering Reality* (Dordrecht, 1983), 225–44; J. Flax, 'Political Philosophy and the Patriarchal Unconscious: A Psychoanalytic Perspective on Epistemology and Metaphysics', in Harding and Hintikka (eds.), *Discovering Reality*, pp. 245–81; and S. Benhabib, 'The Generalized and the Concrete Other: The Kohlberg–Gilligan Controversy and Moral Theory', in E. F. Kittay and D. T. Meyers (eds.), *Women and Moral Theory* (Totowa, NJ, 1987), 154–77.

[2] Cf. D. Gauthier, *Morals by Agreement* (Oxford, 1986).

bond than that of instrumental relations based on calculated self-interest.[3]

Against this abstractive individualist view of the self and of human community, many feminists have asserted a conception of what might be called the 'social self'.[4] This conception fundamentally acknowledges the role of social relationships and human community in constituting both self-identity and the nature and meaning of the particulars of individual lives.[5] The modified conception of the self has carried with it an altered conception of community. Conflict and competition are no longer considered to be the basic human relationships; instead they are being replaced by alternative visions of the foundation of human society derived from nurturance, caring attachment, and mutual interestedness.[6] Some feminists, for example, recommend that the mother–child relationship be viewed as central to human society, and they project major changes in moral theory from such a revised focus.[7]

Some of these anti-individualist developments emerging from feminist thought are strikingly similar to other theoretical developments which are not specifically feminist. Thus, the 'new communitarians', to borrow Amy Gutmann's term,[8] have also reacted critically to various aspects of modern liberal thought, including abstract individualism, rational egoism, and an instrumental conception of social relationships. The communitarian self, or subject, is also not a social atom but is instead a being constituted and defined by its attachments, including the

---

[3] Cf. G. Homans, *Social Behavior: Its Elementary Forms* (New York, 1961); and P. Blau, *Exchange and Power in Social Life* (New York, 1974).

[4] Cf. my 'Autonomy in Social Context', in J. Sterba and C. Peden (eds.), *Freedom, Equality, and Social Change: Problems in Social Philosophy Today* (Lewiston, NY, 1989).

[5] Cf. D. Cornell, 'Toward a Modern/Postmodern Reconstruction of Ethics', *University of Pennsylvania Law Review*, 133 (1985), 291–380.

[6] Cf. A. Baier, 'Trust and Antitrust', *Ethics*, 96 (1986), 231–60; and O. Flanagan and K. Jackson, 'Justice, Care, and Gender: The Kohlberg–Gilligan Debate Revisited', *Ethics*, 97 (1987), 622–37.

[7] Cf. Hartsock, *Money, Sex, and Power*, pp. 41–2; and V. Held, 'Non-Contractual Society', in M. Hanen and K. Nielsen (eds.), *Science, Morality and Feminist Theory* (*Canadian Journal of Philosophy*, 13, suppl. (1987), 111–38).

[8] A. Gutmann, 'Communitarian Critics of Liberalism', *Philosophy and Public Affairs*, 14 (1985), 308–22.

particularities of its social relationships, community ties, and historical context. Its identity cannot be abstracted from community or social relationships.

With the recent feminist attention to values of care, nurturance, and relatedness—values that psychologists call 'communal'[9] and which have been amply associated with women and women's moral reasoning[10]—one might anticipate that communitarian theory would offer important insights for feminist reflection. There is considerable power to the model of the self as deriving its identity and nature from its social relationships, from the way it is intersubjectively apprehended, from the norms of the community in which it is embedded.

However, communitarian philosophy as a whole is a perilous ally for feminist theory. Communitarians invoke a model of community which is focused particularly on families, neighbourhoods, and nations. These sorts of communities have harboured social roles and structures which have been highly oppressive for women, as recent feminist critiques have shown. But communitarians seem oblivious to those criticisms and manifest a troubling complacency about the moral authority claimed or presupposed by these communities in regard to their members. By building on uncritical references to those sorts of communities, communitarian philosophy can lead in directions which feminists should not wish to follow.

This article is an effort to redirect communitarian thought so as to avoid some of the pitfalls which it poses, in its present form, for feminist theory and feminist practice. In the first part of the article, I develop some feminist-inspired criticisms of communitarian philosophy as it is found in writings by Michael Sandel and Alasdair MacIntyre.[11] My brief critique of communitarian thought has the aim of showing that communitarian theory, in the form in which it condones or tolerates traditional communal norms of gender subordination, is unacceptable from any

---

[9] Cf. A. H. Eagly and V. J. Steffen, 'Gender Stereotypes Stem from the Distribution of Women and Men into Social Roles', *Journal of Personality and Social Psychology*, 46 (1984), 735–54.

[10] Cf. C. Gilligan, *In a Different Voice* (Cambridge, Mass., 1989).

[11] In particular, M. Sandel, *Liberalism and the Limits of Justice* (Cambridge, 1982); A. MacIntyre, *After Virtue* (Notre Dame, Ind., 1981).

standpoint enlightened by feminist analysis. This does not preclude agreeing with certain specific communitarian views, for example, the broad metaphysical conception of the individual, self, or subject as constituted by its social relationships and communal ties, or the assumption that traditional communities have some value. But the aim of the first section is critical: to focus on the communitarian disregard of gender-related problems with the norms and practices of traditional communities.

In the second part of the article, I will delve more deeply into the nature of different types of community and social relationship. I will suggest that friendships, on the one hand, and urban relationships and communities, on the other, offer an important clue toward a model of community which usefully counterbalances the family–neighbourhood–nation complex favoured by communitarians. With that model in view, we can begin to transform the communitarian vision of self and community into a more congenial ally for feminist theory.

THE SOCIAL SELF, IN COMMUNITARIAN PERSPECTIVE

[. . .] Despite the feminist concern with a social conception of the self and the importance of social relationships, at least three features of the communitarian version of these notions are troubling from a feminist standpoint. First, a relatively minor point: the communitarian's metaphysical conception of an inherently social self has little usefulness for normative analysis; in particular, it will not support a specifically feminist critique of individualist personality. Second, communitarian theory fails to acknowledge that many communities make illegitimate moral claims on their members, linked to hierarchies of domination and subordination. Third, the specific communities of family, neighbourhood, and nation so commonly invoked by communitarians are troubling paradigms of social relationship and communal life. I will discuss each of these points in turn.

First, the communitarian's metaphysical conception of the social self will not support feminist critiques of ruggedly individualist personality or its associated attributes: the avoidance of intimacy, nonnurturance, social distancing, aggression, or violence. Feminist theorists have often been interested in developing a critique of the norm of the highly individualistic, competitive, aggressive personality type, seeing that personality type as more characteristically male than female and as an important part of the foundation for patriarchy.

Largely following the work of Nancy Chodorow, Dorothy Dinnerstein, and, more recently, Carol Gilligan,[12] many feminists have theorized that the processes of psycho-gender development, in a society in which early infant care is the primary responsibility of women but not men, result in a radical distinction between the genders in the extent to which the self is constituted by, and self-identifies with, its relational connections to others. Males are theorized to seek and value autonomy, individuation, separation, and the moral ideals of rights and justice which are thought to depend on a highly individuated conception of persons. By contrast, females are theorized to seek and value connection, sociality, inclusion, and moral ideals of care and nurturance.

From this perspective, highly individuated selves have been viewed as a problem. They are seen as incapable of human attachments based on mutuality and trust, unresponsive to human needs, approaching social relationships merely as rationally self-interested utility maximizers, thriving on separation and competition, and creating social institutions which tolerate, even legitimize, violence and aggression.

However, a metaphysical view that all human selves are constituted by their social and communal relationships does not itself entail a critique of these highly individualistic selves or yield any indication of what degree of psychological attachment to others is desirable. On metaphysical grounds alone, there would be no reason to suppose that caring, nurturant, relational, sociable selves were better than more autonomous, individualistic, and separate selves. All would be equivalently socially constituted at a metaphysical level. Abstract individualism's failure would be, not that it has produced asocial selves, for, on the communitarian view, such beings are metaphysically

---

[12] D. Dinnerstein, *The Mermaid and the Minotaur: Sexual Arrangements and Human Malaise* (New York, 1976); N. Chodorow, *The Reproduction of Mothering* (Berkeley, Calif., 1978); and Gilligan, *In a Different Voice*.

impossible, but, rather, that it has simply failed theoretically to acknowledge that selves are inherently social. And autonomy, independence, and separateness would become just a different way of being socially constituted, no worse nor better than heteronomy, dependence, or connectedness.

The communitarian conception of the social self, if it were simply a metaphysical view about the constitution of the self (which is what it seems to be), thus provides no basis for regarding nurturant, relational selves as morally superior to those who are highly individualistic. For that reason, it appears to be of no assistance to feminist theorists seeking a normative account of what might be wrong or excessive about competitive self-seeking behaviours or other seeming manifestations of an individualistic perspective. The communitarian 'social self', as a metaphysical account of the self, is largely irrelevant to the array of normative tasks which many feminist thinkers have set for a conception of the self.

My second concern about communitarian philosophy has to do with the legitimacy of the moral influences which communities exert over their members and which are supposed to define the moral starting-points of those members. As a matter of moral psychology, it is common for subjects to regard or presume as binding the moral claims made upon them by the norms of their communities. However, this point about moral psychology does not entail an endorsement of those moral claims, and it leaves open the question of whether, and to what extent, those claims might 'really' be morally binding. Unfortunately, the new communitarians seem sometimes to go beyond the point of moral psychology to a stronger view, namely, that the moral claims of communities really are morally binding, at least as 'moral starting-points'. MacIntyre refers to the 'debts, inheritances, *rightful* expectations and obligations' which we 'inherit' from family, nation, and so forth.[13]

But such inheritances are enormously varied and troubling. Many communities are characterized by practices of exclusion and suppression of non-group members, especially outsiders defined by ethnicity and sexual orientation.[14] If the new com-

---

[13] MacIntyre, *After Virtue*, p. 205 (emphasis added).

[14] A similar point is made by I. Young, 'The Ideal of Community and the Politics of Difference', *Social Theory and Practice*, 12 (1986), 12–13.

munitarians do not recognize legitimate 'debts, inheritances, rightful expectations and obligations' across community lines, then their views have little relevance for our radically hetero-geneous modern society. If people have 'rightful expectations and obligations' across community lines, if, for example, whites have debts to blacks and Native Americans for histories of exploitation, if Germany owed reparations to non-Germans for genocidal practices, and so on, then 'the' community as such, that is, the relatively bounded and local network of relationships which forms a subject's primary social setting, would not singularly determine the legitimate moral values or require-ments which rightfully constitute the self's moral commitments or self-definition.

Besides excluding or suppressing outsiders, the practices and traditions of numerous communities are exploitative and oppressive towards many of their own members. This problem is of special relevance to women. Feminist theory is rooted in a recognition of the need for change in all the traditions and practices which show gender differentiation; many of these are located in just the sorts of communities invoked by communi-tarians, for example, family practices and national political traditions. The communitarian emphasis on communities unfortunately dovetails too well with the current popular emphasis on 'the family' and seems to hark back to the repres-sive world of what some sociologists call communities of 'place', the world of family, neighbourhood, school, and church, which so intimately enclosed women in oppressive gender politics—the peculiar politics which it has been feminism's distinctive contri-bution to uncover. Any political theory which appears to sup-port the hegemony of such communities and which appears to restore them to a position of unquestioned moral authority must be viewed with grave suspicion. I will come back to this issue when I turn to my third objection to communitarian philosophy.

Thus, while admitting into our notion of the self the impor-tant constitutive role played by social and communal relation-ships, we, from a standpoint independent of some particular subject, are not forced to accept as binding on that subject the moral claims made by the social and communal relationships in which that subject is embedded or by which she is identified. Nor are we required to say that any particular subject is herself morally obliged to accept as binding the moral claims made on her by any of the communities which constitute or define her. To evaluate the moral identities conferred by communities on their members, we need a theory of communities, of their inter-relationships, of the structures of power, dominance, and oppression within and among them. Only such a theory would allow us to assess the legitimacy of the claims made by communities upon their members by way of their traditions, practices, and conventions of 'debts, inheritances . . . expectations, and obligations'.

The communitarian approach suggests an attitude of celebrating the attachments which one finds oneself unavoidably to have, the familial ties and so forth. But some relationships compete with others, and some relationships provide standpoints from which other relationships appear threatening or dangerous to oneself, one's integrity, or one's well-being. In such cases, simple formulas about the value of community provide no guidance. The problem is not simply to appreciate community *per se* but, rather, to reconcile the conflicting claims, demands, and identity-defining influences of the variety of communities of which one is a part.

It is worth recalling that liberalism has always condemned, in principle if not in practice, the norms of social hierarchy and political subordination based on inherited or ascribed status. Where liberals historically have applied this tenet at best only to the public realm of civic relationships, feminism seeks to extend it more radically to the 'private' realm of family and other communities of place. Those norms and claims of local communities which sustain gender hierarchies have no intrinsic legitimacy from a feminist standpoint. A feminist interest in community must certainly aim for social institutions and relational structures which diminish and, finally, erase gender subordination.

Reflections such as these characterize the concerns of the modern self, the self who acknowledges no a priori loyalty to any feature of situation or role, and who claims the right to question the moral legitimacy of any contingent moral claim.[15] We can agree with the communitarians that it would be impossible for

---

[15] Cf. Cornell, 'Toward a Modern/Postmodern Reconstruction of Ethics', p. 323.

the self to question all her contingencies at once, yet at the same time, unlike the communitarians, still emphasize the critical importance of morally questioning various communal norms and circumstances.

A third problem with communitarian philosophy has to do with the sorts of communities evidently endorsed by communitarian theorists. Human beings participate in a variety of communities and social relationships, not only across time, but at any one time. However, when people think of 'community', it is common for them to think of certain particular social networks, namely, those formed primarily out of family, neighbourhood, school, and church.[16] MacIntyre and Sandel both emphasize family specifically. MacIntyre cites neighbourhood along with clan, tribe, city, and nation, while Sandel includes 'nation or people . . . bearers of this history . . . sons and daughters of that revolution . . . citizens of this republic'.[17]

But where, one might ask, is the International Ladies Garment Workers' Union, the Teamsters, the Democratic Party, Alcoholics Anonymous, or the Committee in Solidarity with the People of El Salvador?

The substantive examples of community listed by MacIntyre and Sandel fall largely into two groups: one, governmental communities which constitute our civic and national identities in a public world of nation-states, and two, local communities centred around family and neighbourhood. Although MacIntyre does mention professions and, rather archaically, 'guilds',[18] these references are anomalous in his work, which, for the most part, ignores such communities as trade unions, political action groups, associations of hobbyists, and so forth.

Some of the communities cited by MacIntyre and Sandel will resonate with the historical experiences of women, especially the inclusive communities of family and neighbourhood. However, it should not be forgotten that governing communities have, until only recently, excluded the legitimate participation of women. It would seem to follow that they have accordingly not

---

[16] This point is made by Young, 'The Ideal of Community', p. 12.

[17] MacIntyre, *After Virtue*, p. 204; Sandel, *Liberalism and the Limits of Justice*, p. 179.

[18] MacIntyre, *After Virtue*, p. 204.

historically constituted the identities of women in profound ways. As 'daughters' of the American revolution, looking back to the 'fathers of our country', we find that we have inconveniently been deprived of the self-identifying heritage of our cultural mothers. In general, the contribution made to the identities of various groups of people by governing communities is quite uneven, given that they are communities to which many are subject but in which far fewer actively participate.

At any rate, there is an underlying commonality to most of the communities which MacIntyre and Sandel cite as constitutive of self-identity and definitive of our moral starting-points. Sandel himself explicates this commonality when he writes that, for people 'bound by a sense of community', the notion of community describes *'not a relationship they choose (as in a voluntary association) but an attachment they discover*, not merely an attribute but a constituent of their identity'.[19] Not voluntary but 'discovered' relationships and communities are what Sandel takes to define subjective identity for those who are bound by a 'sense of community'. It is the communities to which we are involuntarily bound to which Sandel accords metaphysical pride of place in the constitution of subjectivity. What are important are not simply the 'associations' in which people 'co-operate' but the 'communities' in which people 'participate', for these latter 'describe a form of life in which the members find themselves commonly situated "to begin with"', their commonality consisting less in relationships they have entered than in attachments they have found'.[20] Thus, the social relationships which one finds, the attachments which are discovered and not chosen, become the points of reference for self-definition by the communitarian subject.

For the child maturing to self-consciousness in her community of origin, typically the family–neighbourhood–school–church complex, it seems uncontroversial that 'the' community is found, not entered, discovered, not created. But this need not be true of an adult's communities of mature self-identification. Many of these adult communities are, for at least some of their members, communities of choice to a significant extent: labour

---

[19] Sandel, *Liberalism and the Limits of Justice*, p. 150 (emphasis added).
[20] Ibid. 151–2.

unions, philanthropic associations, political coalitions, and, if one has ever moved or migrated, even the communities of neighbourhood, church, city, or nation-state might have been chosen to an important extent. One need not have simply discovered oneself to be embedded in them in order that one's identity or the moral particulars of one's life be defined by them. Sandel is right to indicate the role of found communities in constituting the unreflective, 'given' identity which the self discovers when *first* beginning to reflect on itself. But, for mature self-identity, we should also recognize a legitimate role for communities of choice, supplementing, if not displacing, the communities and attachments which are merely found.

Moreover, the discovered identity constituted by one's original community of place might be fraught with ambivalences and ambiguities. Thus, poet Adrienne Rich writes about her experiences growing up with a Christian mother, a Jewish father who suppressed his ethnicity, and a family community which taught Adrienne Rich contempt for all that was identified with Jewishness. In 1946, while still a high-school student, Rich saw, for the first time, a film about the Allied liberation of Nazi concentration camps. Writing about this experience in 1982, she brooded: 'I feel belated rage that I was so impoverished by the family and social worlds I lived in, that I had to try to figure out by myself what this did indeed mean for me. That I had never been taught about resistance, only about passing. That I had no language for anti-Semitism itself.'[21] As a student at Radcliffe in the late forties, Rich met 'real' Jewish women who inducted her into the lore of Jewish background and customs, holidays and foods, names and noses. She plunged in with trepidation: 'I felt I was testing a forbidden current, that there was danger in these revelations. I bought a reproduction of a Chagall portrait of a rabbi in striped prayer shawl and hung it on the wall of my room. I was admittedly young and trying to educate myself, but I was also doing something that *is* dangerous: I was flirting with identity.'[22] And she was doing it apart

---

[21] A. Rich, 'Split at the Root: An Essay on Jewish Identity', in her *Blood, Bread, and Poetry* (New York, 1986), 107; repr. from Evelyn Torton Beck (ed.), *Nice Jewish Girls: A Lesbian Anthology* (Trumansburg, NY, 1982), 67–84.
[22] Ibid. 108.

from the family community from which her ambiguous ethnic identity was originally derived.

For Sandel, Rich's lifelong troubled reflections on her ethnic identity might seem compatible with his theory. In his view, the subject discovers the attachments which are constitutive of its subjectivity through reflection on a multitude of values and aims, differentiating what is self from what is not-self. He might say that Rich discriminated among the many loyalties and projects which defined who she was in her original community, that is, her family, and discerned that her Jewishness appeared 'essential'[23] to who she was. But it is not obvious, without question begging, that her original community really defined her as essentially Jewish. Indeed, her family endeavoured to suppress loyalties and attachments to all things Jewish. Thus, one of Rich's quests in life, so evidently not inspired by her community of origin alone, was to re-examine the identity found in that original context. The communitarian view that found communities and social attachments constitute self-identity does not, by itself, explicate the source of such a quest. It seems more illuminating to say that her identity became, in part, 'chosen', that it had to do with social relationships and attachments which she sought out, rather than merely found, created as well as discovered.

Thus, the commitments and loyalties of our found communities, our communities of origin, may harbour ambiguities, ambivalences, contradictions, and oppressions which complicate as well as constitute identity and which have to be sorted out, critically scrutinized. And since the resources for such scrutiny may not be found in all 'found' communities, our theories of community should recognize that resources and skills derived from communities which are not merely found or discovered may equally well contribute to the constitution of identity. The constitution of identity and moral particularity, for the modern self, may well require radically different communities from those so often invoked by communitarians.

The whole tenor of communitarian thinking would change once we opened up the conception of the social self to encompass chosen communities, especially those which lie beyond the

---

[23] This term is used by Sandel, *Liberalism and the Limits of Justice*, p. 180.

typical original community of family–neighbourhood–school–church. No longer would communitarian thought present a seemingly conservative complacency about the private and local communities of place which have so effectively circumscribed, in particular, the lives of most women.

In the second part of this article, I will explore more fully the role of communities and relationships of 'choice', which point the way toward a notion of community more congenial to feminist aspirations.

MODERN FRIENDSHIP, URBAN COMMUNITY, AND BEYOND

My goals are manifold: to retain the communitarian insights about the contribution of community and social relationship to self-identity, yet open up for critical reflection the moral particulars imparted by those communities, and identify the sorts of communities which will provide non-oppressive and enriched lives for women.

Toward this end, it will be helpful to consider models of human relationship and community which contrast with those cited by communitarians. I believe that friendship and urban community can offer us crucial insights into the social nature of the modern self. It is in moving forward from these relationships that we have the best chance of reconciling the communitarian conception of the social self with the longed-for communities of feminist aspiration.

Both modern friendship and the stereotypical urban community share an important feature which is either neglected or deliberately avoided in communitarian conceptions of human relationship. From a liberal, or Enlightenment, or modernist standpoint, this feature would be characterized as voluntariness: those relationships are based partly on choice.

Let us first consider friendship as it is understood in this culture. Friends are supposed to be people whom one chooses on one's own to share activities and intimacies. No particular people are assigned by custom or tradition to be a person's friends. From among the larger number of one's acquaintances, one moves toward closer and more friendlike relationships with some of them, motivated by one's own needs, values, and attractions. No consanguineous or legal connections establish or maintain ties of friendship. As this relationship is widely understood in our culture, its basis lies in voluntary choice.

In this context, 'voluntary choice' refers to motivations arising out of one's own needs, desires, interests, values, and attractions, in contrast to motivations arising from what is socially assigned, ascribed, expected, or demanded. This means that friendship is more likely than many other relationships, such as those of family and neighbourhood, to be grounded in and sustained by shared interests and values, mutual affection, and possibilities for generating mutual respect and esteem.

In general, friendship has had an obvious importance to feminist aspirations as the basis of the bond which is (ironically) called 'sisterhood'.[24] Friendship is more likely than many other close personal relationships to provide social support for people who are idiosyncratic, whose unconventional values and deviant life-styles make them victims of intolerance from family members and others who are unwillingly related to them. In this regard, friendship has socially disruptive possibilities, for out of the unconventional living which it helps to sustain there often arise influential forces for social change. Friendship among women has been the cement not only of the various historical waves of the feminist movement, but as well of numerous communities of women throughout history who defied the local conventions for their gender and lived lives of creative disorder.[25] In all these cases, women moved out of their given or found communities into new attachments with other women by their own choice, that is, motivated by their own needs, desires, attractions, and fears rather than, and often in opposition to, the expectations and ascribed roles of their found communities.

Like friendship, many urban relationships are also based more on choice than on socially ascribed roles, biological connections, or other non-voluntary ties. Voluntary associations,

---

[24] Martha Ackelsberg points out the ironic and misleading nature of this use of the term 'sisterhood' in '"Sisters" or "Comrades"? The Politics of Friends and Families', in I. Diamond (ed.), *Families, Politics, and Public Policy* (New York, 1983), 339–56.

[25] Cf. J. Raymond, *A Passion for Friends* (Boston, 1986), esp. chs. 2 and 3.

such as political action groups, support groups, associations of co-hobbyists, and so on, are a common part of modern urban life, with its large population centres and the greater availability of critical masses of people with special interests or needs. But while friendship is almost universally extolled, urban communities and relationships have been theorized in wildly contradictory ways. Cities have sometimes been taken as 'harbingers' of modern culture *per se*[26] and have been particularly associated with the major social trends of modern life, such as industrialization and bureaucratization.[27] The results of these trends are often thought to have been a fragmentation of 'real' community and the widely lamented alienation of modern urban life: people seldom know their neighbours; population concentration generates massive psychic overload;[28] fear and mutual distrust, even outright hostility, generated by the dangers of urban life, may dominate most daily associations. Under such circumstances, meaningful relationships are often theorized to be rare, if at all possible.

But is this image a complete portrait of urban life? It is probably true, in urban areas, that communities of place are diminished in importance; neighbourhood plays a far less significant role in constituting community than it does in non-urban areas.[29] But this does not mean that the social networks and communities of urban dwellers are inferior to those of non-urban residents.

Much evidence suggests that urban settings do not, as commonly stereotyped, promote only alienation, isolation, and psychic breakdown. The communities available to urban dwellers are different from those available to non-urban dwellers, but not necessarily less gratifying or fulfilling.[30] Communities of place are relatively non-voluntary; one's extended family of origin is given or ascribed, and the relationships found as one grows.

[26] C. Fischer, *To Dwell among Friends* (Chicago, 1982), 1.

[27] Cf. R. Sennett, 'An Introduction', in R. Sennett (ed.), *Classic Essays on the Culture of Cities* (New York, 1969), 3–22.

[28] Cf. S. Milgram, 'The Experience of Living in Cities', *Science*, 167 (1970), 1461–8.

[29] Fischer, *To Dwell among Friends*, pp. 97–103.

[30] Ibid. 193–232.

Sociological research has shown that urban dwellers tend to form their social networks, their communities, out of people who are brought together for reasons other than geographical proximity. As sociologist Claude Fischer has stated it, in urban areas 'population concentration stimulates allegiances to sub-cultures based on more significant social traits' than common locality or neighbourhood.[31] Communities of place, centred around the family–neighbourhood–church–school web, are more likely, for urban dwellers, to be supplanted by other sorts of communities, resulting in what the sociologist Melvin Webber has called 'community without propinquity'.[32] But most important for our purposes, these are still often genuine communities, and not the cesspools of 'Rum, Romanism, and Rebellion' sometimes depicted by anti-urbanists.

Literature reveals that women writers have been both repelled and inspired by cities. The city, as a concentrated centre of male political and economic power, seems to exclude women altogether.[33] However, as literary critic Susan Merrill Squier points out, the city can provide women not only with jobs, education, and the cultural tools with which to escape imposed gender roles, familial demands, and domestic servitude, but can also bring women together, in work or in leisure, and lay the basis for bonds of sisterhood.[34] The quests of women who journey to cities leaving behind men, home, and family are subversive, writes literary critic Blanche Gelfant, and may well be perceived by others 'as assaults upon society'.[35] Thus, cities open up for women possibilities of supplanting communities of place with relationships and communities of choice. These chosen communities can provide the resources for women to

---

[31] Ibid. 273.

[32] M. Webber, 'Order in Diversity: Community without Propinquity', in R. Gutman and D. Popenoe (eds.), *Neighbourhood, City and Metropolis* (New York, 1970), 792–811.

[33] Cf. the essays in C. Stimpson *et al.* (eds.), *Women and the American City* (Chicago, 1980, 1981); and the special issue on 'Women in the City', *Urban Resources*, 3. 2 (Winter 1986).

[34] Introduction to S. M. Squier (ed.), *Women Writers and the City* (Knoxville, Tenn., 1984), 3–10.

[35] B. Gelfant, 'Sister to Faust: The City's "Hungry" Woman as Heroine', in Squier (ed.), *Women Writers and the City*, p. 267.

surmount the moral particularities of family and place which define and limit their moral starting-points.

Social theorists have long decried the interpersonal estrangement of urban life, an observation which seems predominantly inspired by the public world of conflict between various subcultural groups. Urbanism does not create interpersonal estrangement within subcultures but, rather, tends to promote social involvement.[36] This is especially true for people with special backgrounds and interests, for people who are members of small minorities, and for ethnic groups. Fischer has found that social relationships in urban centres are more 'culturally specialized: urbanites were relatively involved with associates in the social world they considered most important and relatively uninvolved with associates, if any, in other worlds'.[37] As Fischer summarizes it, 'Urbanism . . . fosters social involvement in the subculture(s) of *choice*, rather than the subculture(s) of circumstances.'[38] This is doubtless reinforced by the recent more militant expression of group values and group demands for rights and respect on the parts of urban subcultural minorities.

We might describe urban relationships as being characteristically 'modern' to signal their relatively greater voluntary basis. We find, in these relationships and the social networks formed of them, not a loss of community but an increase in importance of community of a different sort from that of family–neighbourhood–church–school complexes. Yet these more voluntary communities may be as deeply constitutive of the identities and particulars of the individuals who participate in them as are the communities of place so warmly invoked by communitarians.

Perhaps it is more illuminating to say that communities of choice foster not so much the constitution of subjects but their reconstitution. They may be sought out as contexts in which people relocate the various constituents of their identities, as Adrienne Rich sought out the Jewish community in her college years. While people in a community of choice may not share a common history, their shared values or interests are likely to

[36] Fischer, *To Dwell among Friends*, pp. 247–8.
[37] Ibid. 230.
[38] Ibid.

manifest backgrounds of similar experiences, as, for example, among the members of a lesbian community. The modern self may seek new communities whose norms and relationships stimulate and develop her identity and self-understanding more adequately than her unchosen community of origin, her original community of place.

In case it is chosen communities which help us to define ourselves, the project of self-definition would not be arising from communities in which we merely found or discovered our immersion. It is likely that chosen communities, lesbian communities, for example, attract us in the first place because they appeal to features of ourselves which, though perhaps merely found or discovered, were inadequately or ambivalently sustained by our unchosen families, neighbourhoods, schools, or churches. Thus, unchosen communities are sometimes communities which we can, and should, leave, searching elsewhere for the resources to help us discern who we really are.

Our communities of origin do not necessarily constitute us as selves who agree or comply with the norms which unify those communities. Some of us are constituted as deviants and resisters by our communities of origin, and our defiance may well run to the foundational social norms which ground the most basic social roles and relationships upon which those communities rest. The feminist challenge to sex/gender arrangements is precisely of this foundational sort.

A community of choice might be a community of people who share a common oppression. This is particularly critical in those instances in which the shared oppression is not concentrated within certain communities of place, as it might be, for example, in the case of ethnic minorities, but, rather, is focused on people who are distributed throughout social and ethnic groupings and who do not themselves constitute a traditional community of place. Women are a prime example of such a distributed group. Women's communities are seldom the original, non-voluntary, found communities of their members.

To be sure, non-voluntary communities of place are not without value. Most lives contain mixtures of relationships and communities, some given/found/discovered and some chosen/created. Most people probably are, to some extent, ineradicably constituted by their communities of place, the community defined by some or all of their family, neighbourhood, school, or church. It is noteworthy that dependent children, elderly persons, and all other individuals whose lives and well-being are at great risk need the support of communities whose other members do not or cannot choose arbitrarily to leave. Recent philosophical investigation into communities and relationships not founded or sustained by choice has brought out the importance of these social networks for the constitution of social life.[39] But these insights should not obscure the additional need for communities of choice to counter oppressive and abusive relational structures in those non-voluntary communities by providing models of alternative social relationships as well as standpoints for critical reflection on self and community.

Having attained a critically reflective stance toward one's communities of origin, one's community of place, toward family, neighbourhood, church, school, and nation, one has probably at the same time already begun to question and distance oneself from aspects of one's 'identity' in that community and, therefore, to have embarked on the path of personal redefinition. From such a perspective, the uncritically assumed communities of place invoked by the communitarians appear deeply problematic. We can concede the influence of those communities without having unreflectively to endorse it. We must develop communitarian thought beyond its complacent regard for the communities in which we once found ourselves toward (and beyond) an awareness of the crucial importance of dislocated communities, communities of choice.

[39] Cf. Baier, 'Trust and Antitrust'; Held, 'Non-Contractual Society'; and Pateman, *The Problem of Political Obligation*.

7

COMMUNITARIAN CRITICS OF
LIBERALISM*

AMY GUTMANN

We are witnessing a revival of communitarian criticisms of liberal political theory. Like the critics of the 1960s, those of the 1980s fault liberalism for being mistakenly and irreparably individualistic. But the new wave of criticism is not a mere repetition of the old. Whereas the earlier critics were inspired by Marx, the recent critics are inspired by Aristotle and Hegel. The Aristotelian idea that justice is rooted in 'a community whose primary bond is a shared understanding both of the good for man and the good of that community' explicitly informs Alasdair MacIntyre in his criticism of John Rawls and Robert Nozick for their neglect of desert;[1] and Charles Taylor in his

Amy Gutmann, from *Philosophy and Public Affairs*, 14/3 (Summer 1985), 308–22. Copyright © 1985 by Princeton University Press. Used by permission.

*This review essay concentrates on the arguments presented in M. Sandel, *Liberalism and the Limits of Justice* (New York, 1982); Sandel, 'Morality and the Liberal Ideal', *The New Republic*, 7 May 1984, pp. 15–17; A. MacIntyre, *After Virtue* (Notre Dame, Ind., 1981); and MacIntyre, 'Is Patriotism a Virtue?' *The Lindley Lecture* (University of Kansas: Department of Philosophy, 26 Mar. 1984). Other works to which I refer are B. Barber, *Strong Democracy: Participatory Politics for a New Age* (Berkeley, Calif., 1984); C. Taylor, 'Atomism', in A. Kontos (ed.), *Powers, Possessions and Freedoms: Essays in Honor of C. B. Macpherson* (Toronto, 1979), 39–61 (ch. 2 in this volume), and 'The Diversity of Goods', in A. Sen and B. Williams (eds.), *Utilitarianism and Beyond* (New York, 1982), 129–44; R. M. Unger, *Knowledge and Politics* (New York, 1975); and M. Walzer, *Spheres of Justice* (New York, 1983). I am grateful to Robert Amdur, Michael Doyle, Steven Lukes, Susan Moller Okin, Judith Shklar, Dennis Thompson, Michael Walzer, Susan Wolf, and the Editors of *Philosophy and Public Affairs* for their helpful suggestions.

[1] MacIntyre, *After Virtue*, pp. 232–3.

attack on 'atomistic' liberals who 'try to defend . . . the priority of the individual and his rights over society'.[2] The Hegelian conception of man as a historically conditioned being implicitly informs both Roberto Unger's and Michael Sandel's rejection of the liberal view of man as a free and rational being.[3]

The political implications of the new communitarian criticisms are correspondingly more conservative. Whereas the good society of the old critics was one of collective property ownership and equal political power, the good society of the new critics is one of settled traditions and established identities. For many of the old critics, the role of women within the family was symptomatic of their social and economic oppression; for Sandel, the family serves as a model of community and evidence of a good greater than justice.[4] For the old critics, patriotism was an irrational sentiment that stood in the way of world peace; for MacIntyre, the particularistic demands of patriotism are no less rational than the universalistic demands of justice.[5] The old critics were inclined to defend deviations from majoritarian morality in the name of non-repression; the new critics are inclined to defend the efforts of local majorities to ban offensive activities in the name of preserving their community's 'way of life and the values that sustain it'.[6]

The subject of the new and the old criticism also differs. The new critics recognize that Rawls's work has altered the premisses and principles of contemporary liberal theory. Contemporary liberals do not assume that people are possessive individualists; the source of their individualism lies at a deeper, more metaphysical level. According to Sandel, the problem is that liberalism has faulty foundations: in order to achieve absolute priority for principles of justice, liberals must hold a set of implausible metaphysical views about the self. They cannot admit, for example, that our personal identities are partly defined by our communal attachments.[7] According to

[2] Taylor, 'Atomism', ch. 2.
[3] Unger, *Knowledge and Politics*, pp. 85, 191–231; Sandel, *Liberalism and the Limits of Justice*, pp. 179–80.
[4] Sandel, *Liberalism and the Limits of Justice*, pp. 30–1, 33–4, 169.
[5] MacIntyre, 'Is Patriotism a Virtue?' pp. 15–18 and *passim*.
[6] Sandel, 'Morality and the Liberal Ideal', p. 17.
[7] Sandel, *Liberalism and the Limits of Justice*, pp. 64–5, 168–73.

MacIntyre, the problem is that liberalism lacks any foundations at all. It cannot be rooted in the only kind of social life that provides a basis for moral judgements, one which 'views man as having an essence which defines his true end'.[8] Liberals are therefore bound either to claim a false certainty for their principles or to admit that morality is merely a matter of individual opinion, that is, is no morality at all.

The critics claim that many serious problems originate in the foundational faults of liberalism. Perhaps the most troubling for liberals is their alleged inability to defend the basic principle that 'individual rights cannot be sacrificed for the sake of the general good'.[9] Because Sandel and MacIntyre make the most detailed and, if true, devastating cases against believing in a liberal politics of rights, I shall focus for the rest of this review on their arguments.

The central argument of Sandel's book is that liberalism rests on a series of mistaken metaphysical and metaethical views: for example, that the claims of justice are absolute and universal; that we cannot know each other well enough to share common ends; and that we can define our personal identity independently of socially given ends. Because its foundations are necessarily flawed, Sandel suggests in a subsequent article that we should give up the 'politics of rights' for a 'politics of the common good'.[10]

MacIntyre begins his book with an even more 'disquieting suggestion': that our entire moral vocabulary, of rights and the common good, is in such 'grave disorder' that 'we have—very largely, if not entirely—lost our comprehension, both theoretical and practical, of morality'.[11] To account for how 'we' have unknowingly arrived at this unenviable social condition, MacIntyre takes us on an intriguing tour of moral history, from Homeric Greece to the present. By the end of the tour we learn that the internal incoherence of liberalism forces us to choose 'Nietzsche or Aristotle', a politics of the will to power or one of communally defined virtue.[12]

---

[8] MacIntyre, *After Virtue*, p. 52.
[9] Sandel, 'Morality and the Liberal Ideal', p. 16.
[10] Ibid. 17.
[11] MacIntyre, *After Virtue*, pp. 1–5.
[12] Ibid. 49, 103–13, 238–45.

THE LIMITS OF COMMUNITARIAN CRITICISM

Do the critiques succeed in undermining liberal politics? If the only foundations available to liberal politics are faulty, then perhaps one need not establish a positive case for communitarian politics to establish the claim that liberal politics is philosophically indefensible.[13] Although this is the logic of Sandel's claim concerning the limits of liberal justice, he gives no general argument to support his conclusion that liberal rights are indefensible.[14] He reaches this conclusion instead on the basis of an interpretation and criticism of Rawls's theory, which he reasonably assumes to be the best theory liberalism has yet to offer.

Sandel argues that, despite Rawls's efforts to distance himself

---

[13] I say 'perhaps' because, if defensibility is relative to our alternatives, then Sandel still would have to establish the positive case for communitarian politics before claiming that the faulty foundations of liberal politics render it indefensible.

[14] The general argument that can be constructed from Sandel's work (using his conceptual framework) is, I think, the following: (1) To accept a politics based on rights entails believing that justice should have absolute priority over all our particular ends (our conception of the good). (2) To accept the priority of justice over our conception of the good entails believing that our identities can be established prior to the good (otherwise our conception of the good will enter into our conception of justice). (3) Since our identities are constituted by our conception of the good, justice cannot be prior. Therefore we cannot consistently believe in the politics of rights. But each of the steps in this argument are suspect: (1) We may accept the politics of rights not because justice is prior to the good, but because our search for the good requires society to protect our right to certain basic freedoms and welfare goods. (2) Justice may be prior to the good not because we are 'antecedently individuated', but because giving priority to justice may be the fairest way of sharing the goods of citizenship with people who do not accept our conception of the good. (3) Our identities are probably not constituted, at least not exclusively, by our conception of the good. If they were, one could not intelligibly ask: 'What kind of person do I want to become?' Yet the question reflects an important part (although not necessarily the whole) of our search for identity. If, however, we assume by definition that our identities are constituted by our good, then we must consider our sense of justice to be part of our identities. My commitment to treating other people as equals, and therefore to respecting their freedom of religion, is just as elemental a part of my identity (on this understanding) as my being Jewish, and therefore celebrating Passover with my family and friends.

from Kantian metaphysics, he fails. Sandel attributes Rawls's failure to his acceptance of the 'central claim' of deontology, 'the core *conviction* Rawls seeks *above all* to defend. It is the claim that "justice is the first virtue of social institutions".'[15] As Rawls presents it, the 'primacy of justice' describes a moral requirement applicable to institutions. Sandel interprets Rawls as also making a metaethical claim: that the foundations of justice must be independent of all social and historical contingencies without being transcendental.[16]

Why saddle Rawls's moral argument for the primacy of justice with this meaning? To be sure, Rawls himself argues that 'embedded in the principles of justice . . . is an ideal of the person that provides an Archimedean point for judging the basic structure of society'.[17] But to translate this passage into a claim that the grounds of justice can be noncontingent ignores most of what Rawls says to explain his Archimedean point, the nature of justification, and Kantian constructivism.[18] 'Justice as fairness is not at the mercy, so to speak, of existing wants and interests. It sets up an Archimedean point . . . *without invoking a priori considerations*.'[19] By requiring us to abstract from our particular but not our shared interests, the original position with its 'veil of ignorance' and 'thin theory of the good' avoids reliance on both existing preferences and a priori considerations in reasoning about justice. The resulting principles of justice,

[15] Sandel, *Liberalism and the Limits of Justice*, p. 15 (emphasis added). See J. Rawls, *A Theory of Justice* (Cambridge, Mass., 1971), 3–4, 586.

[16] Sandel, *Liberalism and the Limits of Justice*, pp. 16–17. Rawls must, in Sandel's words, 'find a standpoint neither compromised by its implication in the world nor dissociated and so disqualified by detachment'.

[17] Rawls, *A Theory of Justice*, p. 584; see also pp. 260–2.

[18] In interpreting Rawls, I rely (as does Sandel) on passages from both *A Theory of Justice* and 'Kantian Constructivism in Moral Theory: The Dewey Lectures 1980', *Journal of Philosophy*, 77 (1980), 515–72. Someone might reasonably argue that not until 'The Dewey Lectures' does Rawls consistently and clearly defend the position on justification that I attribute to him. Had Sandel directed his criticism only against *A Theory of Justice*, his interpretation would have been more credible. But he still could not have sustained his central claim that Rawls's principles and liberalism more generally *must* rest on implausible metaethical grounds.

[19] Rawls, *A Theory of Justice*, p. 261 (emphasis added). See also 'Kantian Constructivism in Moral Theory', esp. pp. 564–7.

then, clearly rely on certain contingent facts: that we share some interests (in primary goods such as income and self-respect), but not others (in a particular religion or form of family life); that we value the freedom to choose a good life or at least the freedom from having one imposed upon us by political authority. If we do not, then we will not accept the constraints of the original position.

Rawls's remarks on justification and Kantian constructivism make explicit the contingency of his principles of justice. The design of the original position must be revised if the resulting principles do not 'accommodate our firmest convictions'.[20] Justification is not a matter of deduction from certain premises, but rather 'a matter of the mutual support of many considerations, of everything fitting together into one coherent view'.[21] Since Rawls accords the view 'that justice is the first virtue of social institutions' the status of a 'common sense conviction',[22] this view is part of what his theory must coherently combine. Rawls therefore does not, nor need he, claim more for justice as fairness than that, 'given our history and the traditions embedded in our public life, it is the most reasonable doctrine for us. We can find no better charter for our social world.'[23]

Rawls could be wrong about our firmest convictions or what is most reasonable for us. But instead of trying to demonstrate this, Sandel argues that Rawls must show that the content and claims of justice are independent of all historical and social particularities.[24] If this is what constitutes deontological

---

[20] Rawls, *A Theory of Justice*, p. 20. The reasoning is circular, but not viciously so, since we must also be prepared to revise our weaker judgements when principles match our considered convictions, until we reach 'reflective equilibrium'.

[21] Ibid. 21, 579.

[22] Ibid. 586.

[23] Rawls, 'Kantian Constructivism in Moral Theory', p. 519. Cf. Sandel, *Liberalism and the Limits of Justice*, p. 30.

[24] Sandel, *Liberalism and the Limits of Justice*, p. 30. Sometimes Sandel comes close to making a more limited but potentially more plausible argument—that Rawls derives his principles of justice from the wrong set of historical and social particularities: from (for example) our identification with all free and rational beings rather than with particular communities. Such an argument, if successful, would establish different limits, and limits of only Rawlsian liberalism.

metaphysics, then it is a metaphysics that Rawls explicitly and consistently denies.

What metaphysics must Rawlsian liberalism then embrace? Several commentators, along with Rawls himself, have argued that liberalism does not presuppose metaphysics.[25] The major aim of liberal justice is to find principles appropriate for a society in which people disagree fundamentally over many questions, including such metaphysical questions as the nature of personal identity. Liberal justice therefore does not provide us with a comprehensive morality; it regulates our social institutions, not our entire lives. It makes claims on us 'not because it expresses our deepest self-understandings', but because it represents the fairest possible *modus vivendi* for a pluralistic society.[26]

The characterization of liberalism as nonmetaphysical can be misleading, however. Although Rawlsian justice does not pre-suppose only *one* metaphysical view, it is not compatible with *all* such views. Sandel is correct in claiming that the Kantian con-ception of people as free and equal is incompatible with the metaphysical conception of the self as 'radically situated' such that 'the good of community . . . [is] so thoroughgoing as to reach beyond the motivations to the subject of motivations'.[27] Sandel seems to mean that communally given ends can so totally constitute people's identities that they cannot appreciate the value of justice. Such an understanding of human identity would (according to constructivist standards of verification) undermine the two principles.[28] To be justified as the *political* ideals most consistent with the 'public culture of a democratic society',[29] Rawlsian principles therefore have to express some (though not all) of our deepest self-understandings. Rawls must

---

[25] See Rawls, 'The Independence of Moral Theory', *Proceedings and Addresses of the American Philosophical Association*, 48 (1975), 5–22.

[26] C. Larmore, 'Review of *Liberalism and the Limits of Justice*', *Journal of Philosophy*, 81/6 (1984), 338. See also Rawls, 'Kantian Constructivism in Moral Theory', p. 542.

[27] Sandel, *Liberalism and the Limits of Justice*, pp. 20–1, 149.

[28] Rawls, 'Kantian Constructivism in Moral Theory', pp. 534–5, 564–7. See also *A Theory of Justice*, p. 260: 'The theory of justice does, indeed, presup-pose a theory of the good, but *within wide limits* this does not prejudge the choice of the sort of persons that men want to be' (emphasis added).

[29] Rawls, 'Kantian Constructivism in Moral Theory', p. 518.

admit this much metaphysics—that we are not radically situated selves—if justification is to depend not on 'being true to an order antecedent to and given to us, but . . . [on] congruence with our deeper understanding of ourselves and our aspirations'.[30]

If this, rather than Kantian dualism, is the metaphysics that liberal justice must admit, Sandel's critique collapses. Rawls need not (and he does not) claim that 'justice is the first virtue of social institutions' in *all* societies to show that the priority of justice obtains *absolutely* in those societies in which people disagree about the good life and consider their freedom to choose a good life an important good.[31] Nor need Rawls assume that human identity is *ever* totally independent of ends and relations to others to conclude that justice must *always* command our moral allegiance unless love and benevolence make it unnecessary.[32] Deontological justice thus can recognize the conditional priority of justice without embracing 'deontological metaethics' or collapsing into teleology. Sandel has failed therefore to show that the foundations of rights are mistaken.

MISSING FOUNDATIONS?

MacIntyre argues that the foundations are missing: 'The best reason for asserting so bluntly that there are no such rights is indeed of precisely the same type as the best reason which we possess for asserting that there are no witches . . . every attempt to give good reasons for believing there *are* such rights has failed.'[33] The analogy, properly drawn, does not support MacIntyre's position. The best reason that people can give for believing in witches is that the existence of witches explains (supposedly) observed physical phenomena. Belief in witches therefore directly competes with belief in physics, and loses out in the competition. The best reason for taking rights seriously is of a different order: believing in rights is one way of regulating

---

[30] Ibid. 519.

[31] Ibid. 516–24. Cf. Sandel, *Liberalism and the Limits of Justice*, pp. 28–40.

[32] Rawls, *A Theory of Justice*, pp. 560–77. Cf. Sandel, *Liberalism and the Limits of Justice*, pp. 47–65.

[33] MacIntyre, *After Virtue*, p. 67.

and constraining our behaviour toward one another in a
desirable manner. This reason does not compete with physics;
it does not require us to believe that rights 'exist' in any sense
that is incompatible with the 'laws of nature' as established by
modern science.[34]

MacIntyre offers another, more historical argument for
giving up our belief in rights. 'Why', he asks, 'should we think
about our modern uses of *good*, *right*, and *obligatory* in any
different way from that in which we think about late eighteenth-
century Polynesian uses of taboo?'[35] Like the Polynesians who
used *taboo* without any understanding of what it meant beyond
'prohibited', we use *human right* without understanding its
meaning beyond 'moral trump'. If the analogy holds, we cannot
use the idea correctly, because we have irretrievably lost the
social context in which its proper use is possible.

But on a contextualist view, it is reasonable for *us* to believe
in human rights: many of the most widely accepted practices
of our society—equality of educational opportunity, careers
open to talent, punishment conditional on intent—treat people
as relatively autonomous moral agents. In so far as we are
committed to maintaining these practices, we are also committed to defending human rights.[36] This argument parallels
MacIntyre's contextualist defence of Aristotelian virtue: that
the established practices of heroic societies supported the
Aristotelian idea that every human life has a socially determined
telos. Each person had a 'given role and status within a well-
defined and highly determinate system of roles and statuses'
which fully defined his identity: 'a man who tried to withdraw
himself from his given position . . . would be engaged in the
enterprise of trying to make himself disappear.'[37]

If moral beliefs depend upon supporting social practices for
their validity, then we have more reason to believe in a liberal
politics of rights than in an Aristotelian politics of the common good. In *our* society it does not logically follow that 'I am

[34] I am grateful to Thomas Scanlon for suggesting this reply.

[35] MacIntyre, *After Virtue*, p. 107.

[36] We need not be committed to a thoroughly deontological moral apparatus. Sophisticated consequentialist theories justify these same practices and
are consistent with believing in rights.

[37] MacIntyre, *After Virtue*, pp. 117, 119.

someone's son or daughter, someone else's cousin or uncle; I am a citizen of this or that city, a member of this or that guild or profession; I belong to this clan, that tribe, this nation[,] *hence* what is good for me *has* to be THE good for one who inhabits these roles.'[38] One reason it does not follow is that none of these roles carries with it only one socially given good. What follows from 'what is good for me has to be the good for someone who was born female, into a first-generation American, working-class Italian, Catholic family'? Had Geraldine Ferraro asked, following Sandel, 'Who am I?' instead of 'What ends should I choose?' an answer would not have been any easier to come by.[39] The Aristotelian method of discovering the good by enquiring into the social meaning of roles is of little help in a society in which most roles are not attached to a single good. Even if there is a single good attached to some social roles (as caring for the sick is to the role of a nurse, or searching for political wisdom to the function of political philosophers, let us suppose), we cannot accurately say that our roles determine our good without adding that we often choose our roles because of the good that is attached to them. The unencumbered self is, in this sense, the encumbrance of our modern social condition.

But the existence of supporting social practices is certainly not a sufficient condition, arguably not even a necessary one, for believing in liberal rights rather than Aristotelian virtue. The practices that support liberal rights may be unacceptable to us for reasons that carry more moral weight than the practices themselves; we may discover moral reasons (even within our current social understandings) for establishing new practices that support a politics of the common good. My point here is not that a politics of rights is the only, or the best, possible politics for our society, but that neither MacIntyre's nor Sandel's critique succeeds in undermining liberal rights, because neither gives an accurate account of their foundations. MacIntyre mistakenly denies liberalism the possibility of foundations; Sandel ascribes to liberalism foundations it need not have.

[38] Ibid. 204–5 (emphasis added). Sandel makes a very similar point in *Liberalism and the Limits of Justice*, p. 179.

[39] Sandel, *Liberalism and the Limits of Justice*, pp. 58–9.

THE TYRANNY OF DUALISMS

The critics' interpretive method is also mistaken. It invites us to see the moral universe in dualistic terms: either our identities are independent of our ends, leaving us totally free to choose our life plans, or they are constituted by community, leaving us totally encumbered by socially given ends; either justice takes absolute priority over the good or the good takes the place of justice; either justice must be independent of all historical and social particularities or virtue must depend completely on the particular social practices of each society; and so on. The critics thereby do a disservice to not only liberal but communitarian values, since the same method that reduces liberalism to an extreme metaphysical vision also renders communitarian theories unacceptable. By interpreting Rawls's conception of community as describing 'just a feeling', for example, Sandel invites us to interpret Aristotle's as describing a fully constituted identity. The same mode of interpretation that permits Sandel to criticize Rawls for betraying 'incompatible commitments' by uneasily combining into one theory 'intersubjective and individualistic images' would permit us to criticize Sandel for suggesting that community is 'a mode of self-understanding *partly* constitutive' of our identity.[40] Neither Sandel's interpretation nor his critique is accurate.

MacIntyre's mode of interpreting modern philosophy similarly divides the moral world into a series of dualisms. The doomed project of modern philosophy, according to MacIntyre, has been to convert naturally egoistical men into altruists. 'On the traditional Aristotelian view such problems do not arise. For what education in the virtues teaches me is that my good as a man is one and the same as the good of those others with whom I am bound up in human community.'[41] But the real, and recognized, dilemma of modern liberalism, as we have seen, is not that people are naturally egoistical, but that they disagree about the nature of the good life. And such problems also arise

---

[40] Ibid. 150. When Sandel characterizes his own preferred 'strong' view of community, it is one in which people conceive their identity 'as defined *to some extent* by the community of which they are a part' (emphasis added).
[41] MacIntyre, *After Virtue*, pp. 212–13.

on any (sophisticated) Aristotelian view, as MacIntyre himself recognizes in the context of distinguishing Aristotelianism from Burkean conservatism: 'when a tradition is in good order it is always partially constituted by an argument about the goods the pursuit of which gives to that tradition its particular point and purpose.'[42]

The dualistic vision thus tyrannizes over our common sense, which rightly rejects all 'easy combinations'—the individualism MacIntyre attributes to Sartre and Goffman 'according to which the self is detachable from its social and historical roles and statuses' such that it 'can have no history',[43] as well as the communitarian vision MacIntyre occasionally seems to share with Roberto Unger according to which the 'conflict between the demands of individuality and sociability would disappear'.[44] Because the critics misinterpret the metaphysics of liberalism, they also miss the appeal of liberal politics for reconciling rather than repressing most competing conceptions of the good life.

BEYOND METAPHYSICS: COMMUNITARIAN POLITICS

Even if liberalism has adequate metaphysical foundations and considerable moral appeal, communitarian politics might be morally better. But MacIntyre and Sandel say almost nothing in their books to defend communitarian politics directly. Sandel makes a brief positive case for its comparative advantage over liberalism in a subsequent article. 'Where libertarian liberals defend the private economy and egalitarian liberals defend the welfare state,' Sandel comments, 'communitarians worry about the concentration of power in both the corporate economy and the bureaucratic state, and the erosion of those intermediate forms of community that have at times sustained a more vital public life.' But these worries surely do not distinguish

---

[42] Ibid. 206.
[43] Ibid. 205. See also Sandel, *Liberalism and the Limits of Justice*, pp. 40, 150; cf. p. 180.
[44] Unger, *Knowledge and Politics*, p. 220.

communitarians from most contemporary liberals, unless (as Sandel implies) communitarians therefore oppose, or refuse to defend, the market or the welfare state.[45] Sandel makes explicit only one policy difference: 'communitarians would be more likely than liberals to allow a town to ban pornographic book-stores, on the grounds that pornography offends its way of life and the values that sustain it'. His answer to the obvious liberal worry that such a policy opens the door to intolerance in the name of communal standards is that 'intolerance flourishes most where forms of life are dislocated, roots unsettled, traditions undone'. He urges us therefore 'to revitalize those civic republi-can possibilities implicit in our tradition but fading in our time'.[46]

What exactly does Sandel mean to imply by the sort of civic republicanism 'implicit within our tradition'? Surely not the mainstream of our tradition that excluded women and minori-ties, and repressed most significant deviations from white, Pro-testant morality in the name of the common good? We have little reason to doubt that a liberal politics of rights is morally better than that kind of republicanism. But if Sandel is arguing that, when members of a society have settled roots and established traditions, they will tolerate the speech, religion, sexual, and associational preferences of minorities, then history simply does not support his optimism. A great deal of intolerance has come from societies of selves so 'confidently situated' that they were sure repression would serve a higher cause.[47] The common good of the Puritans of seventeenth-century Salem commanded them to hunt witches; the common good of the Moral Majority of the twentieth century commands them not to tolerate homo-sexuals. The enforcement of liberal rights, not the absence of

[45] Sandel, 'Morality and the Liberal Ideal', p. 17.

[46] Ibid.

[47] Sandel may be correct in claiming that *more* intolerance has come—in the form of fascism—from societies of 'atomized, dislocated, frustrated selves'. But the truth of this claim does not establish the case for communi-tarian over liberal politics unless our only choice is to support a society of totally 'atomized' or one of totally 'settled' selves. This dualistic interpretation of our alternatives seems to lead Sandel to overlook the moral value of estab-lishing some balance between individualism and community, and to under-estimate the theoretical difficulty of determining where the proper balance lies.

settled community, stands between the Moral Majority and the contemporary equivalent of witch-hunting.

The communitarian critics want us to live in Salem, but not to believe in witches. Or human rights. Perhaps the Moral Majority would cease to be a threat were the United States a communitarian society; benevolence and fraternity might take the place of justice. Almost anything is possible, but it does not make moral sense to leave liberal politics behind on the strengths of such speculations.[48]

Nor does it make theoretical sense to assume away the conflicts among competing ends—such as the conflict between communal standards of sexual morality and individual sexual preference—that give rise to the characteristic liberal concern for rights. In so doing, the critics avoid discussing how morally to resolve our conflicts and therefore fail to provide us with a political theory relevant to our world. They also may overlook the extent to which some of their own moral commitments presuppose the defence of liberal rights.

CONSTRUCTIVE POTENTIAL

Even if the communitarian critics have not given good reasons for abandoning liberalism, they have challenged its defenders. One should welcome their work if for no other reason than this. But there is another reason. Communitarianism has the potential for helping us discover a politics that combines community with a commitment to basic liberal values.

The critics' failure to undermine liberalism suggests not that there are no communitarian values but that they are properly viewed as supplementing rather than supplanting basic liberal values. We can see the extent to which our moral vision already relies on communitarian values by imagining a society in which no one does more or less than respect everyone else's liberal

---

[48] Sandel might want to argue that societies like Salem were not 'settled'. Perfectly settled communities would not be repressive because every individual's identity would be fully constituted by the community or completely compatible with the community's understanding of the common good. This argument, however, is a truism: a perfectly settled society would not be repressive, because perfect settlement would leave no dissent to repress.

rights. People do not form ties of love and friendship (or they do so only in so far as necessary to developing the kind of character that respects liberal rights). They do not join neighbourhood associations, political parties, trade unions, civic groups, synagogues, or churches. This might be a perfectly liberal, arguably even a just society, but it is certainly not the best society to which we can aspire. The potential of communitarianism lies, I think, in indicating the ways in which we can strive to realize not only justice but community through the many social unions of which the liberal state is the super social union.

What might some of those ways be? Sandel suggests one possibility: states might 'enact laws regulating plant closings, to protect their communities from the disruptive effects of capital mobility and sudden industrial change'.[49] This policy is compatible with the priority Rawls gives to liberty and may even be dictated by the best interpretation of the difference principle. But the explicit concern for preventing the disruption of local communities is an important contribution of communitarianism to liberalism. We should also, as Sandel suggests, be 'troubled by the tendency of liberal programs to displace politics from smaller forms of association to more comprehensive ones'. But we should not therefore oppose all programmes that limit—or support all those that expand—the jurisdiction of local governments. We may be able to discover ways in which local communities *and* democracy can be vitalized without violating individual rights. We can respect the right of free speech by opposing local efforts to ban pornographic bookstores, for example, but still respect the values of community and democratic participation by supporting local (democratic) efforts to regulate the location and manner in which pornographic bookstores display their wares. Attuned to the dangers of dualism, we can appreciate the way such a stand combines—uneasily—liberal and communitarian commitments.

Some ways of fostering communal values—I suspect some of the best ways—entail creating new political institutions rather than increasing the power of existing institutions or reviving old ones. By restoring 'those intermediate forms of community

[49] Sandel, 'Morality and the Liberal Ideal', p. 17.

that have at times sustained a more vital public life', we are unlikely to control 'the concentration of power in both the corporate economy and the bureaucratic state' that rightly worries both communitarians and liberals.[50] If large corporations and bureaucracies are here to stay, we need to create new institutions to prevent them from imposing (in the name of either efficiency or expertise) their values on those of potentially more democratic communities. Realizing the relatively old idea of workplace democracy would require the creation of radically new economic institutions.[51] Recently, mandated citizen review boards in areas such as health care, education, and community development have increased interest in democratic participation. Wholehearted political support of such reforms and others yet untried is probably necessary before we can effectively control bureaucratic power.[52] Although the political implications of the communitarian criticisms of liberalism are conservative, the constructive potential of communitarian values is not.

Had they developed the constructive potential of communitarian values, the critics might have moved further toward discovering both the limits of Rawlsian liberalism and a better charter for our social world. Instead, MacIntyre concludes that we should be 'waiting not for a Godot, but for another—doubtless very different—St Benedict'.[53] The critics tend to look toward the future with nostalgia. We would be better off, by both Aristotelian and liberal democratic standards, if we tried to shape it according to our present moral understandings. At the end of his book, Sandel urges us to remember 'the possibility that when politics goes well, we can know a good in common that we cannot know alone'. But he has neglected the possibility that the only common good worth striving for is one

[50] Ibid.
[51] For a communitarian defence of economic democracy that is not based on a rejection of liberal values, see Walzer, *Spheres of Justice*, pp. 161, 291–303.
[52] For a suggestive agenda of democratic reforms, see Barber, *Strong Democracy*, pp. 261–307. Although Barber attacks liberal theory as fundamentally flawed in the first nine chapters, the aim of his agenda for reform in the last chapter is 'to reorient liberal democracy toward civic engagement and political community, not to raze it' (p. 308).
[53] Ibid. 245. Roberto Unger similarly concludes *Knowledge and Politics* waiting for God to speak (p. 235).

that is not 'an unsettling presence for justice'.[54] Justice need not be the only virtue of social institutions for it to be better than anything we are capable of putting in its place. The worthy challenge posed by the communitarian critics, therefore, is not to replace liberal justice, but to improve it.

[54] Cf. Sandel, *Liberalism and the Limits of Justice*, p. 183.

8

DISTRIBUTIVE JUSTICE

ROBERT NOZICK

The minimal state is the most extensive state that can be justified. Any state more extensive violates people's rights. Yet
many persons have put forth reasons purporting to justify a
more extensive state. [. . .] I shall focus upon those generally
acknowledged to be most weighty and influential, to see
precisely wherein they fail. In this essay we consider the claim
that a more extensive state is justified, because necessary (or the
best instrument) to achieve distributive justice [. . .].

The term 'distributive justice' is not a neutral one. Hearing
the term 'distribution', most people presume that some thing or
mechanism uses some principle or criterion to give out a supply
of things. Into this process of distributing shares some error may
have crept. So it is an open question, at least, whether redistribution should take place; whether we should do again what has
already been done once, though poorly. However, we are not
in the position of children who have been given portions of pie
by someone who now makes last-minute adjustments to rectify
careless cutting. There is no *central* distribution, no person or
group entitled to control all the resources, jointly deciding how
they are to be doled out. What each person gets, he gets from
others who give to him in exchange for something, or as a gift.
In a free society, diverse persons control different resources,
and new holdings arise out of the voluntary exchanges and
actions of persons. There is no more a distributing or distribution of shares than there is a distributing of mates in a society in
which persons choose whom they shall marry. The total result is
the product of many individual decisions which the different

Robert Nozick, excerpts from *Anarchy, State and Utopia*. Copyright © 1974 by
Basic Books, Inc. Reprinted by permission of Basic Books, Inc., a division of
Harper Collins Publishers, and Basil Blackwell.

individuals involved are entitled to make. Some uses of the term 'distribution', it is true, do not imply a previous distributing appropriately judged by some criterion (for example, 'probability distribution'); nevertheless, despite the title of this chapter, it would be best to use a terminology that clearly is neutral. We shall speak of people's holdings; a principle of justice in holdings describes (part of) what justice tells us (requires) about holdings. I shall state first what I take to be the correct view about justice in holdings, and then turn to the discussion of alternative views.

THE ENTITLEMENT THEORY

The subject of justice in holdings consists of three major topics. The first is the *original acquisition of holdings*, the appropriation of unheld things. This includes the issues of how unheld things may come to be held, the process, or processes, by which unheld things may come to be held, the things that may come to be held by these processes, the extent of what comes to be held by a particular process, and so on. We shall refer to the complicated truth about this topic, which we shall not formulate here, as the principle of justice in acquisition. The second topic concerns the *transfer of holdings* from one person to another. By what processes may a person transfer holdings to another? How may a person acquire a holding from another who holds it? Under this topic come general descriptions of voluntary exchange, and gift and (on the other hand) fraud, as well as reference to particular conventional details fixed upon in a given society. The complicated truth about this subject (with placeholders for conventional details) we shall call the principle of justice in transfer. (And we shall suppose it also includes principles governing how a person may divest himself of a holding, passing it into an unheld state.)

If the world were wholly just, the following inductive definition would exhaustively cover the subject of justice in holdings.

1. A person who acquires a holding in accordance with the principle of justice in acquisition is entitled to that holding.
2. A person who acquires a holding in accordance with the principle of justice in transfer, from someone else entitled to the holding, is entitled to the holding.

3. No one is entitled to a holding except by (repeated) applications of 1 and 2.

The complete principle of distributive justice would say simply that a distribution is just if everyone is entitled to the holdings they possess under the distribution.

A distribution is just if it arises from another just distribution by legitimate means. The legitimate means of moving from one distribution to another are specified by the principle of justice in transfer. The legitimate first 'moves' are specified by the principle of justice in acquisition.[1] Whatever arises from a just situation by just steps is itself just. The means of change specified by the principle of justice in transfer preserve justice. As correct rules of inference are truth-preserving, and any conclusion deduced via repeated application of such rules from only true premisses is itself true, so the means of transition from one situation to another specified by the principle of justice in transfer are justice-preserving, and any situation actually arising from repeated transitions in accordance with the principle from a just situation is itself just. The parallel between justice-preserving transformations and truth-preserving transformations illuminates where it fails as well as where it holds. That a conclusion could have been deduced by truth-preserving means from premisses that are true suffices to show its truth. That from a just situation a situation *could* have arisen via justice-preserving means does *not* suffice to show its justice. The fact that a thief's victims voluntarily *could* have presented him with gifts does not entitle the thief to his ill-gotten gains. Justice in holdings is historical; it depends upon what actually has happened. We shall return to this point later.

Not all actual situations are generated in accordance with the two principles of justice in holdings: the principle of justice in acquisition and the principle of justice in transfer. Some people steal from others, or defraud them, or enslave them, seizing their product and preventing them from living as they choose, or forcibly exclude others from competing in exchanges. None

---

[1] Applications of the principle of justice in acquisition may also occur as part of the move from one distribution to another. You may find an unheld thing now and appropriate it. Acquisitions also are to be understood as included when, to simplify, I speak only of transitions by transfers.

of these is a permissible mode of transition from one situation to another. And some persons acquire holdings by means not sanctioned by the principle of justice in acquisition. The existence of past injustice (previous violations of the first two principles of justice in holdings) raises the third major topic under justice in holdings: the rectification of injustice in holdings. If past injustice has shaped present holdings in various ways, some identifiable and some not, what now, if anything, ought to be done to rectify these injustices? What obligations do the performers of injustice have toward those whose position is worse than it would have been had the injustice not been done? Or, than it would have been had compensation been paid promptly? How, if at all, do things change if the beneficiaries and those made worse off are not the direct parties in the act of injustice, but, for example, their descendants? Is an injustice done to someone whose holding was itself based upon an unrectified injustice? How far back must one go in wiping clean the historical slate of injustices? What may victims of injustice permissibly do in order to rectify the injustices being done to them, including the many injustices done by persons acting through their government? I do not know of a thorough or theoretically sophisticated treatment of such issues.[2] Idealizing greatly, let us suppose theoretical investigation will produce a principle of rectification. This principle uses historical information about previous situations and injustices done in them (as defined by the first two principles of justice and rights against interference), and information about the actual course of events that flowed from these injustices, until the present, and it yields a description (or descriptions) of holdings in the society. The principle of rectification presumably will make use of its best estimate of subjunctive information about what would have occurred (or a probability distribution over what might have occurred, using the expected value) if the injustice had not taken place. If the actual description of holdings turns out not to be one of the descriptions yielded by the principle, then one of the descriptions yielded must be realized.[3]

---

[2] See, however, the useful book by B. Bittker, *The Case for Black Reparations* (New York, 1973).

[3] If the principle of rectification of violations of the first two principles

The general outlines of the theory of justice in holdings are that the holdings of a person are just if he is entitled to them by the principles of justice in acquisition and transfer, or by the principle of rectification of injustice (as specified by the first two principles). If each person's holdings are just, then the total set (distribution) of holdings is just. To turn these general outlines into a specific theory we would have to specify the details of each of the three principles of justice in holdings: the principle of acquisition of holdings, the principle of transfer of holdings, and the principle of rectification of violations of the first two principles. I shall not attempt that task here. (Locke's principle of justice in acquisition is discussed below.)

HISTORICAL PRINCIPLES AND END-RESULT PRINCIPLES

The general outlines of the entitlement theory illuminate the nature and defects of other conceptions of distributive justice. The entitlement theory of justice in distribution is *historical*; whether a distribution is just depends upon how it came about. In contrast, *current time-slice principles* of justice hold that the justice of a distribution is determined by how things are distributed (who has what) as judged by some *structural* principle(s) of just distribution. A utilitarian who judges between any two distributions by seeing which has the greater sum of utility and, if the sums tie, applies some fixed equality criterion to choose the more equal distribution, would hold a current time-slice principle of justice. As would someone who had a fixed schedule of trade-offs between the sum of happiness and equality. According to a current time-slice principle, all that needs to be looked at, in judging the justice of a distribution, is who ends

---

yields more than one description of holdings, then some choice must be made as to which of these is to be realized. Perhaps the sort of considerations about distributive justice and equality that I argue against play a legitimate role in *this* subsidiary choice. Similarly, there may be room for such considerations in deciding which otherwise arbitrary features a statute will embody, when such features are unavoidable because other considerations do not specify a precise line; yet a line must be drawn.

up with what; in comparing any two distributions one need look only at the matrix presenting the distributions. No further information need be fed into a principle of justice. It is a consequence of such principles of justice that any two structurally identical distributions are equally just. (Two distributions are structurally identical if they present the same profile, but perhaps have different persons occupying the particular slots. My having ten and your having five, and my having five and your having ten are structurally identical distributions.) Welfare economics is the theory of current time-slice principles of justice. The subject is conceived as operating on matrices representing only current information about distribution. This, as well as some of the usual conditions (for example, the choice of distribution is invariant under relabelling of columns), guarantees that welfare economics will be a current time-slice theory, with all of its inadequacies.

Most persons do not accept current time-slice principles as constituting the whole story about distributive shares. They think it relevant in assessing the justice of a situation to consider not only the distribution it embodies, but also how that distribution came about. If some persons are in prison for murder or war crimes, we do not say that to assess the justice of the distribution in the society we must look only at what this person has, and that person has, and that person has . . . at the current time. We think it relevant to ask whether someone did something so that he *deserved* to be punished, deserved to have a lower share. Most will agree to the relevance of further information with regard to punishments and penalties. Consider also desired things. One traditional socialist view is that workers are entitled to the product and full fruits of their labour; they have earned it; a distribution is unjust if it does not give the workers what they are entitled to. Such entitlements are based upon some past history. No socialist holding this view would find it comforting to be told that, because the actual distribution A happens to coincide structurally with the one he desires D, A therefore is no less just than D; it differs only in that the 'parasitic' owners of capital receive under A what the workers are entitled to under D, and the workers receive under A what the owners are entitled to under D, namely very little. This socialist rightly, in my view, holds on to the notions of earning, producing, entitlement, desert, and so forth, and he rejects current time-slice principles that look only to the structure of the resulting set of holdings. (The set of holdings resulting from what? Isn't it implausible that how holdings are produced and come to exist has no effect at all on who should hold what?) His mistake lies in his view of what entitlements arise out of what sorts of productive processes.

We construe the position we discuss too narrowly by speaking of *current* time-slice principles. Nothing is changed if structural principles operate upon a time sequence of current time-slice profiles and, for example, give someone more now to counterbalance the less he has had earlier. A utilitarian or an egalitarian or any mixture of the two over time will inherit the difficulties of his more myopic comrades. He is not helped by the fact that *some* of the information others consider relevant in assessing a distribution is reflected, unrecoverably, in past matrices. Henceforth, we shall refer to such unhistorical principles of distributive justice, including the current time-slice principles, as *end-result principles* or *end-state principles*.

In contrast to end-result principles of justice, *historical principles* of justice hold that past circumstances or actions of people can create differential entitlements or differential deserts to things. An injustice can be worked by moving from one distribution to another structurally identical one, for the second, in profile the same, may violate people's entitlement, or deserts; it may not fit the actual history.

PATTERNING

The entitlement principles of justice in holdings that we have sketched are historical principles of justice. To understand their precise character better, we shall distinguish them from another subclass of the historical principles. Consider, as an example, the principle of distribution according to moral merit. This principle requires that total distributive shares vary directly with moral merit; no person should have a greater share than anyone whose moral merit is greater. (If moral merit could be not merely ordered but measured on an interval or ratio scale, stronger principles could be formulated.) Or consider the principle that results by substituting 'usefulness to society' for 'moral merit' in the previous principle. Or instead of 'distribute according to moral merit', or 'distribute according to useful- ness to society', we might consider 'distribute according to the weighted sum of moral merit, usefulness to society, and need', with the weights of the different dimensions equal. Let us call a principle of distribution *patterned* if it specifies that a distribu- tion is to vary along with some natural dimension, weighted sum of natural dimensions, or lexicographic ordering of natural dimensions. And let us say a distribution is patterned if it accords with some patterned principle. (I speak of natural dimensions, admittedly without a general criterion for them, because for any set of holdings some artificial dimensions can be gimmicked up to vary along with the distribution of the set.) The principle of distribution in accordance with moral merit is a patterned historical principle, which specifies a patterned distribution. 'Distribute according to IQ' is a patterned princi- ple that looks to information not contained in distributional matrices. It is not historical, however, in that it does not look to any past actions creating differential entitlements to evaluate a distribution; it requires only distributional matrices whose columns are labelled by IQ scores. The distribution in a society, however, may be composed of such simple patterned distribu- tions, without itself being simply patterned. Different sectors may operate different patterns, or some combination of patterns may operate in different proportions across a society. A distribu- tion composed in this manner, from a small number of pat- terned distributions, we also shall term 'patterned'. And we extend the use of 'pattern' to include the overall designs put forth by combinations of end-state principles.

Almost every suggested principle of distributive justice is patterned: to each according to his moral merit, or needs, or marginal product, or how hard he tries, or the weighted sum of the foregoing, and so on. The principle of entitlement we have sketched is *not* patterned.[4] There is no one natural dimension or weighted sum or combination of a small number of natural dimensions that yields the distributions generated in accordance

[4] One might try to squeeze a patterned conception of distributive justice into the framework of the entitlement conception, by formulating a gimmicky obligatory 'principle of transfer' that would lead to the pattern. For example,

with the principle of entitlement. The set of holdings that results when some persons receive their marginal products, others win at gambling, others receive a share of their mate's income, others receive gifts from foundations, others receive interest on loans, others receive gifts from admirers, others receive returns on investment, others make for themselves much of what they have, others find things, and so on, will not be patterned. Heavy strands of patterns will run through it; significant portions of the variance in holdings will be accounted for by pattern-variables. If most people most of the time choose to transfer some of their entitlements to others only in exchange for something from them, then a large part of what many people hold will vary with what they held that others wanted. More details are provided by the theory of marginal productivity. But gifts to relatives, charitable donations, bequests to children, and the like, are not best conceived, in the first instance, in this manner. Ignoring the strands of pattern, let us suppose for the moment that a distribution actually arrived at by the operation of the principle of entitlement is random with respect to any pattern. Though the resulting set of holdings will be unpatterned, it will not be incomprehensible, for it can be seen as a rising from the operation of a small number of principles. These principles specify how an initial distribution may arise (the principle of acquisition of holdings) and how distributions may be transformed into others (the principle of transfer of holdings). The process whereby the set of holdings is generated will be intelligible, though the set of holdings itself that results from this process will be unpatterned. [. . .]

---

the principle that if one has more than the mean income one must transfer everything one holds above the mean to persons below the mean so as to bring them up to (but not over) the mean. We can formulate a criterion for a 'principle of transfer' to rule out such obligatory transfers, or we can say that no correct principle of transfer, no principle of transfer in a free society, will be like this. The former is probably the better course, though the latter also is true.

Alternatively, one might think to make the entitlement conception instantiate a pattern, by using matrix entries that express the relative strength of a person's entitlements as measured by some real-valued function. But even if the limitation to natural dimensions failed to exclude this function, the resulting edifice would *not* capture our system of entitlements to *particular* things.

HOW LIBERTY UPSETS PATTERNS

It is not clear how those holding alternative conceptions of distributive justice can reject the entitlement conception of justice in holdings. For suppose a distribution favoured by one of these non-entitlement conceptions is realized. Let us suppose it is your favourite one and let us call this distribution $D1$; perhaps everyone has an equal share, perhaps shares vary in accordance with some dimension you treasure. Now suppose that Wilt Chamberlain is greatly in demand by basketball teams, being a great gate attraction. (Also suppose contracts run only for a year, with players being free agents.) He signs the following sort of contract with a team: In each home game, twenty-five cents from the price of each ticket of admission goes to him. (We ignore the question of whether he is 'gouging' the owners, letting them look out for themselves.) The season starts, and people cheerfully attend his team's games; they buy their tickets, each time dropping a separate twenty-five cents of their admission price into a special box with Chamberlain's name on it. They are excited about seeing him play; it is worth the total admission price to them. Let us suppose that in one season one million persons attend his home games, and Wilt Chamberlain winds up with $250,000, a much larger sum than the average income and larger even than anyone else has. Is he entitled to this income? Is this new distribution $D2$ unjust? If so, why? There is *no* question about whether each of the people was entitled to the control over the resources they held in $D1$; because that was the distribution (your favourite) that (for the purposes of argument) we assumed was acceptable. Each of these persons *chose* to give twenty-five cents of their money to Chamberlain. They could have spent it on going to the movies, or on candy bars, or on copies of *Dissent* magazine, or of *Monthly Review*. But they all, at least one million of them, converged on giving it to Wilt Chamberlain in exchange for watching him play basketball. If $D1$ was a just distribution, and people voluntarily moved from it to $D2$, transferring parts of their shares they were given under $D1$ (what was it for if not to do something with?), isn't $D2$ also just? If the people were entitled to dispose of the resources to which they were entitled (under $D1$), didn't this include their being entitled to give it to, or exchange it with, Wilt

Chamberlain? Can anyone else complain on grounds of justice? Each other person already has his legitimate share under $D1$. Under $D1$, there is nothing that anyone has that anyone else has a claim of justice against. After someone transfers something to Wilt Chamberlain, third parties *still* have their legitimate shares; *their* shares are not changed. By what process could such a transfer among two persons give rise to a legitimate claim of distributive justice on a portion of what was transferred, by a third party who had no claim of justice on any holding of the others *before* the transfer?[5] To cut off objections irrelevant here, we might imagine the exchanges occurring in a socialist society, after hours. After playing whatever basketball he does in his daily work, or doing whatever other daily work he does, Wilt Chamberlain decides to put in *overtime* to earn additional money. (First his work quota is set; he works time over that.) Or imagine it is a skilled juggler people like to see, who puts on shows after hours.

Why might someone work overtime in a society in which it is assumed their needs are satisfied? Perhaps because they care about things other than needs. I like to write in books that I read, and to have easy access to books for browsing at odd hours. It would be very pleasant and convenient to have the resources of Widener Library in my back yard. No society, I assume, will provide such resources close to each person who would like them

---

[5] Might not a transfer have instrumental effects on a third party, changing his feasible options? (But what if the two parties to the transfer independently had used their holdings in this fashion?) I discuss this question below, but note here that this question concedes the point for distributions of ultimate intrinsic non-instrumental goods (pure utility experiences, so to speak) that are transferable. It also might be objected that the transfer might make a third party more envious because it worsens his position relative to someone else. I find it incomprehensible how this can be thought to involve a claim of justice. [. . .]

Here and elsewhere in this essay a theory which incorporates elements of pure procedural justice might find what I say acceptable, *if* kept in its proper place; that is, if background institutions exist to ensure the satisfaction of certain conditions on distributive shares. But if these institutions are not themselves the sum or invisible-hand result of people's voluntary (non-aggressive) actions, the constraints they impose require justification. At no point does *our* argument assume any background institutions more extensive than those of the minimal night-watchman state, a state limited to protecting persons against murder, assault, theft, fraud, and so forth.

as part of his regular allotment (under $D1$). Thus, persons either must do without some extra things that they want, or be allowed to do something extra to get some of these things. On what basis could the inequalities that would eventuate be forbidden? Notice also that small factories would spring up in a socialist society, unless forbidden. I melt down some of my personal possessions (under $D1$) and build a machine out of the material. I offer you, and others, a philosophy lecture once a week in exchange for your cranking the handle on my machine, whose products I exchange for yet other things, and so on. (The raw materials used by the machine are given to me by others who possess them under $D1$, in exchange for hearing lectures.) Each person might participate to gain things over and above their allotment under $D1$. Some persons even might want to leave their job in socialist industry and work full time in this private sector. [. . .] Here I wish merely to note how private property even in means of production would occur in a socialist society that did not forbid people to use as they wished some of the resources they are given under the socialist distribution $D1$.[6] The socialist society would have to forbid capitalist acts between consenting adults.

[6] See the selection from J. H. MacKay's novel, *The Anarchists*, repr. in L. Krimmerman and L. Perry (eds.), *Patterns of Anarchy* (New York, 1966), in which an individualist anarchist presses upon a communist anarchist the following question: 'Would you, in the system of society which you call "free Communism" prevent individuals from exchanging their labor among themselves by means of their own medium of exchange? And further: Would you prevent them from occupying land for the purpose of personal use?' The novel continues: '[the] question was not to be escaped. If he answered "Yes!" he admitted that society had the right of control over the individual and threw overboard the autonomy of the individual which he had always zealously defended; if on the other hand, he answered "No!" he admitted the right of private property which he had just denied so emphatically. . . . Then he answered "In Anarchy any number of men must have the right of forming a voluntary association, and so realizing their ideas in practice. Nor can I understand how any one could justly be driven from the land and house which he uses and occupies . . . every serious man must declare himself: for Socialism, and thereby for force and against liberty, or for Anarchism, and thereby for liberty and against force."' In contrast, we find Noam Chomsky writing, 'Any consistent anarchist must oppose private ownership of the means of production,' 'the consistent anarchist then . . . will be a socialist . . . of a particular sort' (Introduction to D. Guerin, *Anarchism: From Theory to Practice* (New York, 1970), pp. xiii, xv).

The general point illustrated by the Wilt Chamberlain example and the example of the entrepreneur in a socialist society is that no end-state principle or distributional patterned principle of justice can be continuously realized without continuous interference with people's lives. Any favoured pattern would be transformed into one unfavoured by the principle, by people choosing to act in various ways; for example, by people exchanging goods and services with other people, or giving things to other people, things the transferrers are entitled to under the favoured distributional pattern. To maintain a pattern one must either continually interfere to stop people from transferring resources as they wish to, or continually (or periodically) interfere to take from some persons resources that others for some reason chose to transfer to them. (But if some time limit is to be set on how long people may keep resources others voluntarily transfer to them, why let them keep these resources for *any* period of time? Why not have immediate confiscation?) It might be objected that all persons voluntarily will choose to refrain from actions which would upset the pattern. This presupposes unrealistically (1) that all will most want to maintain the pattern (are those who don't, to be 're-educated' or forced to undergo 'self-criticism'?), (2) that each can gather enough information about his own actions and the ongoing activities of others to discover which of his actions will upset the pattern, and (3) that diverse and far-flung persons can co-ordinate their actions to dovetail into the pattern. Compare the manner in which the market is neutral among persons' desires, as it reflects and transmits widely scattered information via prices, and co-ordinates persons' activities.

It puts things perhaps a bit too strongly to say that every patterned (or end-state) principle is liable to be thwarted by the voluntary actions of the individual parties transferring some of their shares they receive under the principle. For perhaps some *very* weak patterns are not so thwarted.[7] Any distributional

---

[7] Is the patterned principle stable that requires merely that a distribution be Pareto-optimal? One person might give another a gift or bequest that the second could exchange with a third to their mutual benefit. Before the second makes this exchange, there is not Pareto-optimality. Is a stable pattern presented by a principle choosing that among the Pareto-optimal positions that

pattern with any egalitarian component is overturnable by the
voluntary actions of individual persons over time; as is every
patterned condition with sufficient content so as actually to have
been proposed as presenting the central core of distributive
justice. Still, given the possibility that some weak conditions or
patterns may not be unstable in this way, it would be better to
formulate an explicit description of the kind of interesting and
contentful patterns under discussion, and to prove a theorem
about their instability. Since the weaker the patterning, the
more likely it is that the entitlement system itself satisfies it, a
plausible conjecture is that any patterning either is unstable or
is satisfied by the entitlement system.

---

satisfies some further condition C? It may seem that there cannot be counter-
example, for won't any voluntary exchange made away from a situation show
that the first situation wasn't Pareto-optimal? (Ignore the implausibility of this
last claim for the case of bequests.) But principles are to be satisfied over time,
during which new possibilities arise. A distribution that at one time satisfies
the criterion of Pareto-optimality might not do so when some new possibilities
arise (Wilt Chamberlain grows up and starts playing basketball); and though
people's activities will tend to move then to a new Pareto-optimal position,
this new one need not satisfy the contentful condition C. Continual interference
will be needed to ensure the continual satisfaction of C. (The theoretical possibility of a pattern's being maintained by some invisible-hand process that
brings it back to an equilibrium that fits the pattern when deviations occur
should be investigated.)

9

THE LIBERAL INDIVIDUAL

DAVID GAUTHIER

1

[. . .] Morality takes on different coloration when viewed in
relation to participation. For asocial seekers and strivers,
morality could be no more than a needed but unwelcome constraint. But for those who value participation, a morality of
agreement, although still a source of constraint, makes their
shared activity mutually welcome and so stable, ensuring the
absence of coercion or deception. [. . .] Agreed constraint is a
condition of the rational acceptability to the actors of the division
of benefits realized by their shared activity. And so it is a condition of their finding participation in such activity intrinsically
valuable.

A person values striving, but only, we have supposed, in so
far as he considers its costs necessary to attain some valued end.
If he believes that it does not satisfy the standard of efficiency
implicit in maximization, then he will consider the striving
misguided. Similarly, a person values participating, again only
in so far as he considers its costs necessary to attain some valued
end. Here it is not enough that it satisfy the standard of efficiency implicit in optimization. For if he believes that its costs
to him are relatively greater than any participant need bear,
then he will consider them excessive and the satisfaction he takes
from participation will be reduced. He might, of course, find
value in participation if the costs to others were excessive, but
if each participant is to find shared activity intrinsically valuable, then it must satisfy the standard of fairness found in
minimax relative concession. And this is to say that it must be

David Gauthier, excerpts from *Morals By Agreement*, 330–55. Reprinted by permission of Oxford University Press.

voluntarily acceptable; the actors must be willing to participate without being coerced or deceived.

If persons develop tuistic values primarily in the context of shared activities, then the acceptance of moral constraints underlies these values. In the absence of a morally acceptable division of benefits, persons will come to view their shared activities as exploitative rather than co-operative, and their fellows as having interests opposed to their own. And this must be inimical to the development or continuation of tuistic bonds. It might seem that, in admitting that persons do come to take an interest in the interests of their co-participants, we undercut the rationale for requiring that moral constraints have a non-tuistic basis. But if moral constraints underlie tuistic values, then they must have a basis independent of those values. Persons come to take an interest in their fellows because they recognize their mutual willingness not to take advantage of each other, and to share jointly produced benefits on a fair basis. In accepting moral constraints they do not express their concern for each other, but rather they bring about the conditions that foster such concern.

But in valuing both participation and their fellow participators, persons come to place a new value on the moral framework within which participation flourishes. Having first engaged their reason, morality now engages their affections. They exhibit the affective capacity for morality that we found lacking in economic man. [. . .] An affective capacity for morality does not give rise to moral constraints but presupposes their prior recognition; the desire to do one's duty cannot determine the content of duty. And this fits our present argument. Persons rationally recognize the constraints of morality as conditions of mutually beneficial co-operation. They then come to value participation in co-operative and shared activities that meet these constraints, and to take an interest in their fellow participants. And finally they come to value the morality that first appeared to them only as a rational constraint.

Our concern here is not with empirical moral psychology. We do not seek to describe the process by which actual individuals come to manifest an affective capacity for morality. Children are not made moral beings by appealing first to their intellects and only thereafter to their feelings. Rather we are engaged in the

philosopher's task of rational reconstruction. We have not supposed that actual moral constraints represent the outcome of real
agreement, but we have argued that, if they are to be justified,
we must be able to consider them as objects of a hypothetical
ex ante agreement, the rationality of which we now recognize
ex post. Similarly, we do not suppose that actual moral feelings
represent the outcome of a prior valuing of participation and an
awareness that voluntary participation requires the acceptance
of moral constraints. Rather our argument is that, if we are to
consider our moral affections to be more than dysfunctional feelings of which we should be well rid, we must be able to show
how they would arise from such a valuing and awareness. We
must show that a person, reflecting on his moral feelings, would
consider them an appropriate extension of his concern for others
in the context of valued participatory activities, and would then
consider those activities appropriately valued in so far as they
were morally constrained. Such a person would find his moral
outlook congruent with his reflection. If morality played in his
life only the role of necessary evil or of convenient deception that
it plays for economic man, then we should expect that awareness
of its role would undermine his moral affections.

A rational morality is contractarian. But this does not imply
that it is of purely instrumental value to us. In relating morality
to the provision of benefits that themselves involve no affective
concern with others, we do not thereby impoverish the moral
feelings of persons who have such concern. It is because we can
give morality a rational basis that we can secure its affective
hold.

2

[. . .] Morals by agreement capture the understanding of
economic man; they capture the affections of the liberal individual. [. . .] First of all, the liberal individual is an active being,
who finds satisfaction in the seeking and striving that constitute
activity as we humans conceive it. Of course [. . .] if one finds
intrinsic value in instrumentally valuable activity, then one
must also find it in the end of that activity; the good life must
combine attainment with striving. But, in so far as the latter is

essential, the habitat of the liberal individual must be one of scarcity, whether material, mental, or emotional.

Second, the liberal individual has her own independent conception of the good. That conception need not rest on purely asocial motivation, for the liberal individual is not an asocial being. But the goods of different individuals characteristically reflect both harmonies and conflicts of interest. The good of each person expresses his preferences, but, we have insisted, his considered preferences. Thus the liberal individual must have the capacity to reflect on her preferences, and to alter them in the light of this reflection; this capacity makes her autonomous.

Thus, third, the liberal individual is fully rational, where rationality embraces both autonomy and the capacity to choose among possible actions on the basis of one's conception of the good as determined by one's reflective preferences. Defining utility as the measure of considered preference, the liberal individual is rational in being a maximizer of expected utility. Here we emphasize the self-critical dimension of practical rationality, since this seems lacking from the crude conception of merely economic rationality.

As an autonomous being, the liberal individual is aware of the reflective process by which her later selves emerge from her present self, so that her preferences are modified, not in a random or uncontrolled way, but in the light of her own experience and understanding. This gives her the sense of a temporally extended being, whose life is a single development, capable of being integrated and unified. Thus, although the liberal individual need not be strictly prudent and take an atemporal view of her preferences and their satisfaction, she views the present, not in isolation, but in relation to both her past and her possible futures. And so she is able to constrain her maximizing behaviour in terms of policies and principles, given that such constraint seems to her rational. She has then the practical capacity for what we have identified as moral behaviour.

But beyond this practical capacity, she also has the emotional or affective capacity. For the liberal individual realizes that she must choose among many possible ways of life, and that the breadth and richness of her choices depend on the existence of other persons choosing in other ways. She therefore sees her life in a social context, as made possible through interaction with others—interaction which of course also makes possible their lives. Valuing this breadth of opportunity and richness of fulfilment, the liberal individual comes to value participation as well as individual seeking and striving, and, although not a natural tuist, comes to value those whom she encounters as fellow participators. Her habitat is then characterized both by scarcity and society, and the intrinsic satisfaction she takes from society is not dissociated from its instrumental role in meeting scarcity. Valuing participation and her fellow participators, she values also the constraints that make it possible; both intellect and emotion make her a moral being.

But there is another characteristic of the liberal individual that demands emphasis here—free affectivity. The liberal individual does not lack emotional ties to other persons, but those she has are of her own volition, or, more properly, represent the joint volition of the persons tied. Just as each individual has her own conception of the good, and makes her own choice among possible ways of life, so each individual makes her own choice of others as objects of affection. She is not bound by fixed social roles, either in her activities or in her feelings. Although social affective relationships are essential to the liberal individual, there are no essential social relationships.

Now the idea of free affectivity should not be confused with traditional notions of 'free love'. In particular, there is no reason for persons whose affections are free, subject to their autonomous control, not to enter into enduring and binding relationships with others. What is essential to free affectivity is that the bonds be of the person's own making. Imposition, not commitment, is incompatible with individual autonomy in the sphere of the emotions.

Free affectivity is linked to essential justice. Only in a society that can be viewed by its members as a genuine co-operative venture for mutual advantage could we expect the purely voluntary relationships formed among persons to be sufficient social cement. There are two related reasons for this. On the one hand, a society recognized as promoting mutual advantage in a fair way needs fewer personal bonds to maintain it; persons interact co-operatively because of the impersonal benefits involved. Recognizing other persons as partners in a mutually beneficial enterprise enables those who take no interest in others' interests nevertheless to interact constructively with them. And on the other hand, in a society viewed as a fair co-operative venture, we may expect a genuine civic friendship to blossom. Interpersonal bonds that would not exist among persons who viewed one another in a traditionally competitive way (a way which we distinguished from market competition), or as enemies, are naturally generated in a framework of mutual benefit. An essentially just society thus fosters interpersonal bonds while being less dependent on them for its continuance. And so an essentially just society can afford to let interpersonal bonds be freely chosen by its members.

In the absence of an affective capacity for morality among its members, free affectivity would prove rapidly destabilizing for any society. An affective capacity for morality is needed if the constraints required by essential justice are to be willingly honoured. Without an emotional commitment by its members to maintain the framework of mutual benefit, a society could ensure its stability only by imposing on them, through processes of socialization, loyalty to a more substantive goal, which would define roles that individuals would not be free to accept or reject. Free love may have arisen as a reaction against emotional responsibility—an understandable reaction in so far as that responsibility was thrust upon persons, independently of their preferences and volitions. But free affectivity is precisely the assumption of personal responsibility for one's emotions.

The idea of free affectivity will no doubt seem threatening to the defenders of substantive community, whether radical or reactionary. Where their concern may seem most justified is, no doubt, in the sphere of purely private or domestic society. Although there is nothing in free affectivity to preclude the assumption of the emotional commitment requisite to the successful raising of children, yet it may be supposed, with some evidence, that too few adults may be prepared to assume this commitment in a freely chosen way. The fair bargain among generations [. . .] was [. . .] essentially a public bargain, concerning social rates of investment. It involved no direct emotional demands. The raising of children, in a society whose technology affords other ways of providing for old age, is a quite different matter.

Free affectivity is not an unproblematic ideal. We may not

assume that a society of liberal individuals would generate the intergenerational concerns that would ensure its viability over time. But equally, we may not assume that it would not. We must suspend judgement.

In defending the normative priority of individual to community we imply nothing about the causal basis of individuality. The self-consciousness necessary for a being to have a genuine self-conception may well be possible only as a result of socialization. And self-consciousness is at the root of our strong sense of individuality; from the perspective of the self-conscious being, grounds for acting must be self-based. In producing a self-conscious being, human society thus finds itself called into question. From the standpoint of the self-conscious being, social practices and institutions appear as the embodiment of norms, standing in need of justification to him if he is voluntarily to acquiesce in them.

But if we admit that individuality may be socially caused, so that persons are social products, then must we not reject the contention that persons are autonomous? And if we sacrifice autonomy, then are we not undermining the conception of the liberal individual, which is at the core of our answer to those who would reject morals by agreement as the pseudo-morality of economic man? The idea that socialization is a threat to autonomy is not a new one, and if we were to suppose that an autonomous being must constitute himself *ex nihilo*, we should be unable to meet it. But autonomy has no such implication. It would be absurd to identify an individual with the formal process of reflection and choice in which autonomy is manifest. This process requires material—preferences and capacity—to serve as inputs, and there is no threat to autonomy in the recognition that these inputs are not, at least initially, autonomously determined. What makes a being autonomous is his capacity to alter given preferences by a rational self-critical, reflective procedure, not a capacity to produce preferences with no prior basis.

We may assume that an individual begins with preferences and capacities that are, at least in part, socially determined. And we assume that the capacity by which an individual reflects self-critically on his preferences and capacities is also in part socially determined. In effect, we assume that human beings are socialized into autonomy. What matters is that their preferences and, within limits, their capacities are not fixed by their socialization, which is not a process by which persons are hard-wired, but rather, at least in part, a process for the development of soft-wired beings, who have the capacity to change the manner in which they are constituted.

[. . .] We [have] characterized an essentially just society as neutral with respect to the aims of its members, adapting itself to enable them to bring about a fair and optimal outcome whatever their particular preferences. We may now add to that characterization, and say that an essentially just society is also neutral with respect to the socialization of its members, in so far as it ensures them the autonomy to alter their preferences through rational reflection. Both neutrality in the production of preferences and neutrality in their satisfaction are required from the Archimedean point.

Neutrality in the production of preferences must, however, be limited. We suppose that persons are soft-wired so that they may change their desires and aims. We cannot suppose that the process of socialization is neutral with respect to what we may, continuing the metaphor, term the initial wiring. The essentially just society may be neutral with respect to the alteration of preferences, but it cannot be neutral with respect to their initial production. The process of socialization brings about determinate persons, not mere possibilities to be constituted by some unimagined, and perhaps unimaginable, act of self-creation. There must then be a non-neutral moment in the socializing activity of even the essentially just society. And this non-neutral moment, even if no threat to autonomy, seems an arbitrary factor that stands in need of justification to the rational autonomous individual.

But does not the assured neutrality of the essentially just society afford this justification? Grant that each person is constituted in part by an initial set of preferences that cannot be subject to his control and that from his standpoint is an arbitrary result of the social process by which he, as an individual with determinate preferences and capacities, was brought into being. Yet if he is a member of an essentially just society, he is assured that this arbitrariness cannot affect his equitable fulfilment; whatever preferences he may have, or come to have as a result of reflection on those initially given, an essentially just society enables him to realize a fair and optimal outcome.

As must be evident, an essentially just society may not socialize its members arbitrarily. [. . .] We [have] noted that an essentially just society is related to a choice reflecting the possible preferences of human beings, given only the general relations between social practices and human concerns that may reasonably be assumed, and the general constraints on circumstances set by the horizon of feasibility. An essentially just society will not encourage yearnings for the impossible; it will not encourage strongly opposed aims that threaten the prospect of mutual advantage. No one has reason to complain of this, for no one has reason to see himself disadvantaged by such restrictions on possible socialization.

Indeed, we must suppose that, in an essentially just society, socialization will strengthen the institutions and practices that its members rationally endorse. While leaving each person free to choose the particular objects of his affections, society must encourage the general sociability of its members, since this facilitates interaction. The assurance that interaction is subject to the constraints of justice meets the concern emphasized in feminist thought, that sociability not be a basis for exploitation. In an essentially just society no individual will be expected to sacrifice her interests to those of others in order to gain the satisfaction of social intercourse.

Furthermore, an essentially just society must be strengthened through the development of the affections and interests of the young in such a way that their mature concerns afford motivational reinforcement to the rational requirements of co-operation. Co-operative activity should be experienced as itself fulfilling. So indeed should market activity, but, in so far as it does not require the constraints on utility-maximizing behaviour that are essential to fair co-operation, non-social satisfactions may be expected to play a more extensive and effective motivational role within the market than beyond it. Socialization, then, should encourage persons to want to co-operate in those situations in which co-operation is otherwise mutually advantageous to them. The desire to co-operate in such circumstances will receive the reflective endorsement of reason; the justification of the essentially just society extends to the justification of the sociability that sustains and strengthens it, and so to the justification of the socialization that instils and encourages this sociability.

Because an essentially just society makes possible the greatest possible breadth of fulfilment, encouraging persons to realize the many and varied potentialities of human beings, we must expect that a division of labour will be built into both the institutions and the socializing procedures of the society. Such a division of labour will not, of course, be expressed in requirements overriding individual autonomy. It will not be coercive. Rather, we might expect an essentially just society to promote a broadly pluralistic conception of human realization that, given the differentiating accidents of circumstance and capacity, leads individuals to choose differing but complementary roles. Neither the objection of Marx, that the division of labour prevents the many-sided development of individual human beings, nor the objection of Rousseau, that the division of labour renders individuals dependent on the alien wills of others and so unfree, can be sustained in the circumstances of essential justice.[1] For [. . .] no human being is capable of realizing all of the possible modes of human activity; the fullest realization possible for each of us is the realization of some mode complementary to the realization of other modes by other persons. And, in the essentially just society, no one is disadvantaged or exploited by dependence on others; the insufficiency of the individual, both in terms of producing the material goods of human life, and in terms of realizing the varied modes of human life, is most fully overcome by the shared, fair, optimal activities that such a society makes possible.

But there are more problematic aspects to socialization that may seem to threaten the very possibility of an essentially just society. All known human societies embrace both gender differentiation and status differentiation, and the two are linked; males are consistently status-superior to females.[2] Now the content of both gender and status differentiation is highly

---

[1] [. . .] Rousseau's underlying idea is clearly formulated in *Projet de constitution pour la corse*, in *Political Writings*, ed. C. E. Vaughan (Oxford, 1962), ii. 308; 'Whoever depends on another, and lacks resources in himself, cannot be free' (my translation).

[2] See, e.g., E. Friedl, *Women and Men: An Anthropologist's View* (New York,

(although not totally) variable; what is constant is the form of differentiation. But, given this constancy, it would be a bold person who would suppose that either gender differentiation, or its linkage with status, is eliminable. Even if we were to suppose that genderization, the conceptual differentiation and identification of human beings corresponding to physiological sexual differences, is itself entirely a social product, yet it may result from a hard-wired difference in the behavioural responses of adult human beings to sexual differences in infants and children. To treat children as male or as female, and to socialize them so that they regard themselves as essentially male or female, may be fixed.

Genderization itself threatens essential justice. Its effect is to relativize the expectations of females and males to separate ideals or standards. Social institutions and practices encourage, if they do not actually require, role differences between women and men. And these are related to affective differences; socialization promotes different forms of sociability for women and men. Even if none of these differences were related to status, yet the imposition of gendering in determining the fulfilment appropriate to women and men may be seen as inconsistent with the requirements of Archimedean choice that determine essential justice.

Differential status leaves the issue in no doubt. A society that assigns it on the basis of imposed standards cannot be supposed to satisfy the neutrality of satisfaction required for essential justice. But, if the assignment of differential status is one of the fixed points of human society, essential justice is impossible. The non-neutral moment in socialization may then seem to undermine the idea of a society of autonomous, affectively free, liberal individuals.

3

We may read the first sustained enquiry into justice, Plato's *Republic*, as an attempt to defend the Greek *polis* by representing

---

1975); 'We begin with the evidence that a degree of male dominance exists in all known societies' (p. 7).

its ideal nature and showing the congruence of that nature with reason. A similar concern may be seen to inform our enquiry, as an attempt to defend Western market society by representing its ideal nature in relation to reason. But as the actual *polis* fell irredeemably short of the city that comes into being in speech, so market society falls short of the society that would manifest essential justice.[3] Plato no doubt hoped to recall the *polis* to its ideal, but his articulation came too late. Is there a further parallel here?

In concluding *The Order of Things*, Michel Foucault writes, 'As the archaeology of our thought easily shows, man is an invention of recent date. And one perhaps nearing its end.'[4] Whether invention or discovery, the liberal individual is indeed of recent date; is she the mere creature of an historical moment, her maximizing rationality and free affectivity variants on some larger theme? We have found her ecological niche in the essentially just society, which is in the fullest sense 'a cooperative venture for mutual advantage'. Her morality and her sociability are elicited and sustained by, and only by, her sense of herself as interacting with others in ways that afford fair mutual benefit. In other habitats, lacking essential justice, persons would be constrained, not autonomously by reason, but heteronomously by socially conditioned beliefs and affections. So we may ask for the prospects of the liberal individual; can her ecological niche be realized and sustained?

Historically, the individual has emerged, both practically and conceptually, in an environment in which there has been a strong positive correlation between the pursuit of individualized interest and a continuing increase in the provision of goods and services to all. However fair or unfair the distribution of benefits may be, Western society has maintained the appearance of affording its members mutual advantage. And we may attribute significant roles in the creation of this environment to the perfection of social instruments for exchange and investment, and to the development of a technology oriented to

---

[3] For the idea of the 'city that comes into being in speech', see *Republic*, 369a.

[4] M. Foucault, *The Order of Things: An Archaeology of the Human Sciences* (New York, 1971), 387.

increasing production and diversification. But we lack the expertise to form a sensible expectation about the prospects for the continuation, much less the improvement, of these circumstances favourable to liberal individuality.

Equally we lack the expertise to form any reasonable expectation about the conceptual future of the individual. If our present self-understanding emerges from the disappearance of the belief that man is a creature, taking his goals and values from a divinely established order, yet it may be no more than an uneasy transitional stage to the emergence of the sense that man is an artefact, constructed through an increasingly known and alterable process of genetic engineering. And man as engineered may be no more compatible with the ideas of individuality and autonomy which underlie our enquiry than man as created.

Perhaps then we have constructed, not a theory linking morality to rational choice, but a portrayal of moral constraints and maximizing choice in an ephemeral market society. Yet we have hope of a better conclusion. Nietzsche begins the second essay of *On the Genealogy of Morals* with the question, 'To breed an animal *with the right to make promises*—is not this the paradoxical task that nature has set itself in the case of man? is it not the real problem regarding man?'[5] Nature sets itself no tasks, but in Nietzsche's metaphor we may find the core of a self-understanding that, once attained, is not lightly to be sacrificed. An animal with the right to make promises must be able to commit itself, giving itself a reason for choice and action that overrides its usual concern with fulfilling its preferences. Such an animal is able to interact with its world in a new and distinctive way, which we have sought to capture in the conception of constrained maximization. Economic man would be no more than 'a globally maximizing machine'.[6] But the liberal individual is surely 'aware of his superiority over all those who lack the right to make promises and stand as their own guarantors . . . and of how this mastery over himself also necessarily gives him

---

[5] F. Nietzsche, *On the Genealogy of Morals* (1887), second essay, sect. 1; trans. W. Kaufmann and R.J. Hollingdale and ed. W. Kaufmann (New York, 1967), 57.

[6] The phrase, italicized in the original, is from J. Elster, *Ulysses and the Sirens: Studies in Rationality and Irrationality* (Cambridge, 1979), 10.

mastery over circumstances, over nature, and over all more short-willed and unreliable creatures'.[7] And this mastery over self is expressed when, recognizing the need for community, the individual human being, woman or man among women and men, embraces morals by agreement.

[7] Nietzsche, second essay, sect. 2; pp. 59–60.

10

LIBERAL INDIVIDUALISM AND LIBERAL NEUTRALITY

WILL KYMLICKA

A distinctive feature of contemporary liberal theory is its emphasis on 'neutrality'—the view that the state should not reward or penalize particular conceptions of the good life but, rather, should provide a neutral framework within which different and potentially conflicting conceptions of the good can be pursued. Liberal neutrality has been criticized from many angles, but I will be concerned here only with the connection critics draw between neutrality and individualism, particularly in the context of Rawls's theory of justice. One of the most persistent criticisms of Rawls's theory is that it is excessively individualistic, neglecting the way that individual values are formed in social contexts and pursued through communal attachments. I will distinguish three different ways that critics have attempted to connect neutrality and individualism and argue that all rest on misinterpretations of Rawls's theory. However, there are important aspects of the relationship between individual values and social contexts which Rawls does not discuss, and I hope to show that the dispute over liberal neutrality would be more fruitful if both sides moved away from general questions of 'individualism' toward more specific questions about the relationship between state, society, and culture in liberal democracies.

DEFINING LIBERAL NEUTRALITY

What sort of neutrality is present, or aspired to, in Rawls's theory? Raz distinguishes two principles which he believes are

Will Kymlicka, excerpted from *Ethics*, 99 (1989), 883–905. Copyright © by The University of Chicago Press 1989. All rights reserved. Used by permission.

present, and inadequately distinguished, in liberal writings on neutrality. One, which Raz calls 'neutral political concern', requires that the state seek to help or hinder different life-plans to an equal degree—that is, government action should have neutral consequences. The other, which Raz calls the 'exclusion of ideals', allows that government action may help some ways of life more than others but denies that government should act in order to help some ways of life over others. The state does not take a stand on which ways of life are most worth living, and the desire to help one way of life over another is precluded as a justification of government action. The first requires neutrality in the consequences of government policy; the second requires neutrality in the justification of government policy. I will call these two conceptions consequential and justificatory neutrality, respectively.

Which conception does Rawls defend? Raz argues that Rawls endorses consequential neutrality,[1] and some of Rawls's formulations are undoubtedly consistent with that interpretation. But there are two basic tenets of Rawls's theory which show that he could not have endorsed consequential neutrality. First, respect for civil liberties will necessarily have non-neutral consequences. Freedom of speech and association allow different groups to pursue and advertise their way of life. But not all ways of life are equally valuable, and some will have difficulty attracting or maintaining adherents. Since individuals are free to choose between competing visions of the good life, civil liberties have non-neutral consequences—they create a market-place of ideas, as it were, and how well a way of life does in this market depends on the kinds of goods it can offer to prospective adherents. Hence, under conditions of freedom, satisfying and valuable ways of life will tend to drive out those which are worthless and unsatisfying.

Rawls endorses such a cultural market-place, despite its non-neutral consequences. Moreover, the prospect that trivial and degrading ways of life fare less well in free competition is not something he regrets or views as an unfortunate side-effect. On the contrary, the liberal tradition has always endorsed civil

---

[1] Raz, *The Morality of Freedom* (Oxford, 1986), 117.

liberties precisely because they make it possible 'that the worth of different modes of life should be proved practically'.[2]

Consequential neutrality is also inconsistent with Rawls's explanation of the role of 'primary goods'. They are supposed to be employable in the pursuit of diverse conceptions of the good. But not all ways of life have the same costs, and so an equal distribution of resources will have non-neutral consequences. Those who choose expensive ways of life—valuing leisure over work, or champagne over beer—will get less welfare out of an equal bundle of resources than will people with more modest tastes. This is unlike an equality of welfare scheme, in which those with expensive tastes would be subsidized by others in order to achieve equality of welfare. On an equality of welfare scheme, resources would be unequally distributed so that every way of life is equally helped, no matter how expensive—those who wish beer get enough money for beer, those who wish champagne get enough money for champagne.

Rawls favours equality of resources, despite its non-neutral consequences and, indeed, because it prohibits excess demands on resources by those with expensive desires:

It is not by itself an objection to the use of primary goods that it does not accommodate those with expensive tastes. One must argue in addition that it is unreasonable, if not unjust, to hold people responsible for their preferences and to require them to make out as best they can. But to argue this seems to presuppose that citizens' preferences are beyond their control as propensities or cravings which simply happen. Citizens seem to be regarded as passive carriers of desires. The use of primary goods, however, relies on a capacity to assume responsibility for our ends. This capacity is part of the moral power to form, to revise, and rationally to pursue a conception of the good. . . . In any particular situation, then, those with less expensive tastes have presumably adjusted their likes and dislikes over the course of their lives to the income and wealth they could reasonably expect; and it is regarded as unfair that they now should have less in order to spare others from the consequences of their lack of foresight or self-discipline.[3]

[2] J. S. Mill, *On Liberty*, ed. D. Spitz (New York, 1975), 54.
[3] Rawls, 'Social Unity and Primary Goods', in A. Sen and B. Williams (eds.), *Utilitarianism and Beyond* (Cambridge, 1982), 168–9; see also Rawls, 'Fairness to Goodness', *Philosophical Review*, 84 (1975), 553.

Since individuals are responsible for forming 'their aims and ambitions in the light of what they can reasonably expect', they recognize that 'the weight of their claims is not given by the strength or intensity of their wants and desires'.[4] Those people who have developed expensive tastes in disregard of what they can reasonably expect have no claim to be subsidized by others, no matter how strongly felt those desires are.[5]

So the two fundamental components of liberal justice—respect for liberty and fairness in the distribution of material resources—both preclude consequential neutrality. However ambiguous his terminology is, Rawls has to be interpreted as endorsing justificatory neutrality.[6] As Rawls puts it, govern-

---

[4] J. Rawls, 'Kantian Constructivism in Moral Theory: The Dewey Lectures 1980', *Journal of Philosophy*, 77 (1980), 545.

[5] This principle of responsibility is also central to Dworkin's equality of resources scheme: the cost to others of the resources we claim should 'figure in each person's sense of what is rightly his and in each person's judgement of what life he should lead, given that command of justice' (R. Dworkin, 'What Is Equality? Part 2', *Philosophy and Public Affairs*, 10 (1981), 289). Indeed, Dworkin's scheme does a better job than Rawls's difference principle of distinguishing the costs that people are responsible for from the costs that are an unchosen part of people's circumstances. Some people argue that an accurate assessment of individual responsibility requires going beyond either primary goods or equality of resources to 'equal opportunity for welfare' (R. Arneson, 'Equality and Equal Opportunity for Welfare', *Philosophical Studies*, 55 (1989), 79–95), or 'equal access to advantage' (G. A. Cohen, 'On the Currency of Egalitarian Justice', *Ethics*, 99 (July 1989)). While these critiques of Rawls's account of primary goods are important, they are not moves away from justificatory neutrality.

[6] Although I cannot argue the point here, I believe that the other major statements of liberal neutrality must similarly be interpreted as endorsing justificatory neutrality—e.g., B. Ackerman, *Social Justice in the Liberal State* (New Haven, Conn., 1980), 11, 61; C. Larmore, *Patterns of Moral Complexity* (Cambridge, 1987), ch. 3, esp. pp. 44–7; R. Dworkin, 'Liberalism', in S. Hampshire (ed.), *Public and Private Morality* (Cambridge, 1978), 127, and *A Matter of Principle* (London, 1985), 222; R. Nozick, *Anarchy, State and Utopia* (New York, 1974), 272–3 (for an extended exegetical discussion of these passages, see D. Knott, 'Liberalism and the Justice of Neutral Political Concern' (D.Phil. thesis, Oxford University, 1989), ch. 2). Hence, I will be using 'liberal neutrality' and 'justificatory neutrality' interchangeably. It is quite possible that 'neutrality' is not the best word to describe the policy at issue. Rawls himself has avoided the term until recently because of its multiple and often misleading meanings—e.g., neutrality in its everyday usage usually implies neutral consequences (J. Rawls, 'The Priority of Right

ment is neutral between different conceptions of the good, 'not in the sense that there is an agreed public measure of intrinsic value or satisfaction with respect to which all these conceptions come out equal, but in the sense that they are not evaluated at all from a social standpoint'.[7] The state does not justify its actions by reference to some public ranking of the intrinsic value of different ways of life, for there is no public ranking to refer to. This kind of neutrality is consistent with the legitimate non-neutral consequences of cultural competition and individual responsibility. Indeed, and I'll return to this point, one might think that good ways of life are most likely to establish their greater worth, and individuals are most likely to accept responsibility for the costs of their choices, when the state is constrained by justificatory neutrality—that is, when individuals cannot 'use the coercive apparatus of the state to win for themselves a greater liberty or larger distributive share on the grounds that their activities are of more intrinsic value'.[8] [. . .]

NEUTRALITY AND ATOMISTIC INDIVIDUALISM

The second and third versions of the claim that neutrality is excessively individualistic accept Rawls's emphasis on the capacity for autonomous choice. But autonomous choices are only possible in certain contexts, and these two objections claim that liberal neutrality is incapable of ensuring the existence and flourishing of that context. While both objections attribute this

---

and Ideas of the Good', *Philosophy and Public Affairs*, 17 (1988), 260, 265; cf. Raz, ch. 5). He has instead used the term 'priority of the right over the good'. But that too has multiple and misleading meanings, since it is used by Rawls to describe both the affirming of neutrality over perfectionism, and the affirming of deontology over teleology. These issues need to be kept distinct, and neither, viewed on its own, is usefully called a matter of the 'priority of the right'; see my 'Rawls on Teleology and Deontology', *Philosophy and Public Affairs*, 17 (1988), 173–90, for a critique of Rawls's usage of 'priority of the right'. Given the absence of any obviously superior alternative, I will continue to use the term 'neutrality'.

[7] Rawls, 'Social Unity', p. 172; cf. Rawls, *A Theory of Justice* (Oxford, 1971), 94.

[8] Rawls, *A Theory of Justice*, p. 329.

failure of neutrality to a certain kind of atomistic individualism, they locate the failure in different places—the second objection centres on the need for a shared cultural structure that provides individuals with meaningful options, and the third centres on the need for shared forums in which to evaluate these options.

Neutrality and a Pluralist Culture

The second objection claims that liberal neutrality is incapable of guaranteeing the existence of a pluralistic culture which provides people with the range of options necessary for meaningful individual choice. Autonomy requires pluralism, but

> any collective attempt by a liberal state to protect pluralism would itself be in breach of liberal principles of justice. The state is not entitled to interfere in the movement of the cultural market place except, of course, to ensure that each individual has a just share of available necessary means to exercise his or her moral powers. The welfare or demise of particular conceptions of the good and, therefore, the welfare or demise of social unions of a particular character is not the business of the state.[9]

The state is not allowed to protect pluralism, yet if the cultural market-place proceeds on its own it will eventually undermine the cultural structure which supports pluralism. Neutrality may ensure that government does not denigrate a way of life that some individuals think is worthy of support, but

> whatever else can be said about this argument one point is decisive. Supporting valuable ways of life is a social rather than an individual matter . . . perfectionist ideals require public action for their viability. Anti-perfectionism in practice would lead not merely to a political stand-off from support for valuable conceptions of the good. It would undermine the chances of survival of many cherished aspects of our culture.[10]

The problem, then, is not that liberal neutrality fails to achieve its aim of genuine neutrality (as the possessive individualism objection claimed) but, rather, that neutrality undermines the very conditions in which it is a worthwhile aim.

---

[9] W. Cragg, 'Two Concepts of Community', *Dialogue*, 25 (1986), 47.
[10] Raz, *The Morality of Freedom*, p. 162.

Liberal neutrality is therefore self-defeating. There seem to be two possible ways out of this dilemma. One is to deny that the value of autonomous choice depends on a viable and flourishing culture. This is the 'atomist' route which accepts 'the utterly facile moral psychology of traditional empiricism',[11] according to which an individual's capacity for meaningful choice is self-sufficient outside of society and culture. This route is inadequate, since our dependence on the cultural structure for worthwhile ways of life is undeniable, and few if any liberals have ever been 'concerned purely with individual choices . . . to the neglect of the matrix in which such choices can be open or closed, rich or meagre'.[12]

The second response is to accept that meaningful autonomous choice requires a viable culture but insist that good ways of life will sustain themselves in the cultural market-place without state assistance.[13] But this too is an inadequate response. In conditions of freedom, people are able to assess and recognize the worth of good ways of life and will support them. But the interests people have in a good way of life, and the forms of support they will voluntarily provide, do not necessarily involve sustaining its existence for future generations. My interest in a valuable social practice may be best promoted by depleting the resources which the practice requires to survive beyond my lifetime. Even if the cultural market-place can be relied on to ensure that existing people can identify valuable ways of life, there is no reason to assume that it can be relied on to ensure that future people have a valuable range of options.

So let us grant Raz's argument that state support may be needed to ensure the survival of an adequate range of options for those who have not yet formed their aims in life. Why does that require rejecting neutrality? Consider two possible cultural policies. In the first case, the government ensures an adequate

[11] C. Taylor, *Philosophy and the Human Sciences: Philosophical Papers* (Cambridge, 1985), ii. 197.

[12] Ibid. 207. See, e.g., Rawls, *A Theory of Justice*, pp. 563–4; Dworkin, *A Matter of Principle*, pp. 220–4.

[13] Rawls, *A Theory of Justice*, pp. 331–2; J. Waldron, 'Autonomy and Perfectionism in Raz's *Morality of Freedom*', *University of Southern California Law Review*, 62 (1989); R. Nozick, 'Commentary on "Art as a Public Good"', *Art and the Law*, 9 (1985), 162–4.

range of options by providing tax credits to individuals who make culture-supporting contributions in accordance with their personal perfectionist ideals. The state acts to ensure that there is an adequate range of options, but the evaluation of these options occurs in civil society, outside the coercive apparatus of the state.[14] In the second case, the evaluation of different conceptions of the good becomes a political question, and the government intervenes, not simply to ensure an adequate range of options, but to promote particular options. Now Raz's argument simply does not address this choice. What is 'decisive' in Raz's argument is that one or the other of these policies must be implemented, but he has not given a decisive reason, or any reason at all, to prefer one policy over the other.

A perfectionist state might hope to improve the quality of people's options by encouraging the replacement of less valuable options by more valuable ones. But it is worth repeating that liberal neutrality also hopes to improve the range of options, and the cultural market-place is valued because it helps good ways of life displace bad. Each side aims to secure and improve the range of options from which individuals make their autonomous choices. What they disagree on is where perfectionist values and arguments should be invoked. Are good ways of life more likely to establish their greater worth when they are evaluated in the cultural market-place of civil society, or when the preferability of different ways of life is made a matter of political advocacy and state action? Hence the dispute should perhaps be seen as a choice, not between perfectionism and neutrality, but between social perfectionism and state perfectionism—for

---

[14] This is endorsed by Dworkin in *A Matter of Principle*, ch. 11. This use of tax credits would only be fair if the distribution of resources in society was in fact just. Indeed, it might not be fair even if the difference principle was honoured, since it gives disproportionate power in shaping cultural development to those who are endowed with (undeserved) natural talents, as they are likely to have more disposable income. I assume there are ways to ensure that this operates fairly while still leaving the evaluation of cultural options outside the political sphere. For a discussion of the problem of fairness in influence over culture, in the context of the neutrality/perfectionist debate, see A. Gutmann, *Democratic Education* (Princeton, NJ, 1987), ch. 9, esp. pp. 263–4.

the flip side of state neutrality is support for the role of perfectionist ideals and arguments in civil society.[15]

Neutrality and Collective Deliberations

The third and final objection accepts that liberal neutrality recognizes the necessity of having a secure cultural structure. But it claims that a different sort of atomistic individualism is found in the liberal account of how cultural options should be evaluated. The liberal preference for the cultural market-place over the state as the appropriate arena for evaluating different life-styles stems from an individualistic belief that judgements about the good should be made by isolated individuals, whose autonomy is ensured by protecting them from social pressures. Liberals think that autonomy is promoted when judgements about the good are taken out of the political realm. But in reality individual judgements require the sharing of experiences and the give and take of collective deliberations. Individual judgements about the good always depend on, and flow from, the collective evaluation of shared practices. They become a matter of purely subjective and arbitrary whim if they are cut off from collective deliberations:

Self-fulfillment and even the working out of personal identity and a

---

[15] Failure to recognize this undermines Beiner's argument against liberal neutrality, which he concludes by saying: 'Even if the state is or tries to be neutral (which likely proves impossible), in any case the wider social order in which the individual is nourished is *not*. Liberal "neutralism" is therefore a mirage. It is hard to see why the *state* is constrained to be neutral (whatever that might mean) if social life as a whole is and must be, however much denied by liberals, strongly partial towards a particular way of life' (R. Beiner, 'What's Wrong with Liberalism?', in L. Green and A. Hutchinson (eds.), *Law and Community* (Toronto, 1989)). This is entirely off target. The best reason for state neutrality is precisely that social life is non-neutral, that people can and do make discriminations among competing ways of life in their social life, affirming some and rejecting others, without using the state apparatus. If individuals are unable to make these arguments in social life, then state perfectionism might be the appropriate way to enable people to discriminate among different conceptions of the good (although it is unclear how moving from the cultural market-place to the state would remove the disability). So the argument for state neutrality presupposes, rather than denies, social non-neutrality.

sense of orientation in the world depend upon a communal enterprise. This shared process is the civic life, and its root is involvement with others: other generations, other sorts of persons whose differences are significant because they contribute to the whole upon which our particular sense of self depends. Thus mutual interdependency is the foundational notion of citizenship . . . outside a linguistic community of shared practices, there would be biological *homo sapiens* as logical abstraction, but there could not be human beings. This is the meaning of the Greek and medieval dictum that the political community is ontologically *prior* to the individual. The *polis* is, literally, that which makes man, as human being, possible.[16]

Or, as Crowley puts it, state perfectionism is

an affirmation of the notion that men living in a community of shared experiences and language is the only context in which the individual and society can discover and test their values through the essentially political activities of discussion, criticism, example, and emulation. It is through the existence of organised public spaces, in which men offer and test ideas against one another . . . that men come to understand a part of who they are.[17]

The state should be the proper arena in which to formulate and pursue our visions of the good, because the good for individuals requires collective interaction and inquiry—it cannot be pursued, or even known, presocially.

But this misconstrues the sense in which Rawls claims that the evaluation of ways of life should not be a public concern. Liberal neutrality does not restrict the scope of perfectionist ideals in the collective activities of individuals and groups. Perfectionist ideals, although excluded from a liberal state, 'have an important place in human affairs' and, hence, an important place in a liberal society.[18] Collective activity and shared experiences concerning the good are at the heart of the 'free internal life of the various communities of interests in which persons and groups seek to achieve, in modes of social

---

[16] W. Sullivan, *Reconstructing Public Philosophy* (Berkeley, Calif., 1982), 158, 173.

[17] B. L. Crowley, *The Self, the Individual, and the Community: Liberalism in the Political Thought of F. A. Hayek and Sidney and Beatrice Webb* (Oxford, 1987), 282; see also R. Beiner, *Political Judgment* (London, 1983), 152.

[18] Rawls, *A Theory of Justice*, p. 543.

union consistent with equal liberty, the ends and excellences to which they are drawn'.[19] Rawls's argument for the priority of liberty is grounded in the importance of this 'free social union with others'.[20] He simply denies that 'the coercive apparatus of the state' is an appropriate forum for those deliberations and experiences:

While justice as fairness allows that in a well-ordered society the values of excellence are recognized, the human perfections are to be pursued within the limits of the principle of free association . . . [Persons] do not use the coercive apparatus of the state to win for themselves a greater liberty or larger distributive shares on the grounds that their activities are of more intrinsic value.[21]

Unfortunately, civic republicans, who make this objection most frequently, rarely distinguish between collective activities and political activities. It is, of course, true that participation in shared linguistic and cultural practices is what enables individuals to make intelligent decisions about the good life. But why should such participation be organized in and through the state, rather than through the free association of individuals? It is true that we should 'create opportunities for men to give voice to what they have discovered about themselves and the world and to persuade others of its worth'.[22] But a liberal society does create opportunities for people to express and develop these social aspects of individual deliberation. After all, freedom of assembly, association, and speech are fundamental *liberal* rights. The opportunities for collective enquiry simply occur within and between groups and associations below the level of the state—friends and family, in the first instance, but also churches, cultural associations, professional groups and trade unions, universities, and the mass media. These are some of the 'organized public spaces of appearance' and 'communication communities' of a liberal society.[23] Liberals do not deny that 'the public display of character and judgement and the exchange of experience and insight' are needed to make

---

[19] Ibid.
[20] Ibid.
[21] Ibid. 328–9.
[22] Crowley, *The Self, the Individual, and the Community*, p. 295.
[23] Ibid. 7, 239.

intelligent judgements about the good, or to show others that I 'hold [my] notion of the good responsibly'.[24] Indeed, these claims fit comfortably in many liberal discussions of the value of free speech and association.[25] What the liberal denies is that I should have to give such an account of myself *to the state*.

A similar failure to confront the distinctive role of the state weakens radical critiques of liberalism, like that of Habermas. Habermas, in his earlier writings at least, wants the evaluation of different ways of life to be a political question, but, unlike communitarians and civic republicans, he does not hope or expect that this political deliberation will serve to promote people's embeddedness in existing practices.[26] Indeed, he thinks that political deliberation is required precisely because in its absence people will tend to accept existing practices as givens and thereby perpetuate the false needs and false consciousness which accompany those historical practices.[27] Only when existing ways of life are 'the objects of discursive will-formation' can people's understanding of the good be free of deception. Rawls's view of distributive justice does not demand the scrutiny of these practices and, hence, does not recognize the emancipatory interest people have in escaping false needs and ideological distortions.

But why should the evaluation of people's conceptions of the good be tied to their claims on resources, and hence to the

---

[24] Ibid. 287.

[25] See, e.g., T. Scanlon, 'Freedom of Expression and Categories of Expression', in D. Copp and S. Wendell (eds.), *Pornography and Censorship* (Buffalo, NY, 1983), 141–7; L. Lomasky, *Persons, Rights, and the Moral Community* (Oxford, 1987), 111.

[26] Habermas seems to endorse this position when he says that the need for a 'discursive desolidification of the (largely externally controlled or traditionally fixed) interpretation of our needs' is the heart of his disagreement with Rawls (J. Habermas, *Communication and the Evolution of Society*, trans. T. McCantry (Boston, 1979), 198–9). However, he now rejects the idea of politically evaluating people's conceptions of the good (J. Habermas, 'Questions and Counterquestions', in R. Bernstein (ed.), *Habermas and Modernity* (Cambridge, Mass., 1985), 214–16). For discussion of the (apparent) shift, see S. Benhabib, *Critique, Norm, and Utopia* (New York, 1986), ch. 8; and N. Funk, 'Habermas and the Social Goods', *Social Text*, 18 (1988), 29–31.

[27] Habermas, *Communication and the Evolution of Society*, pp. 198–9; Benhabib, *Critique, Norm, and Utopia*, pp. 312–14.

state apparatus? Communities smaller than the entire political society, groups and associations of various sizes, might be more appropriate forums for those forms of discursive will-formation which involve evaluating the good and interpreting one's genuine needs. While Habermas rejects the communitarian tendency to uncritically endorse existing social practices as the basis for political deliberations about the good, he shares their tendency to assume that anything which is not politically deliberated is thereby left to an individual will incapable of rational judgement.

So the liberal commitment to state neutrality does not manifest abstract individualism either in regard to the importance of a shared cultural context for meaningful individual options, or in regard to the importance of the sharing of experiences and arguments for meaningful individual evaluation of those options. Liberal neutrality does not deny these shared social requirements of individual autonomy but, rather, provides an interpretation of them.

EVALUATING THE NEUTRALITY DEBATE

I have argued that liberal neutrality is not excessively individualistic, either in terms of the way it conceives the content of people's ends, or in the way that people evaluate and pursue those ends. Of course neutrality may be indefensible for other reasons. Neutrality requires a certain faith in the operation of non-state forums and processes for individual judgement and cultural development, and a distrust of the operation of state forums and processes for evaluating the good. Nothing I have said so far shows that this optimism and distrust are warranted. Indeed, just as critics of neutrality have failed to defend their faith in political forums and procedures, so liberals have failed to defend their faith in non-state forums and procedures. The crucial claims have not been adequately defended by either side.

In fact, it is hard to avoid the conclusion that each side in the neutrality debate has failed to learn the important lesson taught by the other side. Despite centuries of liberal insistence on the importance of the distinction between society and the state, communitarians still seem to assume that whatever is properly social must become the province of the political. They have not confronted the liberal worry that the all-embracing authority and coercive means which characterize the state make it a particularly inappropriate forum for the sort of genuinely shared deliberation and commitment that they desire. Despite centuries of communitarian insistence on the historically fragile and contingent nature of our culture, and the need to consider the conditions under which a free culture can arise and sustain itself, liberals still tend to take the existence of a tolerant and diverse culture for granted, as something which naturally arises and sustains itself, the ongoing existence of which is therefore simply assumed in a theory of justice. Hegel was right to insist that a culture of freedom is a historical achievement, and liberals need to explain why the cultural market-place does not threaten that achievement, either by failing to connect people in a strong enough way to their communal practice (as communitarians fear), or, conversely, by failing to detach people in a strong enough way from the expectations of existing practices and ideologies (as Habermas fears). A culture of freedom requires a mix of both exposure and connection to existing practices, and also distance and dissent from them. Liberal neutrality may provide that mix, but that is not obviously true, it may be true only in some times and places. So both sides need to give us a more comprehensive comparison of the opportunities and dangers present in state and non-state forums and procedures for evaluating the good.

While both sides have something to learn from the other, that is not to say that the truth is somewhere in between the two. I cannot provide here the sort of systematic comparison of the empirical operation of state and non-state forums and procedures that is required for a proper defence of neutrality, but I want to suggest a few reasons why state perfectionism would have undesirable consequences for our society. I will assume, for the moment, that the public ranking of the value of different ways of life which a perfectionist state appeals to would be arrived at through the collective political deliberation of citizens, rather than through the secret or unilateral decisions of political elites.

What are the consequences of having a collectively determined ranking of the value of different conceptions of the good? One consequence is that more is at stake when people publicly formulate and defend their conception of the good. If people do not advance persuasive arguments for their conception of the good, then a perfectionist state may take action which will make their way of life harder to maintain. In a liberal society with a neutral state, on the other hand, people who cannot persuade others of the value of their way of life will lose out in the competition with other conceptions of the good being advanced in the cultural market-place, but they will not face adverse state action.

Why is that an undesirable consequence? In principle, it is not undesirable—it may simply intensify the patterns of cultural development, since the pros and cons of different ways of life might be revealed more quickly under the threat of state action than would occur in the cultural market-place, where people are sometimes reluctant to confront opposing values and arguments. However, I believe that state perfectionism would in fact serve to distort the free evaluation of ways of life, to rigidify the dominant ways of life, whatever their intrinsic merits, and to unfairly exclude the values and aspirations of marginalized and disadvantaged groups within the community.

First, state perfectionism raises the prospect of a dictatorship of the articulate and would unavoidably penalize those individuals who are inarticulate. But being articulate, in our society, is not simply an individual variable. There are many culturally disadvantaged groups whose beliefs and aspirations are not understood by the majority. Recent immigrants are an obvious example whose disadvantage is partly unavoidable. But there are also groups which have been deliberately excluded from the mainstream of American society, and whose cultural disadvantage reflects prejudice and insensitivity. The dominant cultural practices of our community were defined by one section of the population—that is, the male members of the upper classes of the white race—and were defined so as to exclude and denigrate the values of subordinate groups. Members of these excluded groups—women, blacks, Hispanics—have been unable to get recognition for their values from the cultural mainstream and have developed (or retained) subcultures for the expression of these values, subcultures whose norms, by necessity, are incommensurable with those of the mainstream. It is unfair to ask them to defend the value of their way of life by reference to cultural standards and norms that were defined by and for others. Even where these historical factors are absent, the majority is likely to use state perfectionism to block valuable social change that threatens their preferred cultural practices. This cultural conservatism need not be malicious—the majority may simply not see the value of cultural change, partly due to incomprehension, partly from fear of change.

State perfectionism would also affect the kinds of arguments given. Minority groups whose values conflict with those of the majority often put a high value on the integrity of their practices and aim at gaining adherents from within the majority slowly, one by one. But where there is state perfectionism, the minority must immediately aim at persuading the majority, and so they will describe their practices in such a way as to be most palatable to the majority, even if that misdescribes the real meaning and value of the practice, which often arose precisely in opposition to dominant practices. There would be an inevitable tendency for minorities to describe and debate conceptions of the good in terms of dominant values, which then reinforces the cultural conservatism of the dominant group itself.

In these and other ways, the threats and inducements of coercive power would distort rather than improve the process of individual judgement and cultural development. Some of these problems also arise in the cultural market-place (i.e. penalizing the inarticulate, social prejudice). Insensitivity and prejudice will be problems no matter which model we choose, since both models reward those groups who can make their way of life attractive to the mainstream. But state perfectionism intensifies these problems, since it dictates to minority groups when and how they will interact with majority norms, and it dictates a time and place—political deliberation over state policy—in which minorities are most vulnerable. State neutrality, on the other hand, gives culturally disadvantaged groups a greater ability to choose the time and place in which they will confront majority sensitivities and to choose an audience with whom they are most comfortable. There will always be an imbalance in the interaction between culturally dominant and subordinate groups.

State neutrality ensures that the culturally subordinate group has as many options as possible concerning that interaction, and that the costs of that imbalance for the subordinate groups are minimized. State perfectionism, I think, does just the opposite.

Some of these problems could be avoided if the public ranking of ways of life was determined by political elites, insulated from popular debate and prejudice. Indeed, an enlightened and insulated political elite could use state perfectionist policies to promote the aims and values of culturally disadvantaged groups. Just as the Supreme Court is supposed to be more able to protect the rights of disadvantaged groups because of its insulation from political pressures, so an insulated political elite may be able to give a fairer hearing to minority values than they get in the cultural market-place. But this raises troubling questions about accountability and the danger of abuse (after all, if majority groups are insensitive to minority aspirations, why won't they elect leaders who are similarly insensitive?). And, in any event, why shouldn't the aim of the political elite be to counteract the biases of the cultural market-place, which affect the public evaluation of all minority values, rather than deciding for themselves which minority values are worth promoting? Using state power to counteract biases against minority values may be legitimate, not because of a general principle of perfectionism, but because of a general principle of redressing biases against disadvantaged groups.

These are some of the reasons why liberals distrust state perfectionism for our society.[28] Communitarians are right to

---

[28] There are other reasons for opposing state perfectionism. I have been discussing the difficulty of finding acceptable procedures for formulating a public ranking of different ways of life. There are also difficulties about how the state should go about promoting its preferred ways of life, once those are identified. Even if the state can be relied on to come up with an accurate ranking and can get people to pursue the right ways of life, it may not be able to get people to pursue them *for the right reasons*. Someone who acts in a certain way in order to avoid state punishment, or to gain state subsidies, is not guided by an understanding of the genuine value of the activity (Waldron, 'Autonomy and Perfectionism'; Lomasky, *Persons, Rights, and the Moral Community*, pp. 253–4). This criticism is important and precludes various coercive and manipulative forms of perfectionism, but it does not preclude short-term state intervention designed to introduce people to valuable ways of life. One way to get people to pursue something for the right reasons is to get them

insist that we examine the history and structure of a particular culture, but it is remarkable how little communitarians themselves undertake such an examination of our culture. They wish to use the ends and practices of our cultural tradition as the basis for a politics of the common good, but they do not mention that these practices were historically defined by a small segment of the population, nor do they discuss how that exclusionary history would affect the politicization of debates about the value of different ways of life. If we look at the history of our society, surely liberal neutrality has the great advantage of its potential inclusiveness, its denial that marginalized and subordinate groups must fit into the historical practices, the 'way of life', which have been defined by the dominant groups. Forcing subordinate groups to defend their ways of life, under threat or promise of coercive power, is inherently exclusive. Communitarians simply ignore this danger and the cultural history which makes it so difficult to avoid.[29]

While liberalism need not be committed to neutrality in all times and places, the relationship between the culture and the state in our society makes neutrality particularly appropriate for us. However, certain features of that relationship also make neutrality particularly difficult to implement. I have discussed different ways a neutral state might protect and promote its culture. But, if we look at actual states and actual cultures, we will quickly notice that most liberal democracies contain more than one cultural community. Most countries contain many cultures, like the French, English, and aboriginal cultures in Canada. When we say that the cultural context can be enriched

---

to pursue it for the wrong reasons and hope they will then see its true value. This is not inherently unacceptable, and it occurs often enough in the cultural market-place. Hence a comprehensive defence of neutrality may need to focus on a prior stage of state perfectionism—i.e., the problems involved in formulating a public ranking of conceptions of the good.

[29] On the exclusionary tendencies of communitarianism, see A. Gutmann, 'Communitarian Critics of Liberalism', *Philosophy and Public Affairs*, 14 (1985), 318–22; D. Herzog, 'Some Questions for Republicans', *Political Theory*, 14 (1986), 481–90; H. Hirsch, 'The Threnody of Liberalism: Constitutional Liberty and the Renewal of Community', *Political Theory*, 14 (1986), 435–8; N. Rosenblum, *Another Liberalism: Romanticism and the Reconstruction of Liberal Thought* (Cambridge, Mass., 1987), 178–81.

or diminished, whose culture are we discussing? Whose language should be used in the schools and courts and media? If immigration policy should give consideration to the consequences of immigration on the cultural structure, as most liberals have agreed, then shouldn't we accept demands by Francophones in Quebec, or the Inuit in Northern Canada, to have some control over immigration into their cultural communities? What does liberal neutrality require when the state contains more than one culture?

The dominant view among contemporary liberals, to which Rawls apparently subscribes, is that liberalism requires the 'absence, even prohibition, of any legal or governmental recognition of racial, religious, language or [cultural] groups as corporate entities with a standing in the legal or governmental process, and a prohibition of the use of ethnic criteria of any type for discriminatory purposes, or conversely for special or favored treatment'.[30] But this view, which achieved its current prominence during the American struggle against racial segregation, has only limited applicability. Once we recognize the importance of the cultural structure and accept that there is a positive duty on the state to protect the cultural conditions which allow for autonomous choice, then cultural membership does have political salience. Respect for the autonomy of the members of minority cultures requires respect for their cultural structure, and that in turn may require special linguistic, educational, and even political rights for minority cultures. Indeed, there are a number of circumstances in which liberal theories of equality should recognize the special status of minority cultures (as pre-war liberal theories often did).[31] The attempt to answer questions about the rights of cultural communities

[30] M. Gordon, 'Toward a General Theory of Racial and Ethnic Group Relations', in N. Glazer and D. Moynihan (eds.), *Ethnicity: Theory and Experience* (Cambridge, Mass., 1975), 105.

[31] Minority rights were a common feature of prewar liberalism, both in theory (e.g., L. T. Hobhouse, *Social Evolution and Political Theory* (New York, 1928), 146–7) and practice (e.g., the League of Nations). I attempt to provide a liberal theory of the rights of minority cultures in 'Liberalism, Individualism, and Minority Rights', in L. Green and A. Hutchinson (eds.), *Law and Community* (Toronto, 1989) and *Liberalism, Community and Culture* (Oxford, 1989), chs. 7–10.

with the formula of colour-blind laws applying to persons of all races and cultures is hopelessly inadequate once we look at the diversity of cultural membership which exists in contemporary liberal democracies.[32] However, the alternatives have rarely been considered in contemporary liberal writings, which are dominated (often unconsciously) by the model of the nation-state.[33]

CONCLUSION

The real issue concerning neutrality is not individualism: nothing in Rawls's insistence on state neutrality is inconsistent with recognizing the importance of the social world to the development, deliberation, and pursuit of individuals' values. It is commonly alleged that liberals fail to recognize that people are naturally social or communal beings. Liberals supposedly think that society rests on an artificial social contract, and that a coercive state apparatus is needed to keep naturally a social people together in society. But there is a sense in which the opposite is true—liberals believe that people naturally form and join social relations and forums in which they come to understand and pursue the good. The state is not needed to provide that communal context and is likely to distort the normal

[32] Even in a genuine 'nation-state', there are questions about how to deal with immigrants from other cultures. Liberals have historically disagreed over the extent to which respect for the autonomy of existing members of the polity requires restrictions on immigration which might damage the cultural structure. They have also disagreed over the extent to which respect for the autonomy of immigrants requires encouraging or compelling their assimilation to the cultural structure of the new country. Again, the requirements of liberal neutrality are not at all obvious.

[33] The assumption that the political community is culturally homogeneous is clear in a number of passages in Rawls and Dworkin—e.g., J. Rawls, 'The Basic Structure as Subject', in A. Goldman and J. Kim (eds.), *Values and Morals* (Dordrecht, 1978), 55, and 'On the Idea of Free Public Reason' (1988, photocopy), 8; Dworkin, *A Matter of Principle*, pp. 230-3. While revising that assumption would affect the conclusions they go on to draw about the distribution of rights and responsibilities, Rawls and Dworkin never discuss what changes would be required in culturally plural countries. Indeed, they do not seem to recognize that any changes would be required. For a criticism of Rawls's inattention to cultural pluralism, see V. van Dyke, 'Justice as Fairness: For Groups?', *American Political Science Review*, 69 (1975), 607-14.

processes of collective deliberations and cultural development. It is communitarians who seem to think that individuals will drift into anomic and detached isolation without the state actively bringing them together to collectively evaluate and pursue the good.[34]

The question is not whether individuals' values and autonomy need to be situated in social relations but whether the relevant relations are necessarily or desirably political ones. This should be the real issue in debates over neutrality, and settling that issue requires a closer examination of the relationship between society, culture, and the state than either defenders or critics have so far provided.

[34] E.g., Crowley says that politics makes possible 'a context within which our own self-understanding *may* be articulated and compared with others' (p. 290; emphasis added). But it would be more accurate to say, as he indeed goes on to say, that 'politics both *makes* us test dialogically the adequacy of our present self-awareness and makes us aware of other dimensions articulated by other people' (p. 290; emphasis added). Since Crowley never discusses this shift, it seems that he believes that individuals are only able to deliberate collectively when they are made to do so. A similar belief may explain why Sullivan thinks that state perfectionism is needed to ensure that no one is 'cut off' from collective deliberations (Sullivan, p. 158). Since people in a liberal society are only cut off from the associations and forums of civil society if they cut themselves off, state perfectionism is needed only if one is assuming that uncoerced people will choose not to participate in collective deliberations. Liberals make the opposite assumption that uncoerced individuals will tend to form and join collective associations, and participate in collective deliberations (the suggestion that non-political activity is inherently solitary is also present in Sandel's claim that under communitarian politics 'we can know a good in common that we cannot know alone' (M. Sandel, *Liberalism and the Limits of Justice* (Cambridge, 1982), p. 183).

11

JUSTICE AS FAIRNESS: POLITICAL NOT METAPHYSICAL

JOHN RAWLS

In this discussion I shall make some general remarks about how I now understand the conception of justice that I have called 'justice as fairness' (presented in my book *A Theory of Justice*).[1] I do this because it may seem that this conception depends on philosophical claims I should like to avoid, for example, claims to universal truth, or claims about the essential nature and identity of persons. My aim is to explain why it does not. I shall first discuss what I regard as the task of political philosophy at the present time and then briefly survey how the basic intuitive ideas drawn upon in justice as fairness are combined into a political conception of justice for a constitutional democracy. Doing this will bring out how and why this conception of justice avoids certain philosophical and metaphysical claims. Briefly, the idea is that in a constitutional democracy the public conception of justice should be, so far as possible, independent of controversial philosophical and religious doctrines. Thus, to formulate such a conception, we apply the principle of toleration to philosophy itself: the public conception of justice is to be political, not metaphysical. Hence the title.

I want to put aside the question whether the text of *A Theory of Justice* supports different readings from the one I sketch here. Certainly on a number of points I have changed my views, and there are no doubt others on which my views have changed in ways that I am unaware of.[2] I recognize further that certain

[1] J. Rawls, *A Theory of Justice* (Cambridge, Mass., 1971).

[2] A number of these changes, or shifts of emphasis, are evident in three

faults of exposition as well as obscure and ambiguous passages in *A Theory of Justice* invite misunderstanding; but I think these matters need not concern us and I shan't pursue them beyond a few footnote indications. For our purposes here, it suffices, first, to show how a conception of justice with the structure and content of justice as fairness can be understood as political and not metaphysical, and, second, to explain why we should look for such a conception of justice in a democratic society.

1

One thing I failed to say in *A Theory of Justice*, or failed to stress sufficiently, is that justice as fairness is intended as a political conception of justice. While a political conception of justice is, of course, a moral conception, it is a moral conception worked out for a specific kind of subject, namely, for political, social,

---

lectures entitled 'Kantian Constructivism in Moral Theory: The Dewey Lectures 1980', *Journal of Philosophy*, 77 (1980). For example, the account of what I have called 'primary goods' is revised so that it clearly depends on a particular conception of persons and their higher-order interests; hence this account is not a purely psychological, sociological, or historical thesis. See pp. 526–7. There is also throughout those lectures a more explicit emphasis on the role of a conception of the person as well as on the idea that the justification of a conception of justice is a practical social task rather than an epistemological or metaphysical problem. See pp. 518–19. And in this connection the idea of 'Kantian constructivism' is introduced, especially in the third lecture. It must be noted, however, that this idea is not proposed as Kant's idea: the adjective 'Kantian' indicates analogy not identity, that is, resemblance in enough fundamental respects so that the adjective is appropriate. These fundamental respects are certain structural features of justice as fairness and elements of its content, such as the distinction between what may be called the Reasonable and the Rational, the priority of right, and the role of the conception of the persons as free and equal, and capable of autonomy, and so on. Resemblances of structural features and content are not to be mistaken for resemblances with Kant's views on questions of epistemology and metaphysics. Finally, I should remark that the title of those lectures, 'Kantian Constructivism in Moral Theory', was misleading; since the conception of justice discussed is a political conception, a better title would have been 'Kantian Constructivism in Political Philosophy'. Whether constructivism is reasonable for moral philosophy is a separate and more general question.

and economic institutions. In particular, justice as fairness is framed to apply to what I have called the 'basic structure' of a modern constitutional democracy.[3] (I shall use 'constitutional democracy' and 'democratic regime', and similar phrases, interchangeably.) By this structure I mean such a society's main political, social, and economic institutions, and how they fit together into one unified system of social co-operation. Whether justice as fairness can be extended to a general political conception for different kinds of societies existing under different historical and social conditions, or whether it can be extended to a general moral conception, or a significant part thereof, are altogether separate questions. I avoid prejudging these larger questions one way or the other.

It should also be stressed that justice as fairness is not intended as the application of a general moral conception to the basic structure of society, as if this structure were simply another case to which that general moral conception is applied.[4] In this respect justice as fairness differs from traditional moral doctrines, for these are widely regarded as such general conceptions. Utilitarianism is a familiar example, since the principle of utility, however it is formulated, is usually said to hold for all kinds of subjects ranging from the actions of individuals to the law of nations. The essential point is this: as a practical political matter no general moral conception can provide a publicly recognized basis for a conception of justice in a modern democratic state. The social and historical conditions of such a state have their origins in the Wars of Religion following the Reformation and the subsequent development of the principle of toleration, and in the growth of constitutional government and the institutions of large industrial market economies. These conditions profoundly affect the requirements of a workable conception of political justice: such a conception must allow for a diversity of doctrines and the plurality of conflicting, and indeed incommensurable, conceptions of the good affirmed by the members of existing democratic societies.

---

[3] *A Theory of Justice*, Sect. 2, and see the index; see also 'The Basic Structure as Subject', in A. Goldman and J. Kim (eds.), *Values and Morals* (Dordrecht, 1978), 47–71.

[4] See 'Basic Structure as Subject', pp. 48–50.

Finally, to conclude these introductory remarks, since justice as fairness is intended as a political conception of justice for a democratic society, it tries to draw solely upon basic intuitive ideas that are embedded in the political institutions of a constitutional democratic regime and the public traditions of their interpretation. Justice as fairness is a political conception in part because it starts from within a certain political tradition. We hope that this political conception of justice may at least be supported by what we may call an 'overlapping consensus', that is, by a consensus that includes all the opposing philosophical and religious doctrines likely to persist and to gain adherents in a more or less just constitutional democratic society.[5]

2

There are, of course, many ways in which political philosophy may be understood, and writers at different times, faced with different political and social circumstances, understand their work differently. Justice as fairness I would now understand as a reasonably systematic and practicable conception of justice for a constitutional democracy, a conception that offers an alternative to the dominant utilitarianism of our tradition of political thought. Its first task is to provide a more secure and acceptable basis for constitutional principles and basic rights and liberties than utilitarianism seems to allow.[6] The need for such a political conception arises in the following way.

There are periods, sometimes long periods, in the history of any society during which certain fundamental questions give rise to sharp and divisive political controversy, and it seems difficult, if not impossible, to find any shared basis of political agreement. Indeed, certain questions may prove intractable and may never be fully settled. One task of political philosophy in a democratic society is to focus on such questions

[5] This idea was introduced in *A Theory of Justice*, pp. 387-8, as a way to weaken the conditions for the reasonableness of civil disobedience in a nearly just democratic society. Here and later in sects. VI and VII it is used in a wider context.

[6] *A Theory of Justice*, Preface, p. viii.

and to examine whether some underlying basis of agreement can be uncovered and a mutually acceptable way of resolving these questions publicly established. Or, if these questions cannot be fully settled, as may well be the case, perhaps the divergence of opinion can be narrowed sufficiently so that political co-operation on a basis of mutual respect can still be maintained.[7]

The course of democratic thought over the past two centuries or so makes plain that there is no agreement on the way basic institutions of a constitutional democracy should be arranged if they are to specify and secure the basic rights and liberties of citizens and answer to the claims of democratic equality when citizens are conceived as free and equal persons (as explained in the last three paragraphs of Section 3). A deep disagreement exists as to how the values of liberty and equality are best realized in the basic structure of society. To simplify, we may think of this disagreement as a conflict within the tradition of democratic thought itself, between the tradition associated with Locke, which gives greater weight to what Constant called 'the liberties of the moderns', freedom of thought and conscience, certain basic rights of the person and of property, and the rule of law, and the tradition associated with Rousseau, which gives greater weight to what Constant called 'the liberties of the ancients', the equal political liberties and the values of public life. This is a stylized contrast and historically inaccurate, but it serves to fix ideas.

Justice as fairness tries to adjudicate between these contending traditions, first, by proposing two principles of justice to serve as guidelines for how basic institutions are to realize the

[7] Ibid. 582-3. On the role of a conception of justice in reducing the divergence of opinion, see pp. 44-5, 53, 314, and 564. At various places the limited aims in developing a conception of justice are noted: see p. 364 on not expecting too much of an account of civil disobedience; pp. 200-1 on the inevitable indeterminacy of a conception of justice in specifying a series of points of view from which questions of justice can be resolved; pp. 89-90 on the social wisdom of recognizing that perhaps only a few moral problems (it would have been better to say: problems of political justice) can be satisfactorily settled, and thus of framing institutions so that intractable questions do not arise; on pp. 53, 87-8, 320-1 the need to accept simplifications is emphasized. Regarding the last point, see also 'Kantian Constructivism in Moral Theory', pp. 560-4.

values of liberty and equality, and, second, by specifying a point of view from which these principles can be seen as more appropriate than other familiar principles of justice to the nature of democratic citizens viewed as free and equal persons. What it means to view citizens as free and equal persons is, of course, a fundamental question and is discussed in the following sections. What must be shown is that a certain arrangement of the basic structure, certain institutional forms, are more appropriate for realizing the values of liberty and equality when citizens are conceived as such persons, that is (very briefly), as having the requisite powers of moral personality that enable them to participate in society viewed as a system of fair co-operation for mutual advantage. So, to continue, the two principles of justice (mentioned above) read as follows:

1. Each person has an equal right to a fully adequate scheme of equal basic rights and liberties, which scheme is compatible with a similar scheme for all.
2. Social and economic inequalities are to satisfy two conditions: first, they must be attached to offices and positions open to all under conditions of fair equality of opportunity; and, second, they must be to the greatest benefit of the least advantaged members of society.

Each of these principles applies to a different part of the basic structure; and both are concerned not only with basic rights, liberties, and opportunities, but also with the claims of equality; while the second part of the second principle underwrites the worth of these institutional guarantees.[8] The two principles together, when the first is given priority over the second, regulate the basic institutions which realize these values.[9] But these details, although important, are not our concern here.

---

[8] The statement of these principles differs from that given in *A Theory of Justice* and follows the statement in 'The Basic Liberties and their Priority', *Tanner Lectures on Human Values*, iii (Salt Lake City, 1982), 5. The reasons for the changes are discussed at pp. 46–55 of that lecture. They are important for the revisions made in the account of the basic liberties found in *A Theory of Justice* in the attempt to answer the objections of H. L. A. Hart; but they need not concern us here.

[9] The idea of the worth of these guarantees is discussed in 'The Basic Liberties and their Priority', *Tanner Lectures*, pp. 40–1.

We must now ask: how might political philosophy find a shared basis for settling such a fundamental question as that of the most appropriate institutional forms for liberty and equality? Of course, it is likely that the most that can be done is to narrow the range of public disagreement. Yet even firmly held convictions gradually change: religious toleration is now accepted, and arguments for persecution are no longer openly professed; similarly, slavery is rejected as inherently unjust, and, however much the aftermath of slavery may persist in social practices and unavowed attitudes, no one is willing to defend it. We collect such settled convictions as the belief in religious toleration and the rejection of slavery and try to organize the basic ideas and principles implicit in these convictions into a coherent conception of justice. We can regard these convictions as provisional fixed points which any conception of justice must account for if it is to be reasonable for us. We look, then, to our public political culture itself, including its main institutions and the historical traditions of their interpretation, as the shared fund of implicitly recognized basic ideas and principles. The hope is that these ideas and principles can be formulated clearly enough to be combined into a conception of political justice congenial to our most firmly held convictions. We express this by saying that a political conception of justice, to be acceptable, must be in accordance with our considered convictions, at all levels of generality, on due reflection (or in what I have called 'reflective equilibrium').[10]

The public political culture may be of two minds even at a very deep level. Indeed, this must be so with such an enduring controversy as that concerning the most appropriate institutional forms to realize the values of liberty and equality. This suggests that, if we are to succeed in finding a basis of public agreement, we must find a new way of organizing familiar ideas and principles into a conception of political justice so that the claims in conflict, as previously understood, are seen in another light. A political conception need not be an original creation but may only articulate familiar intuitive ideas and principles so that they can be recognized as fitting together in a somewhat different way from before. Such a conception may, however,

[10] *A Theory of Justice*, pp. 20-1, 48-51, and 120-1.

go further than this: it may organize these familiar ideas and principles by means of a more fundamental intuitive idea within the complex structure of which the other familiar intuitive ideas are then systematically connected and related. In justice as fairness, as we shall see in the next section this more fundamental idea is that of society as a system of fair social co-operation between free and equal persons. The concern of this section is how we might find a public basis of political agreement. The point is that a conception of justice will only be able to achieve this aim if it provides a reasonable way of shaping into one coherent view the deeper bases of agreement embedded in the public political culture of a constitutional regime and acceptable to its most firmly held considered convictions.

Now suppose justice as fairness were to achieve its aim and a publicly acceptable political conception of justice is found. Then this conception provides a publicly recognized point of view from which all citizens can examine before one another whether or not their political and social institutions are just. It enables them to do this by citing what are recognized among them as valid and sufficient reasons singled out by that conception itself. Society's main institutions and how they fit together into one scheme of social co-operation can be examined on the same basis by each citizen, whatever that citizen's social position or more particular interests. It should be observed that, on this view, justification is not regarded simply as valid argument from listed premisses, even should these premisses be true. Rather, justification is addressed to others who disagree with us, and therefore it must always proceed from some consensus, that is, from premisses that we and others publicly recognize as true; or better, publicly recognize as acceptable to us for the purpose of establishing a working agreement on the fundamental questions of political justice. It goes without saying that this agreement must be informed and uncoerced, and reached by citizens in ways consistent with their being viewed as free and equal persons.[11]

Thus, the aim of justice as fairness as a political conception is practical, and not metaphysical or epistemological. That is, it presents itself not as a conception of justice that is true, but

[11] Ibid. 580–3.

one that can serve as a basis of informed and willing political
agreement between citizens viewed as free and equal persons.
This agreement when securely founded in public political and
social attitudes sustains the good of all persons and associations
within a just democratic regime. To secure this agreement we
try, so far as we can, to avoid disputed philosophical, as well
as disputed moral and religious, questions. We do this, not
because these questions are unimportant or regarded with indifference,[12] but because we think them too important and recognize that there is no way to resolve them politically. The only
alternative to a principle of toleration is the autocratic use of
state power. Thus, justice as fairness deliberately stays on the
surface, philosophically speaking. Given the profound differences in belief and conceptions of the good, at least since the
Reformation, we must recognize that, just as on questions of
religious and moral doctrine, public agreement on the basic
questions of philosophy cannot be obtained without the state's
infringement of basic liberties. Philosophy as the search for
truth about an independent metaphysical and moral order
cannot, I believe, provide a workable and shared basis for a
political conception of justice in a democratic society.

We try, then, to leave aside philosophical controversies whenever possible, and look for ways to avoid philosophy's long-
standing problems. Thus, in what I have called 'Kantian
constructivism', we try to avoid the problem of truth and the
controversy between realism and subjectivism about the status
of moral and political values. This form of constructivism
neither asserts nor denies these doctrines.[13] Rather, it recasts
ideas from the tradition of the social contract to achieve a practicable conception of objectivity and justification founded on
public agreement in judgement on due reflection. The aim is
free agreement, reconciliation through public reason. And
similarly [. . .], a conception of the person in a political view,
for example, the conception of citizens as free and equal persons,
need not involve, so I believe, questions of philosophical psychology or a metaphysical doctrine of the nature of the self.

---

[12] Ibid. 214–15.
[13] On Kantian constructivism, see especially the third lecture in 'Kantian
Constructivism in Moral Theory'.

No political view that depends on these deep and unresolved matters can serve as a public conception of justice in a constitutional democratic state. As I have said, we must apply the principle of toleration to philosophy itself. The hope is that, by this method of avoidance, as we might call it, existing differences between contending political views can at least be moderated, even if not entirely removed, so that social co-operation on the basis of mutual respect can be maintained. Or, if this is expecting too much, this method may enable us to conceive how, given a desire for free and uncoerced agreement, a public understanding could arise consistent with the historical conditions and constraints of our social world. Until we bring ourselves to conceive how this could happen, it can't happen.

3

Let's now survey briefly some of the basic ideas that make up justice as fairness in order to show that these ideas belong to a political conception of justice. As I have indicated, the overarching fundamental intuitive idea, within which other basic intuitive ideas are systematically connected, is that of society as a fair system of co-operation between free and equal persons. Justice as fairness starts from this idea as one of the basic intuitive ideas which we take to be implicit in the public culture of a democratic society.[14] In their political thought, and in the context of public discussion of political questions, citizens do not view the social order as a fixed natural order, or as an institutional hierarchy justified by religious or aristocratic values. Here it is important to stress that, from other points of view, for example, from the point of view of personal morality, or from the point of view of members of an association, or of one's religious or philosophical doctrine, various aspects of the world and one's relation to it may be regarded in a different way.

[14] Although *A Theory of Justice* uses this idea from the outset (it is introduced on p. 4), it does not emphasize, as I do here and in 'Kantian Constructivism in Moral Theory', that the basic ideas of justice as fairness are regarded as implicit or latent in the public culture of a democratic society

But these other points of view are not to be introduced into political discussion.

We can make the idea of social co-operation more specific by noting three of its elements:

1. Co-operation is distinct from merely socially co-ordinated activity, for example, from activity co-ordinated by orders issued by some central authority. Co-operation is guided by publicly recognized rules and procedures which those who are co-operating accept and regard as properly regulating their conduct.

2. Co-operation involves the idea of fair terms of co-operation: these are terms that each participant may reasonably accept, provided that everyone else likewise accepts them. Fair terms of co-operation specify an idea of reciprocity or mutuality: all who are engaged in co-operation and who do their part as the rules and procedures require, are to benefit in some appropriate way as assessed by a suitable benchmark of comparison. A conception of political justice characterizes the fair terms of social co-operation. Since the primary subject justice is the basic structure of society, this is accomplished in justice as fairness by formulating principles that specify basic rights and duties within the main institutions of society, and by regulating the institutions of background justice over time so that the benefits produced by everyone's efforts are fairly acquired and divided from one generation to the next.

3. The idea of social co-operation requires an idea of each participant's rational advantage, or good. This idea of good specifies what those who are engaged in co-operation, whether individuals, families, or associations, or even nation-states, are trying to achieve, when the scheme is viewed from their own standpoint.

Now consider the idea of the person.[15] There are, of course,

---

[15] It should be emphasized that a conception of the person, as I understand it here, is a normative conception, whether legal, political, or moral, or indeed also philosophical or religious, depending on the overall view to which it belongs. In this case the conception of the person is a moral conception, one that begins from our everyday conception of persons as the basic

many aspects of human nature that can be singled out as especially significant depending on our point of view. This is witnessed by such expressions as *homo politicus*, *homo oeconomicus*, *homo faber*, and the like. Justice as fairness starts from the idea that society is to be conceived as a fair system of co-operation and so it adopts a conception of the person to go with this idea. Since Greek times, both in philosophy and law, the concept of the person has been understood as the concept of someone who can take part in, or who can play a role in, social life, and hence exercise and respect its various rights and duties. Thus, we say that a person is someone who can be a citizen, that is, a fully co-operating member of society over a complete life. We add the phrase 'over a complete life' because a society is viewed as a more or less complete and self-sufficient scheme of co-operation, making room within itself for all the necessities and activities of life, from birth until death. A society is not an association for more limited purposes; citizens do not join society voluntarily but are born into it, where, for our aims here, we assume they are to lead their lives.

Since we start within the tradition of democratic thought, we also think of citizens as free and equal persons. The basic intuitive idea is that, in virtue of what we may call their moral powers, and the powers of reason, thought, and judgement connected with those powers, we say that persons are free. And, in virtue of their having these powers to the requisite degree to be fully co-operating members of society, we say that persons are equal.[16] We can elaborate this conception of the person as follows. Since persons can be full participants in a fair system of social co-operation, we ascribe to them the two moral powers connected with the elements in the idea of social co-operation noted above: namely, a capacity for a sense of justice and a capacity for a conception of the good. A sense of justice is the

---

units of thought, deliberation, and responsibility, and adapted to a political conception of justice and not to a comprehensive moral doctrine. It is in effect a political conception of the person, and given the aims of justice as fairness, a conception of citizens. Thus, a conception of the person is to be distinguished from an account of human nature given by natural science or social theory. On this point, see 'Kantian Constructivism in Moral Theory', pp. 534–5.

[16] *A Theory of Justice*, sect. 77.

capacity to understand, to apply, and to act from the public conception of justice which characterizes the fair terms of social co-operation. The capacity for a conception of the good is the capacity to form, to revise, and rationally to pursue a conception of one's rational advantage, or good. In the case of social co-operation, this good must not be understood narrowly but rather as a conception of what is valuable in human life. Thus, a conception of the good normally consists of a more or less determinate scheme of final ends, that is, ends we want to realize for their own sake, as well as of attachments to other persons and loyalties to various groups and associations. These attachments and loyalties give rise to affections and devotions, and therefore the flourishing of the persons and associations who are the objects of these sentiments is also part of our conception of the good. Moreover, we must also include in such a conception a view of our relation to the world—religious, philosophical, or moral—by reference to which the value and significance of our ends and attachments are understood.

In addition to having the two moral powers, the capacities for a sense of justice and a conception of the good, persons also have at any given time a particular conception of the good that they try to achieve. Since we wish to start from the idea of society as a fair system of co-operation, we assume that persons as citizens have all the capacities that enable them to be normal and fully co-operating members of society. This does not imply that no one ever suffers from illness or accident; such misfortunes are to be expected in the ordinary course of human life; and provision for these contingencies must be made. But for our purposes here I leave aside permanent physical disabilities or mental disorders so severe as to prevent persons from being normal and fully co-operating members of society in the usual sense.

Now the conception of persons as having the two moral powers, and therefore as free and equal, is also a basic intuitive idea assumed to be implicit in the public culture of a democratic society. Note, however, that it is formed by idealizing and simplifying in various ways. This is done to achieve a clear and uncluttered view of what for us is the fundamental question of political justice: namely, what is the most appropriate conception of justice for specifying the terms of social co-operation between citizens regarded as free and equal persons, and as normal and fully co-operating members of society over a complete life. It is this question that has been the focus of the liberal critique of aristocracy, of the socialist critique of liberal constitutional democracy, and of the conflict between liberals and conservatives at the present time over the claims of private property and the legitimacy (in contrast to the effectiveness) of social policies associated with the so-called welfare state.

4

I now take up the idea of the original position.[17] This idea is introduced in order to work out which traditional conception of justice, or which variant of one of those conceptions, specifies the most appropriate principles for realizing liberty and equality once society is viewed as a system of co-operation between free and equal persons. Assuming we had this purpose in mind, let's see why we would introduce the idea of the original position and how it serves its purpose.

Consider again the idea of social co-operation. Let's ask: how are the fair terms of co-operation to be determined? Are they simply laid down by some outside agency distinct from the persons co-operating? Are they, for example, laid down by God's law? Or are these terms to be recognized by these persons as fair by reference to their knowledge of a prior and independent moral order? For example, are they regarded as required by natural law, or by a realm of values known by rational intuition? Or are these terms to be established by an undertaking among these persons themselves in the light of what they regard as their mutual advantage? Depending on which answer we give, we get a different conception of co-operation.

Since justice as fairness recasts the doctrine of the social contract, it adopts a form of the last answer: the fair terms of social co-operation are conceived as agreed to by those engaged in it, that is, by free and equal persons as citizens who are born into the society in which they lead their lives. But their agreement, like any other valid agreement, must be entered into under

---

[17] Ibid., sect. 4, ch. 3, and the index.

appropriate conditions. In particular, these conditions must situate free and equal persons fairly and must not allow some persons greater bargaining advantages than others. Further, threats of force and coercion, deception and fraud, and so on, must be excluded.

So far so good. The foregoing considerations are familiar from everyday life. But agreements in everyday life are made in some more or less clearly specified situation embedded within the background institutions of the basic structure. Our task, however, is to extend the idea of agreement to this background framework itself. Here we face a difficulty for any political conception of justice that uses the idea of a contract, whether social or otherwise. The difficulty is this: we must find some point of view, removed from and not distorted by the particular features and circumstances of the all-encompassing background framework, from which a fair agreement between free and equal persons can be reached. The original position, with the feature I have called 'the veil of ignorance', is this point of view.[18] And the reason why the original position must abstract from and not be affected by the contingencies of the social world is that the conditions for a fair agreement on the principles of political justice between free and equal persons must eliminate the bargaining advantages which inevitably arise within background institutions of any society as the result of cumulative social, historical, and natural tendencies. These contingent advantages and accidental influences from the past should not influence an agreement on the principles which are to regulate the institutions of the basic structure itself from the present into the future.

Here we seem to face a second difficulty, which is, however, only apparent. To explain: from what we have just said it is clear that the original position is to be seen as a device of representation and hence any agreement reached by the parties must be regarded as both hypothetical and non-historical. But if so, since hypothetical agreements cannot bind, what is the significance of the original position?[19] The answer is implicit in what

[18] On the veil of ignorance, see ibid., sect. 24, and the index.
[19] This question is raised by Ronald Dworkin in the first part of his very illuminating, and to me highly instructive essay 'Justice and Rights' (1973),

has already been said: it is given by the role of the various features of the original position as a device of representation. Thus, that the parties are symmetrically situated is required if they are to be seen as representatives of free and equal citizens who are to reach an agreement under conditions that are fair. Moreover, one of our considered convictions, I assume, is this:

---

repr. in *Taking Rights Seriously* (Cambridge, Mass., 1977). Dworkin considers several ways of explaining the use of the original position in an account of justice that invokes the idea of the social contract. In the last part of the essay (pp. 173–83), after having surveyed some of the constructivist features of justice as fairness (pp. 159–68) and argued that it is a right-based and not a duty-based or a goal-based view (pp. 168–77), he proposes that the original position with the veil of ignorance be seen as modelling the force of the natural right that individuals have to equal concern and respect in the design of the political institutions that govern them (p. 180). He thinks that this natural right lies as the basis of justice as fairness and that the original position serves as a device for testing which principles of justice this right requires. This is an ingenious suggestion but I have not followed it in the text. I prefer not to think of justice as fairness as a right-based view; indeed, Dworkin's classification scheme of right-based, duty-based, and goal-based views (pp. 171f.) is too narrow and leaves out important possibilities. Thus, as explained in sect. 2 above, I think of justice as fairness as working up into idealized conceptions certain fundamental intuitive ideas such as those of the person as free and equal, of a well-ordered society and of the public role of a conception of political justice, and as connecting these fundamental intuitive ideas with the even more fundamental and comprehensive intuitive idea of society as a fair system of co-operation over time from one generation to the next. Rights, duties, and goals are but elements of such idealized conceptions. Thus, justice as fairness is a conception-based, or, as Elizabeth Anderson has suggested to me, an ideal-based view, since these fundamental intuitive ideas reflect ideals implicit or latent in the public culture of a democratic society. In this context the original position is a device of representation that models the force, not of the natural right of equal concern and respect, but of the essential elements of these fundamental intuitive ideas as identified by the reasons for principles of justice that we accept on due reflection. As such a device, it serves first to combine and then to focus the resultant force of all these reasons in selecting the most appropriate principles of justice for a democratic society. (In doing this the force of the natural right of equal concern and respect will be covered in other ways.) This account of the use of the original position resembles in some respects an account Dworkin rejects in the first part of his essay, especially pp. 153–4. In view of the ambiguity and obscurity of *A Theory of Justice* on many of the points he considers, it is not my aim to criticize Dworkin's valuable discussion, but rather to indicate how my understanding of the original position differs from his. Others may prefer his account.

the fact that we occupy a particular social position is not a good reason for us to accept, or to expect others to accept, a conception of justice that favours those in this position. To model this conviction in the original position, the parties are not allowed to know their social position; and the same idea is extended to other cases. This is expressed figuratively by saying that the parties are behind a veil of ignorance. In sum, the original position is simply a device of representation: it describes the parties, each of whom is responsible for the essential interests of a free and equal person, as fairly situated and as reaching an agreement subject to appropriate restrictions on what are to count as good reasons.[20]

Both of the above mentioned difficulties, then, are overcome by viewing the original position as a device of representation: that is, this position models what we regard as fair conditions under which the representatives of free and equal persons are to specify the terms of social co-operation in the case of the basic structure of society; and, since it also models what, for this case, we regard as acceptable restrictions on reasons available to the parties for favouring one agreement rather than

---

[20] The original position models a basic feature of Kantian constructivism, namely, the distinction between the Reasonable and the Rational, with the Reasonable as prior to the Rational. (For an explanation of this distinction, see 'Kantian Constructivism in Moral Theory', pp. 528–32, and *passim*.) The relevance of this distinction here is that *A Theory of Justice* more or less consistently speaks not of rational but of reasonable (or sometimes of fitting or appropriate) conditions as constraints on arguments for principles of justice (see pp. 18–19, 20–1, 120–1, 130–1, 138, 446, 516–17, 578, 584–5). These constraints are modelled in the original position and thereby imposed on the parties: their deliberations are subject, and subject absolutely, to the reasonable conditions, the modelling of which makes the original position fair. The Reasonable, then, is prior to the Rational, and this gives the priority of right. Thus, it was an error in *A Theory of Justice* (and a very misleading one) to describe a theory of justice as part of the theory of rational choice, as on pp. 16 and 583. What I should have said is that the conception of justice as fairness uses an account of rational choice subject to reasonable conditions to characterize the deliberations of the parties as representatives of free and equal persons; and all of this within a political conception of justice, which is, of course, a moral conception. There is no thought of trying to derive the content of justice within a framework that uses an idea of the rational as the sole normative idea. That thought is incompatible with any kind of Kantian view.

another, the conception of justice the parties would adopt identifies the conception we regard—*here and now*—as fair and supported by the best reasons. We try to model restrictions on reasons in such a way that it is perfectly evident which agreement would be made by the parties in the original position as citizens' representatives. Even if there should be, as surely there will be, reasons for and against each conception of justice available, there may be an overall balance of reasons plainly favouring one conception over the rest. As a device of representation, the idea of the original position serves as a means of public reflection and self-clarification. We can use it to help us work out what we now think, once we are able to take a clear and uncluttered view of what justice requires when society is conceived as a scheme of co-operation between free and equal persons over time from one generation to the next. The original position serves as a unifying idea by which our considered convictions at all levels of generality are brought to bear on one another so as to achieve greater mutual agreement and self-understanding.

To conclude: we introduce an idea like that of the original position because there is no better way to elaborate a political conception of justice for the basic structure from the fundamental intuitive idea of society as a fair system of co-operation between citizens as free and equal persons. There are, however, certain hazards. As a device of representation the original position is likely to seem somewhat abstract and hence open to misunderstanding. The description of the parties may seem to presuppose some metaphysical conception of the person, for example, that the essential nature of persons is independent of and prior to their contingent attributes, including their final ends and attachments, and, indeed, their character as a whole. But this is an illusion caused by not seeing the original position as a device of representation. The veil of ignorance, to mention one prominent feature of that position, has no metaphysical implications concerning the nature of the self; it does not imply that the self is ontologically prior to the facts about persons that the parties are excluded from knowing. We can, as it were, enter this position any time simply by reasoning for principles of justice in accordance with the enumerated restrictions. When, in this way, we simulate being in this position, our reasoning no more commits us to a metaphysical doctrine about the nature of the self than our playing a game like Monopoly commits us to thinking that we are landlords engaged in a desperate rivalry, winner take all.[21] We must keep in mind that we are trying to show how the idea of society as a fair system of social co-operation can be unfolded so as to specify the most appropriate principles for realizing the institutions of liberty and equality when citizens are regarded as free and equal persons. [. . .]

[21] *A Theory of Justice*, pp. 138–9, 147. The parties in the original position are said (p. 147) to be theoretically defined individuals whose motivations are specified by the account of that position and not by a psychological view about how human beings are actually motivated. This is also part of what is meant by saying (p. 121) that the acceptance of the particular principles of justice is not conjectured as a psychological law or probability but rather follows from the full description of the original position. Although the aim cannot be perfectly achieved, we want the argument to be deductive, 'a kind of moral geometry'. In 'Kantian Constructivism in Moral Theory' (p. 532) the parties are described as merely artificial agents who inhabit a construction. Thus I think R. B. Brandt mistaken in objecting that the argument from the original position is based on defective psychology. See his *A Theory of the Good and the Right* (Oxford, 1979), 239–42. Of course, one might object to the original position that it models the conception of the person and the deliberations of the parties in ways that are unsuitable for the purposes of a political conception of justice; but for these purposes psychological theory is not directly relevant. On the other hand, psychological theory is relevant for the account of the stability of a conception of justice, as discussed in *A Theory of Justice*, pt. III. [. . .] Similarly, I think Michael Sandel mistaken in supposing that the original position involves a conception of the self 'shorn of all its contingently-given attributes', a self that 'assumes a kind of supra-empirical status . . . and given prior to its ends, a pure subject of agency and possession, ultimately thin'. See *Liberalism and the Limits of Justice* (Cambridge, 1982), 93–5. I cannot discuss these criticisms in any detail. The essential point (as suggested in the introductory remarks) is not whether certain passages in *A Theory of Justice* call for such an interpretation (I doubt that they do), but whether the conception of justice as fairness presented therein can be understood in the light of the interpretation I sketch in this article and in the earlier lectures on constructivism, as I believe it can be.

12

LIBERAL COMMUNITY

RONALD DWORKIN

This symposium considers an old problem; should conventional ethics be enforced through the criminal law?[1] We discuss the problem against the background of the Supreme Court's recent decision in *Bowers* v. *Hardwick*,[2] which upheld Georgia's law making sodomy a crime against constitutional challenge. I consider the role that the concept of community might play in arguments about the enforcement of ethics. It is widely thought that liberalism as a political theory is hostile to, or anyway not sufficiently appreciative of, the value or importance of community, and that liberal tolerance, which insists that it is wrong of government to use its coercive power to enforce ethical homogeneity, undermines community. I shall try to test these assumptions.

Very different arguments, using very different concepts of community, have been used to attack liberal tolerance in different ways. I distinguish four such arguments. The first is an argument from democratic theory which associates community with majority. In *Bowers*, Justice White suggested that the community has a right to use the law to support its vision of ethical decency:[3] it has a right to impose its views about ethics just because it is the majority. The second is an argument

Ronald Dworkin, from *California Law Review*, 77 (1989), 479–504. © 1989 by California Law Review Inc. Used by permission.

[1] Throughout this essay I distinguish ethics from morality. Ethics, as I use the term, includes convictions about which kinds of lives are good or bad for a person to lead, and morality includes principles about how a person should treat other people. So the question I consider is whether a political community should use criminal law to force its members to lead what a majority deems good lives, not whether it should use the law to force them to behave justly to others.

[2] 478 US 186 (1986).

[3] Ibid. at 192–6.

of *paternalism*. It holds that in a genuine political community each citizen has a responsibility for the well-being of other members and should therefore use his political power to reform those whose defective practices will ruin their lives. The third is an argument of *self-interest*, broadly conceived. It condemns atomism, the view that individuals are self-sufficient unto themselves, and emphasizes the wide variety of ways—material, intellectual, and ethical—in which people need community. It insists that liberal tolerance undermines the community's ability to serve these needs. The fourth, which I shall call *integration*, argues that liberal tolerance depends on an illegitimate distinction between the lives of individual people within the community and the life of the community as a whole. According to this argument, the value or goodness of any individual citizen's life is only a reflection and function of the value of the life of the community in which he lives. So citizens, in order to make their own lives successful, must vote and work to make sure that their fellow citizens lead decent lives.

Each of these arguments uses the concept of community in an increasingly more substantial and less reductive way. The first argument, that a democratic majority has a right to define ethical standards for all, uses community only as a shorthand symbol for a particular, numerically defined, political grouping. The second argument, which encourages paternalism, gives the concept more substance: it defines community, not as just a political group, but as the dimensions of a shared and distinct responsibility. The third argument, that people need community, recognizes community as an entity in its own right, as a source of a wide variety of influences and benefits not reducible to the contributions of particular people one by one. The fourth argument, about identification, further personifies community and describes a sense in which a political community is not only independent of, but prior to, individual citizens. In this article I focus on this fourth argument, partly because I have not discussed it before, but also because I find its root idea, that people should identify their own interests with those of their political community, true and valuable. Properly understood, the idea furnishes no argument against liberal tolerance, and no support for *Bowers*. On the contrary, liberalism supplies the best interpretation of this concept of community, and liberal theory the best account of its importance. [. . .]

INTEGRATION WITH COMMUNITY

Integration

I come [. . .] to the [. . .] communitarian argument against liberal tolerance. Liberalism, according to many of its critics, presupposes a sharp distinction between people's own welfare or well-being and the well-being of the political community to which they belong. The fourth argument against tolerance denies that distinction. It claims that the lives of individual people and that of their community are integrated, and that the critical success of any one of their lives is an aspect of, and so is dependent on, the goodness of the community as a whole. I shall call people who accept this view (adopting a fashionable phrase) civic republicans. They take the same attitude toward the moral and ethical health of the community as they do toward their own. Liberals understand the question whether the law should tolerate homosexuality as asking whether some people have the right to impose their own ethical convictions on others. Civic republicans understand it as asking whether the common life of the community, on which the critical value of their own lives depends, should be healthy or degenerate.

According to the argument from integration, once the distinction between personal and communal well-being is recognized as mistaken and civic republicanism flourishes, citizens will necessarily be as concerned for the soundness of the community's ethical health, including the views of sexual morality that it sponsors or discourages, as for the fairness or generosity of its tax system or foreign-aid programme. Both are aspects of the community's overall health, and an integrated citizen, who recognizes that his own well-being is derived from the community's well-being must be concerned with the community's overall health, not with one selected aspect of it. This is an important argument, even though it ends in serious error. I should say at once what I regard as good in the argument, and where, in my view, it goes wrong. Its most fundamental premiss is right and important: political communities have a communal life, and the success or failure of a community's communal life is part of what determines whether its members' lives are good or bad. The argument's most fundamental mistake lies in misunderstanding the *character* of the communal life that a political community can have. The argument succumbs to anthropomorphism; it supposes that a communal life is the life of an outsize person, that it has the same shape, encounters the same moral and ethical watersheds and dilemmas, and is subject to the same standards of success and failure, as the several lives of the citizens who make it up. The illiberal force of the overall argument depends on this fallacy, which forfeits much of the advantage gained by the argument's sound and attractive premiss.

A Community's Communal Life

We need, to begin, a more detailed account of what the phenomenon of integration is supposed to be. The civic republican, who recognizes that he is integrated with his community, is not the same as the altruistic citizen for whom the interests of others are of capital importance. This is a crucial distinction, because the argument from integration, which we are now considering, is different from the argument of paternalism and other arguments that begin in the idea that a virtuous citizen will be concerned for the well-being of others. The argument from integration does not suppose that the good citizen will be concerned for the well-being of fellow citizens; it argues that he must be concerned for his *own* well-being, and that, just in virtue of *that* concern, he must take an interest in the moral life of the community of which he is a member. So the integrated citizen differs from the altruistic citizen, and we need some further distinctions to see how and why.

We associate actions with what I shall call a unit of agency: the person or group or entity treated as the author of and held responsible for the action. We normally consider ourselves, as individuals, to be the agency unit of—and only of—actions or decisions we initiate or take on our own. I take myself to be responsible for only what I do. I take no pride or satisfaction or remorse or shame in what you do, no matter how interested I might be in your life or in its consequences. Often a person directs his actions at his own well-being, in either a volitional or critical sense. The unit of agency and what we might call the unit of the agent's concern are then identical. When someone acts altruistically, whether out of charity or a sense of justice, he continues to regard himself as the unit of agency, but the unit of his concern migrates or expands. Paternalism, including moral paternalism, is a sub-case of altruism. If I believe that homosexuals lead degraded lives, I might think that I act in their interests when I campaign for laws making their conduct criminal.

Integration is a different phenomenon, according to the argument I am considering, because it supposes that the appropriate unit of agency, for some actions affecting the well-being of an individual, is not the individual but some community to which he belongs. He belongs to that unit of agency *ethically*: he shares in the success or failure of acts or achievements or practices which may be completely independent of anything he himself, considered as an individual, has done. Some examples are familiar; many Germans born well after the Second World War feel shame, and a responsibility to compensate, for Nazi atrocities, for instance. John Rawls offers, in a slightly different context, an example that is much more illuminating for our purposes.[4] A healthy orchestra is itself a unit of agency. The various musicians who compose it are exhilarated, in the way personal triumph exhilarates, not by the quality or brilliance of their individual contributions, but by the performance of the orchestra as a whole. It is the orchestra that succeeds or fails, and the success or failure of that community is the success or failure of each of its members.

So integration is strikingly different from altruism and paternalism. It is also different from vicarious or indirect pride or regret. When parents take pride in the achievements of their children, or friends rejoice in each other's success, or brothers (in some cultures) are dishonoured by a sister's shame, the unit of agency—the actor whose acts have brought pride or rejoicing or dishonour—remains individual. The vicarious emotion is second order and parasitic; the success or failure, achievement or disgrace, remains primarily and distinctly that of someone else, and the vicarious concern reflects not participation in any act but a particular connection with the actor.

The argument from integration escapes the objection I made to the second, paternalistic argument because it rejects the

[4] J. Rawls, *A Theory of Justice* (Oxford, 1971), 520-9.

whole structure of agency and concern on which the paternalistic argument rests. The argument from integration forbids us to think in Millian terms about whether we intervene to protect other people, or only the agent himself, from some harm the agent's conduct inflicts. It rejects that whole, individuated way of thinking. Its unit of agency is the community itself, and it only asks how the community's decisions about liberty and regulation will affect *the community's* life and character. It insists that citizens' lives are bound up in their communal life, and that there can be no private accounting of the critical success or failure or their individual lives one by one. So the personification latent in the idea of integration is genuine and deep. The more familiar ideas of altruism, paternalism, and vicarious emotion are built around individual units of agency and concern. Integration supposes a very different structure of concepts, in which the community, and not the individual, is fundamental.

All this may suggest that integration depends on a baroque metaphysics which holds that communities are fundamental entities in the universe and that individual human beings are only abstractions or illusions. But integration can be understood in a different way, as depending not on the ontological primacy of the community, but on ordinary and familiar facts about the social practices that human beings develop. An orchestra has a collective life not because it is ontologically more fundamental than its members, but secure of their practices and attitudes. They recognize a personified unit of agency in which they no longer figure as individuals, but as components; the community's collective life consists in the activities they treat as constituting its collective life. I shall call this interpretation of integration, which assumes that integration depends on social practices and attitudes, the practice view, to distinguish it from the metaphysical view which assumes that integration depends on the ontological primacy of community. I do not mean to suggest that the practice view is reductionist. When an integrated community exists, the statements citizens make within it, about its success or failure, are not simply statistical summaries of their own successes or failures as individuals. An integrated community has interests and concerns of its own—its own life to lead. Integration and community are genuine phenomena, even on the practice view. But on that view they are created by and embedded in attitudes and practices, and do not precede them.

On the practice view, therefore, a special kind of case must be made before integration can be claimed. It must be shown that social practice has in fact created a composite unit of agency. It would be nonsense for someone to claim integration with some community or institution by personal fiat, that is, simply be declaring and believing that he is part of it. I cannot just declare myself integrated with the Berlin Symphony Orchestra and thereafter share in that institution's triumphs and occasional lapses. Nor can I bring a common unit of agency into existence by fiat. I may declare and believe, for example, that philosophers whose surname starts with 'D' are a common unit of agency in philosophical work, and that I can properly take pride and credit in Donald Davidson's and Michael Dummett's work the way a cymbal player can take pride and credit in his orchestra's performance. But I would be wrong. There must already be a common unit of agency, to which I am already attached, for it to be appropriate for me to regard myself as ethically integrated with its actions.

So the argument from integration must rely on some theory about how collective units of agency are established, and how individual membership in them is fixed. On the metaphysical view of integration, collective units of agency just exist: they are more real than their members. But on the practice view collective units of agency are not primitive; they are constituted by social practices and attitudes, and anyone defending this view of integration must identify and describe these practices. Our orchestra example is instructive, because it indicates the features that provide a common unit of agency in central or paradigmatic cases. First, collective agency presupposes acts socially denominated as collective, that is, acts identified and individuated as those of a community as a whole rather than of members of the community as individuals. An orchestral performance is treated as a collective act, in that sense, both by its members and by the community as a whole. Second, the individual acts that constitute collective acts are concerted. They are performed self-consciously, as contributing to the collective act, rather than as isolated acts that happen to coincide in some way. The orchestra performs a particular concerto only when its members play with a co-operative intention; it would not perform at all if its musicians played exactly the notes assigned to them in the score, at exactly the designated moments, and in the same room, but with no intention of playing together as an orchestra. Third, the composition of the community—who is treated as a member of it—is tailored to its collective acts, so that a community's collective acts explain its composition, and vice versa. Since an orchestra is a common unit of agency for the production of music, its members are musicians.

The collective acts of a community constitute its communal life. On the metaphysical view of integration, a community is a super-person, and its collective life embodies all the features and dimensions of a human life. But the practice view defines a community's communal life more narrowly; it includes only the acts treated as collective by the practices and attitudes that create the community as a collective agent. The communal life of an orchestra is limited to producing orchestral music: it is *only* a musical life. This fact determines the character and limits of the ethical integration of the musicians' lives into the communal life. The musicians treat their performances together as the performance of their orchestra personified, and they share in its triumphs and failures as their own. But they do not suppose that the orchestra also has a sex life, in some way composed of the sexual activities of its members. Or that it has headaches, or high blood pressure, or responsibilities of friendship, or crises over whether it should care less about music and take up photography instead. Though the first violinist may be concerned about a colleague's sexual habits or deviance, this is concern for a friend that reflects altruism, not self-concern for any composite unit of agency which includes him. His moral integrity is not compromised by the drummer's adultery.

A Political Community's Communal Life

How far can we regard a political community—a nation or a state—as having a communal life on the practice view? The formal political acts of a political community—the acts of its government through its legislative, executive, and judicial institutions—meet all the conditions of collective agency we identified when we considered why an orchestra has a communal life. Our practices identify these formal political acts as acts of a distinct legal person rather than of some collection of individual citizens. The United States, rather than particular officials and soldiers, fought a war in Vietnam. The United States, rather than particular officials or citizens, imposes taxes at particular rates, distributes some of the funds it collects in welfare programmes, and declines to distribute funds for other programmes. Though the acts of particular people—votes of members of Congress, for example, and commands of generals—constitute these collective acts, this is only because these officials act self-consciously under a constitutional structure that transforms their individual behaviour into national decisions. There is at least a rough fit, moreover, between the membership of a decent, democratic political community and those formal collective acts. In a creditable democracy, every citizen who reaches a certain age and meets other conditions can participate indirectly in formal political decisions by voting, speaking, lobbying, demonstrating, and so forth.[5] And the citizens of a political community are those who are particularly affected by its formal political acts. So treating the legislative, executive, and judicial decisions as a political community's communal acts helps to explain the community's composition; it is composed of those who play some role in those decisions and who are most directly affected by them.

That much seems relatively uncontroversial. If a community has a communal life at all, its formal political decisions must be part of that life. But we must ask what else, in addition to those formal political acts, is part of its communal life. The communitarian argument from integration which we are exploring claims that formal political acts do not exhaust the nation's communal life. The argument supposes that the political

---

[5] I do not mean, of course, that these participatory acts are themselves collective acts of the political community as a whole: they are not. But they may be collective acts of some smaller community within it: a demonstration, for example, may be part of the communal life of a political action group, which, though political in its aims, is not in itself a political community because it does not administer its affairs through a monopoly of coercive power over its members.

community also has a communal sex life. It supposes that the sexual activities of individual citizens somehow combine into a national sex life in the way in which the performances of individual musicians combine into an orchestral performance, or the distinct acts of the citizens and officials of a political community combine in legislation. For only if this were true could one citizen's life be defiled by the sexual practices of another.

If we accept the anthropomorphic, metaphysical view of the political community, then we can begin, at least, to persuade ourselves that a state or nation has a sex life towards which the sexual activity of individual citizens contributes in some mysterious way. But if we insist instead on the practice view, then the argument from integration must defend the proposition that the community has a sex life in a very different way. It must show that our social practices and attitudes and conventions in fact create and recognize a national sexual act. You will have anticipated my judgement about the project. Consider the three features we identified as supporting the claim of a communal musical life in the case of an orchestra. None of them is satisfied for the claim of a national sex life. Our conventions recognize no distinctly collective national sexual activity. When we speak of a nation's sexual preferences and habits, we speak statistically, not, as in the case of an orchestra's performance, of some collective achievement or disgrace.[6] Nor do we have conventions or practices that provide structures for co-operative sexual activity on a national scale, in the way our constitution provides a mechanism for electing presidents.

Nor is the composition of a political community in any way related to the idea that its communal life has a sexual side. The criteria of citizenship can neither explain nor be explained by the assumption of any collective sexual venture. Citizens are by and large born into their political communities and most have no real prospect of leaving the one they are born into.[7]

---

[6] Of course, as I emphasize later, that is not to say that no community does or could recognize a collective sex act.

[7] Citizens are not mutually self-selected, like members of a fraternal organization, nor are they chosen for some particular talent or ambition, like musicians in an orchestra, nor are they identified by some independently given

People of every race, faith, and ambition are often born into the same political community, and it is deeply implausible that the characterization of communal life that best fits such a community could be one that assumes that it must choose one faith or set of personal ambitions or ethnic allegiance, or one set of standards of sexual responsibility, as a healthy individual person must. That characterization not only does not fit the criteria of citizenship; it makes them close to nonsensical.

Perhaps we cannot rule out, a priori, the possibility that some other social grounds might be found to support the claim that a nation has a collective sex life—grounds very different from those to which we naturally appeal in explaining why a symphony or a piece of legislation is a collective, communal act. But I cannot see what those other grounds could be. If none can be suggested, then the communitarian argument from integration can succeed, if at all, only by falling back on the anthropomorphic view of a political community most readers would be anxious to disavow.

I should add two clarifications here. First, I have not claimed that there are no communities whose collective life has a sexual aspect. There are all kinds of communities—there are associations of stamp fanatics who engage in collective projects of collection, for example—and some might be in the nature of sexual rather than musical orchestras. It has been suggested, for example, that some families do—and that others might—see themselves as communities for propagation, in which case the sexual acts of family members might well be seen as collective in the sense that the integration argument assumes. My point is only that neither the United States nor its several states are communities that have a communal sex life, and that the argument from integration, used to justify illiberal political decisions by and across those political communities, accordingly fails.

Second, I have not considered the argument that the members of a political community should develop whatever practices would be needed in order that it would *then* be true that the

---

religious faith or sexual conviction or even, in the modern world of immigration and boundary shifts, by racial or ethnic or linguistic type or background,

community had a collective sex life. I have no idea how such an argument could be defended or made to seem plausible. Someone might say, for example, that people should try to expand the communal life of their political community because the phenomenological sensation of integration is itself desirable in the way some people think sensual pleasure or the exhilaration of danger is desirable. But if the value of integration lies in a particular sensation, it would hardly be necessary to seek integration with a political community to achieve it. People belong to a variety of communities and most people can belong to many more if they choose. They belong—or may belong—to families, neighbourhood, alumni groups, fraternal associations, factories, colleges, teams, orchestras, ethnic groups, expatriate communities, and so forth. So there would be ample opportunity for people to have whatever degree of the experience of integration they might think valuable without having to seek that experience in the political community, where it is inevitably harder to secure. In any case, however, the argument that we should try to create a community with a collective sex life is very different from the integration argument we have been considering. For the latter argument begins in, and draws its force from, the claim that we are already in such a community—that we have no choice now but to look after the sex life of others because, if their lives are degraded, ours are too.[8]

LIBERAL COMMUNITY

Liberal Civic Republicans

The illiberal argument from integration assumes that a political community has a life that includes a sex life. The assumption

---

[8] It does not follow, of course, from my claim that ethical integration is possible only when social practices create the necessary conceptual background, that ethical integration is mandatory or even defensible on every occasion when they do. No one should think his own critical interests tied to the success or failure of a community that does not recognize him as an equal member, or that denies him the most basic human rights, for example. Compare, in this connection, the parallel conditions of political obligations discussed in R. Dworkin, *Law's Empire* (London, 1986).

is half right. A political community does have a life, but not *that* life. If so, the argument from integration collapses as a critique of liberal tolerance in sexual matters. I shall now explore the part of the argument that is right: its important underlying premiss that political integration is of great ethical importance. I shall try to show that, although liberals have not emphasized the ethical importance of integration, recognizing its importance does not threaten, but rather nourishes, liberal principles.

First, I must caution against a misreading of my argument so far. I have not said that people should not fully identify with their own political community, or that full identification is impossible because its conditions cannot be met. I have argued rather for a particular view of what identifying with community means. Citizens identify with their political community when they recognize that the community has a communal life, and that the success or failure of their own lives is ethically dependent on the success or failure of that communal life. So what counts as full identification depends on what the communal life is understood to be. The liberal view of integration I shall describe takes a limited view of the dimensions of a political community's communal life. But it is not therefore a watered-down conception of identification with community. It is a full, genuine, intense conception exactly because it is discriminatory. Those who argue that identification with community requires illiberal legislation are not arguing for a deeper level of identification than liberalism allows. They only argue for a different account of what a community's collective life really is. If the liberal account is correct, and theirs is wrong, liberalism provides a more genuine form of identification than its critics can.

What then *is* the communal life of a political community? I said that the collective life of a political community includes its official political acts: legislation, adjudication, enforcement, and the other executive functions of government. An integrated citizen will count his community's success or failure in these formal political acts as resonating in his own life, as improving or diminishing it. On the liberal view, nothing more should be added. These formal political acts of the community as a whole should be taken to exhaust the communal life of a political body, so that citizens are understood to act together, as a collective, only in that structured way. This view of a political community's communal life will seem too meagre to many, and it is not necessary to the argument for liberal tolerance I have been developing. But it is worth exploring why the meagre view might be enough after all.

The idea that a community's collective life is only its formal political life appears disappointing because it seems to emasculate the idea of integration, to leave it with no work to do. The idea that people's lives should be seen as integrated with the life of their community suggests, at first sight, an exciting expansion of political theory. It seems to promise a politics devoted to advancing the collective good as well as, or perhaps instead of, protecting individual rights. The anthropomorphic conception of communal life—that the life of the community reflects all parts of the lives of individuals including their sexual choices and preferences—appears to fulfil that promise. It claims that an integrated citizen will reject liberal tolerance in favour of a commitment to healthy sexual standards imposed on all, because caring for community means caring that its life be good as well as just. But my suggestion—that communal life is limited to political activities—does not expand political justification beyond what liberals already accept. If the life of a community is limited to formal political decisions, if the critical success of a community therefore depends only on the success or failure of its legislative, executive, and adjudicative decisions, then we can accept the ethical primacy of the community's life without abandoning or compromising liberal tolerance and neutrality about the good life. We simply repeat that success at political decisions requires tolerance. Of course *that* proposition can be and has been challenged. The argument for integration presents a *new* challenge to those for liberal tolerance, however, only if it assumes an anthropomorphic picture of community, or at least one that includes more than the community's purely formal political activities. If we limit a political community's communal life to its formal political decisions, integration offers no threat to liberal principles, and it seems disappointing exactly for that reason.

It would be a mistake, however, to conclude that integration is an idea of no consequence, that it adds nothing to political morality. A citizen who identifies with the political community, by accepting the community's ethical priority, will offer no new arguments about the justice or wisdom of any political decision. He will, however, take a very different attitude towards politics. We can see the difference by contrasting his attitude, not with the selfish individual of invisible-hand fantasies, but with the person supposed to be the paragon of liberalism by its critics, the person who rejects integration but is moved by a sense of justice. That person will vote and work and lobby, only for the political decisions he believes justice demands. He will nevertheless draw a sharp line between what justice requires of him and the critical success of his own life. He will not count his own life as any less successful if, in spite of his best efforts, his community accepts great economic inequality, or racial or other forms of unfair discrimination, or unjust constraints on individual freedom.[9]

The integrated liberal will not separate his private and public lives in that way. He will count his own life as diminished—a less good life than he might have had—if he lives in an unjust community, no matter how hard he has tried to make it just. That fusion of political morality and critical self-interest seems to me to be the true nerve of civic republicanism, the important way in which individual citizens should merge their interests and personality into political community. It states a distinctly liberal ideal, one that flourishes only within a liberal society. I cannot assure you, of course, that a society of integrated citizens will inevitably achieve a more just society than a non-integrated community would. Injustice is the upshot of too many other factors—of failures of energy or industry, of weakness of the will, of philosophical error.

A community of people who accept integration in this sense will always have one important advantage over communities whose citizens deny integration. An integrated citizen accepts that the value of his own life depends on the success of his community in treating everyone with equal concern. Suppose this sense is public and transparent: everyone understands that everyone else shares that attitude. Then the community will have an important source of stability and legitimacy even though its members disagree greatly about what justice is. They

---

[9] Unless, of course, he is himself the victim of these various forms of discrimination.

will share an understanding that politics is a joint venture in a particularly strong sense: that everyone, of every conviction and economic level, has a personal stake—a *strong* personal stake for someone with a lively sense of his critical interests—in justice not only for himself but for everyone else as well. That understanding provides a powerful bond underlying even the most heated argument over particular policies and principles. People who think of justice in the non-integrated way, as requiring necessary compromises of their own interests for the sake of others, will tend to suspect that those who resist programmes that require evident sacrifices from them, because they reject the conception of justice on which those programmes are based, act out of self-interested bias, whether deliberate or subconscious. Political argument will then degenerate into the sullen trading that destroys civic republicanism.

That kind of suspicion has no place to root among people who take political disagreement to be disagreement, not about what sacrifices are required from each, but about how to serve the common interests of all in securing a genuinely just solution. Disagreement persists against that background, as it is desirable that it should. But it is a healthy disagreement among partners whose interests coalesce, who know that they are not antagonists in interest, who know that they win or lose together. Integration, so understood, gives a fresh meaning to the old idea of a commonweal, a genuine interest people share in politics, even when political disagreements are profound. Of course all this is utopian. We can scarcely hope that a thoroughly integrated political society will ever be realized. It will not be realized in coming decades. But we are now exploring utopia, an ideal of community we can define, defend, and perhaps even grope our way towards, in good moral and metaphysical conscience.

Ethical Priority

The consequences of civic republicanism in the liberal mode are therefore attractive. But there is a considerable gap in the argument I have offered you, because I have offered no reason, so far, why people should accept integration in the liberal sense, why they should regard the success of their lives as dependent, in the way I just described, on the justice of their community's political decisions. We cannot hope to provide a knock-down demonstration by way of answer to that question. But we can try to make the idea of liberal community more attractive by identifying aspects of the good life that are made possible or are nourished in a just state.

I shall describe only one strand of that project—and that in skeletal form. It begins in a weak form of Plato's view that morality and well-being are interdependent in an adequate ethics, that someone who does not behave in a just way leads a worse life in consequence.[10] That is hardly a plausible view if we have in mind what I call volitional well-being. There seems no inherent connection between my being just and my having what I want. But Plato's view seems more plausible when we have critical well-being in mind. The criteria of a life good in the critical sense cannot be defined acontextually, as if the same standards held for all people in all stages of history. Someone lives well when he responds appropriately to his circumstances. The ethical question is not how should human beings live, but how should someone in my position live? A great deal turns, therefore, on how my position is to be defined, and it seems compelling that justice should figure in the description. The ethical question becomes: what is a good life for someone entitled to the share of resources I am entitled to have? And against that background Plato's view of critical success is appealing. Someone does *pro tanto* a poorer job of living— responds *pro tanto* more poorly to his circumstances—if he acts unjustly. We need not accept the strong view that Plato in fact defended, that no one ever profits from injustice. Perhaps the great lives of some artists would not have been possible in a fully just society, and it would not follow that they had bad lives. But it does follow that it counts against the goodness of any life, even theirs, that it was supported by injustice.

Now notice what might seem to be a contradiction between two ethical ideals most of us embrace. The first dominates our private lives. We believe we have particular responsibilities towards those with whom we have special relationships: ourselves, our family, friends, and colleagues. We spend more of our time and other resources on them than on strangers, and

---

[10] See Plato, *The Republic.*

we think this right. We believe that someone who showed equal
concern for all members of his political community, in his
private life, would be defective. The second ideal dominates
our political life. The just citizen, in his political life, insists
on equal concern for all. He votes and works for policies that
he thinks treat every citizen as an equal. He shows no more
concern, in choosing among candidates and programmes, for
himself or his own family than for people who are only statistics
to him.

A competent overall ethics must reconcile these two ideals.
They can be reconciled adequately, however, only when politics
actually succeeds in distributing resources in the way justice
requires. If a just distribution has been secured, then the
resources people control are morally as well as legally theirs;
using them as they wish, and as special attachments and projects
require, in no way derogates from their recognizing that all
citizens are entitled to a just share. But when injustice is substantial, people who are drawn to both the ideals—of personal
projects and attachments on the one hand and equality of
political concern on the other—are placed in a kind of ethical
dilemma. They must compromise one of the two ideals, and
each direction of compromise impairs the critical success of
their lives.

Acting justly is not entirely a passive matter; it means not only
not cheating, but also doing what one can to reduce injustice.
So someone acts unjustly when he fails to devote resources he
knows he is not entitled to have to the needs of those who have
less. That failure will hardly be redeemed by occasional charity,
limited and arbitrary in the way charity inevitably is. So, if the
critical value of a life is diminished by a failure to act as justice
requires, then it is diminished by ignoring the injustice in one's
own political community. A life entirely devoted to reducing
injustice so far as one can, on the other hand, would be at least
equally diminished. When injustice is substantial and pervasive
in a political community, any private citizen who accepts a
personal responsibility to do whatever he possibly can to repair
it will end by denying himself the personal projects and attachments, as well as the pleasures and frivolities, that are essential
to a decent and rewarding life.

So someone with a vivid sense of his own critical interests is

inevitably thwarted when his community fails in its responsibilities of justice, and this is so even when he, for his own part,
has done all he personally can to encourage it to succeed. Each
of us shares that powerful reason for wanting our community to
be a just one. A just society is a prerequisite for a life that respects
both of two ideals, neither of which should be abandoned.
So our private lives, our success or failure in leading the lives
people like us should have, are in that limited but powerful way
parasitic on our success together in politics. Political community
has that ethical primacy over our individual lives.

NOTES ON CONTRIBUTORS

RONALD DWORKIN is Professor of Jurisprudence at the University of Oxford, and Professor of Law at New York University. He has published many articles (among them 'What is Equality?' in *Philosophy and Public Affairs*) and several books, among them *Taking Rights Seriously* (1977), *Law's Empire* (1986), and *A Matter of Principle* (1986).

MARILYN FRIEDMAN was the director of women's studies at Bowling Green State University, and now teaches philosophy at Purdue University, Indiana. She is currently working on a book on friendship, justice, and gender.

DAVID GAUTHIER is Professor of Philosophy at the University of Pittsburgh. He is the editor of *Morality and Rational Self-Interest* (1970) and the author of *The Logic of Leviathan* (1969) and *Morals by Agreement* (1986).

AMY GUTMANN is Professor at Princeton University. She is the author of *Liberal Equality* (1980), *Democratic Education* (1987), and *Democracy and the Welfare State* (1988).

WILL KYMLICKA is a policy analyst with the Canadian Royal Commission on New Reproductive Technologies. He has taught philosophy at the University of Toronto. He is the author of *Liberalism, Community and Culture* (Oxford, 1989) and *Contemporary Political Philosophy* (Oxford, 1990).

ALASDAIR MACINTYRE was a Fellow of University College, Oxford, and is now W. Alton Jones Distinguished Professor of Philosophy at Vanderbilt University, Tennessee. His publications include *A Short History of Ethics* (1967), *Against the Self Image of the Age* (1971), *After Virtue* (1981), and *Whose Justice? Which Rationality?* (1988).

DAVID MILLER is Official Fellow at Nuffield College, Oxford. His publications include *Social Justice* (1976), *Hume's Political Thought* (1981), *Market, State and Community* (1989), and (as an editor) *The Nature of Political Theory* (1983).

ROBERT NOZICK is Professor of Philosophy at Harvard University. He is the author of *Anarchy, State and Utopia* (1974) and *Philosophical Explanation* (1981).

JOHN RAWLS is Professor of Philosophy at Harvard University. He is the author of *A Theory of Justice* (1971), and many articles in *Philosophy and Public Affairs* and other journals.

226   NOTES ON CONTRIBUTORS

MICHAEL SANDEL is Associate Professor of Government at Harvard University. He is the author of *Liberalism and the Limits of Justice* (1982) and the editor of *Liberalism and its Critics* (1984).

CHARLES TAYLOR was formerly Chichele Professor of Social and Political Theory at Oxford University, and has taught at many universities, among them Princeton University and L'Université de Montreal. He is now Professor at McGill University. Among his books are *Hegel* (1975), *Philosophical Papers* (1985), and *Sources of the Self* (1989).

MICHAEL WALZER is Professor at the Institute of Advanced Studies, Princeton. His books include *Obligations* (1970), *Just and Unjust Wars* (1977), *Spheres of Justice* (1983), *Interpretations and Social Criticism* (1987), and *The Company of Critics* (1989).

SELECT BIBLIOGRAPHY

Two interesting and reasonably brief essays which offer a general assessment of the communitarian argument and the response by Rawls are the works by Buchanan (1989) and Galston (1982). Both philosophers are respectful but critical at one and the same time towards communitarianism (Buchanan) and Rawls's new works (Galston).

For further criticism of individualism and of the individualist concept of the self, the immediate work to be consulted is Sandel (1982), where he puts forward his argument that deontological liberalism is mistaken in its conception of the 'unencumbered' self. The book edited by Sandel (1984) is a collection of liberal arguments and the response by some communitarians. Charles Taylor's books (1973 and 1989) are more ambitious and difficult works. The former reveals some of Taylor's reflections on the liberal society when he studied the works of Hegel. The latter is a philosophical and historical examination of the concept of the self. MacIntyre's (1989) survey of the concept of justice through history follows his earlier book (1981) in which he offers a diagnosis of the poor state of moral philosophy in contemporary liberal societies.

For the individualist answer and the liberal defence on the concept of the individual, the reader may wish to consult Rawls's Dewey lectures (1980), in which Rawls reconstructed the original position by relating it to the Kantian ideal of the person and to the Western democratic societies. Also of great importance are the two essays by Rawls (1987 and 1988) in which he answers the communitarian challenges, especially the claim that liberals attribute priority to the right over the good. Doppelt (1989) is original in his response to the communitarian attack on deontological liberalism. He argues that Rawls's theory does not tie in with Sandel's description of the liberal self. This line of denying the communitarian interpretation of liberalism is taken also by Kymlicka (1989). The latter is, perhaps, one of the clearest assessments of the communitarian and individualist arguments.

An important concept in Rawls's theory is that of the primary goods. Among the many articles written about it we would specifically recommend the works by Schwartz (1973) and Nagel (1987) as criticisms of the individualistic bias that is built into this concept. The two argue that by using this concept Rawls fails to base his theory on neutrality, since the primary goods serve to advance many different individual plans but they are less useful in implementing views that

228   SELECT BIBLIOGRAPHY

hold a good life to be achievable only in certain social structures. Rawls's modification of the concept can be found in Rawls (1982), where he redefines the concept and argues that, 'while the determination of primary goods invokes a knowledge of the general circumstances and requirements of social life, it does so only in the light of a conception of the person given in advance'.

Concerning the implications of the communitarian criticism of liberal individualism, in particular the implications for the politics of neutral concern, we recommend the book by Nagel (1986) and Raz's works (1982 and 1986), although the two scholars are far from being 'communitarian'. Raz offers three interpretations of political neutrality and argues that neutrality is not always desirable. Nagel discusses the claim that morality requires a view from nowhere, that is to say that human beings will consider policies in a detached way. An illuminating discussion of the implications of the communitarian standpoint for the political and moral theorist and his role in society can be found in Walzer (1987), while Miller (1989) refers to the idea of community in the context of socialist thought rather than the tradition of liberal thought.

A coherent theory about what liberalism is can be found in Dworkin (1986). In this essay Dworkin puts forward the interesting argument that modern liberalism is about equality (including equal liberties and individual rights to be treated as equals), rather than simply a theory of liberty, as it used to be seen in the nineteenth century. If liberalism is seen this way, it might be less vulnerable to attacks from socialist communitarians. Finally, in addition to the above items, we suggest reading Lukes's book (1973) for an historical review of the idea of individualism.

REFERENCES

BARRY, B. (1990), 'Social Criticism and Political Philosophy', *Philosophy and Public Affairs*, 19: 4, 360–73.
BUCHANAN, A. (1989), 'Assessing Communitarian Critique of Liberalism', *Ethics*, 99, 852–82.
DOPPELT, G. (1989), 'Is Rawls's Kantian Liberalism Coherent and Defensible?', *Ethics*, 99: 4, 815–52.
DWORKIN, R. (1986), 'Liberalism', in his *A Matter of Principle* (Oxford).
GALSTON, W. (1982), 'Moral Personality and Liberal Theory: John Rawls's Dewey Lectures', *Political Theory*, 10, 492–519.
KYMLICKA, W. (1989), *Liberalism, Community and Culture* (Oxford).

LARMORE, C. (1987), *Patterns of Moral Complexity* (Cambridge).
LUKES, S. (1973), *Individualism* (Oxford).
MACINTYRE, A. (1981), *After Virtue* (London).
—— (1989), *Whose Justice, Which Rationality?* (London).
MILLER, D. (1989), 'In What Sense Must Socialism be Com-
munitarian?', *Social Philosophy and Politics*, 6, 57–74.
NAGEL, T. (1986), *A View From Nowhere* (Oxford).
—— (1987), 'Moral Conflict and Political Legitimacy', *Philosophy and
Public Affairs*, 16, 215–40.
RAWLS, J. (1980), 'Kantian Constructivism in Moral Theory: The
Dewey Lectures 1980', *Journal of Philosophy*, 77, 515–72.
—— (1982), 'Social Unity and Primary Goods', in A. Sen and
B. Williams (eds.), *Utilitarianism and Beyond* (Cambridge).
—— (1987), 'The Idea of Overlapping Consensus', *Oxford Journal of
Legal Studies*, 7, 1–25.
—— (1988), 'The Priority of Right and Ideas of the Good', *Philosophy
and Public Affairs*, 17, 251–76.
RAZ, J. (1982), 'Liberalism, Autonomy and the Politics of Neutral
Concern', *Midwest Studies in Philosophy*, 7, 89–120.
—— (1986), *The Morality of Freedom* (Oxford).
RORTY, R. (1988), 'The Priority of Democracy to Philosophy' in
M. Peterson and R. Vaughan (eds.), *The Virginia Statute for Religious
Freedom* (Madison, Wisconsin).
SANDEL, M. (1982), *Liberalism and the Limits of Justice* (Cambridge).
—— (ed.) (1984), *Liberalism and its Critics* (Oxford).
SCHWARTZ, A. (1973), 'Moral Neutrality and Primary Goods',
Ethics, 83, 294–307.
TAYLOR, C. (1973), *Hegel and Modern Society* (Cambridge).
—— (1989) *Sources of the Self: The Making of Modern Identity* (Cambridge).
WALZER, M. (1987), *Interpretations and Social Sciences* (Cambridge,
Mass.).
—— (1990), 'The Communitarian Critique of Liberalism', *Political
Theory*, 18: 1, 6–23.

INDEX

Ackelsberg, Martha 114 n.
Ackerman, B. 168 n.
acquisitions 139–41, 145
affective capacity, of liberal
   individual 154–7
agency, units of 208–12
altruism 208–10, 212
anarchism 46–7, 48, 64, 148 n.
Anderson, Elizabeth 191 n., 201 n.
Aquinas, St Thomas 1
Arendt, H. 9 n., 99 n.
Aristotle 1, 15, 32, 51, 61, 120,
   128, 130–1
Arneson, R. 168 n.
atomism 206
   definition 29, 31–2
   and neutrality 171
Augustine, St 1
autonomy 7, 43–6, 49, 83, 157–8
   and neutrality 169–73
   and rationality 154
   see also freedom; person, concept
   of

Baier, A. 102 n., 119 n.
Bakke case (US) 62
Barber, B. 99 n., 120 n., 135
Barry, B. 87 n.
Bauer, O. 80, 83 n.
Beer, Samuel 26
Beiner, R. 173 n.
Benditt, T. M. 67 n.
Benhabib, S. 101 n., 176 n.
Berry, C. 99 n.
Bittker, B. 140 n.
Blau, P. 102 n.
Bosanquet, Bernard 72
Bottomore, T., and Goode, P.
   80 n.
Bowers v. Hardwick case (US)
   205–6
Brandt, R. B. 204 n.

Buchanan, A. 11 n., 85 n.
Burke, Edmund 1

Chamberlain, Wilt 146–7, 149
child-rearing, and free affectivity
   156–7
Chodorow, Nancy 105
choice, freedom of, see autonomy;
   freedom
Chomsky, n. 148 n.
Cicero 1
citizenship 65–6, 83–4, 197–8,
   214–15, 217, 222
   and community 7–8
   and equality 83–4
   and nationality 93–100
   and political involvement 96–7,
   98–9
   and rights 94–5
   see also immigration; membership;
   society; state
civic republicans 207, 208
   liberal 216–20
civil disobedience 190
civilization, and human
   development 43–6
clubs, membership of 75–7
co-operation 159–60
   society as system of 193–6,
   199–204
Cohen, G. A. 168 n.
communitarianism:
   and ambiguity 10–11
   and conservatism 9–10
   criticism of liberalism 120–36,
   207–16
   endorsement of existing social
   practices 177
   and family obligations 107–8
   and feminism 103–19
   methodological 2–6
   and moral claims 106–7, 207–16

communitarianism (*cont.*)
  normative 2–3, 6–11
  politics of 131–3, 205–16
  and 'social self' 105–6
community:
  and autonomy of
    individuals 158–61
  of choice 116–19
  and citizenship 7–8
  communal life 208–16, 217–20
  concept of 1–2, 4, 6–7
  and enforcement of ethics
    205–16
  'health' of 207–8
  as identity 100, 121–2
  local 109
  and markets 85
  moral claims of 106–7
  and nationality 24–8, 85–93, 109
  non-voluntary 118–19
  and role of women 121
  seen in political terms 7–8
  'settled' 133 n.
  and sexual freedoms 205,
    214–17, 218
  urban 113, 114–17
consequential neutrality 166–9
Constant 190
constructivism, Kantian 187 n.,
    202 n.
Cornell, D. 102 n., 108
Cottingham, J. 89 n.
Cragg, W. 170 n.
Croly, Herbert 25–6
Crowley, B. L. 174, 175 n., 185 n.
cultural structure:
  and neutrality 173–7, 178
  subcultures 179–85
current time-slice principles of
    justice 141–3

democracy 213
  and justice as fairness 188,
    189–99
desert, concept of 57–61, 142–3
development:
  and family 42, 43, 45, 110
  of morality 152–3

and 'social self' 105–6
difference principle 21–4
Dinnerstein, Dorothy 105
discrimination 179–81
  positive 62, 183–4
distributive justice 1, 55–64,
    137–50, 222
  entitlement theory 138–41
  and nationality 81
  and patterning 143–50
dualisms 130–1, 134
Dworkin, R. 8, 11, 62
  'Justice and Rights' 200–1 n.
  Law's Empire 216 n.
  'Liberalism' 27 n.
  A Matter of Principle 171 n.,
    172 n., 184 n.
  'What is Equality? Part 2'
    168 n.

Eagly, A. H., and Steffen, V. J.
    103 n.
Eisenstein, Z. 101 n.
Elster, J. 92 n., 163 n.
emigration 75, 78–9
end-result principles of justice 143,
    149–50
entitlement, principle of 144–50
equality, and citizenship 83–4
  and justice 52–64
  of resources 167–8
ethics:
  distinguished from morality
    205 n.
  enforcement of 205–23
  see also good, conceptions of;
    justice; moral tradition

family:
  and communitarian philosophy
    105–10
  and human development 42, 43,
    45
  membership of 71, 77–8
  as model of community 121
  obligations to 42–3, 77, 221–2
  and self-interest 59

feminism 121
  and communitarian philosophy
    103–19
  and individualism 101–2
Ferguson, Adam 62–3
Ferraro, Geraldine 129
Fischer, C. 115 n., 116, 117
Flanagan, O., and Jackson, K.
  102 n.
Flax, J. 101 n.
Foucault, Michel, *The Order of
  Things* 162
fraternity 100
free affectivity 162
freedom:
  and political deliberation 47–50
  right to 35, 40–1, 43, 125, 190
  and self-understanding 49
Friedl, E. 160–1 n.
Friedman, M. 10, 102 n.
friendship 91, 104, 113–14, 221–2
Funk, N. 176 n.

Gauthier, D. 5, 7, 101 n.
Gelfant, B. 116
gender differentiation 160–1
  see also discrimination; feminism
Germany 78, 107, 209
Gilligan, C. 103 n., 105
Godwin, W. 88 n.
Goffman 131
Goldman, A., and Kini, J. 188 n.
good:
  conceptions of 154, 176 n., 196,
    197–9
  relationship to right 13–20
Goodin, R. E. 6 n., 99 n.
Gordon, M. 183 n.
Green, P. 99 n.
Greenberg, E. S. 96 n.
groups, constitution of 65–6
  see also membership
Gutman, A. 10, 11, 102, 172 n.,
  182 n.

Habermas, J. 176, 178
Harris, D. 94 n.
Hart, H. L. A. 191 n.

Hartsock, N. C. M. 101 n., 102 n.
Hegel, G. 1, 2, 7, 120, 121, 178
Held, V. 102 n.
Herzog, D. 182 n.
Higham, J. 76 n.
Hirsch, H. 182 n.
Hobbes, T. 20, 29–40, 59, 79
Hobhouse, L. T. 183 n.
Homans, G. 102 n.
Huntinton, S. 12 n.

identity 100, 110
  ethnic 111–12
immigration 66, 69–70, 74–6,
  78–84, 179, 183, 184 n.
individual, liberal 151–64
individualism:
  causal basis 157–61
  feminist criticism of 101–2
  and neutrality 165–85
  political theory 1–2, 5–11
  see also atomism
integration, and liberal tolerance
  206, 207–23
intolerance 7
  and communitarian politics
    132–3
  see also liberal tolerance;
    toleration

Jagger, A. M. 101 n.
justice:
  in acquisition and transfer
    139–41, 145
  as basis of social life 51–64
  capacity for sense of 197–9
  and community 20–4
  current time-slice principles
    141–3
  deontological 123–7
  and desert 57–61
  distributive 55–64, 137–50
  economic factors 61–2
  end-result principles 143, 149–50
  as fairness 186–204
  and free affectivity 155–7
  and gender differentiation 161
  historical principles 143

justice (*cont.*)
　in holdings 138–41
　and individual behaviour 220–3
　and integrated liberal 219–20
　and membership 83–4
　moral tradition 60–1
　and participation 151–3
　political conception of 186–204
　primacy of 123–7, 124–7
　and principle of entitlement
　　144–50
　and rationality 202
　and socialization 158–61
　theories of 15
justificatory neutrality 166–9

Kant, I. 13, 14–18
　Critique of Pure Reason 17
Kantian constructivism 187 n.,
　202 n.
King, D. S., and Waldron, J. 96 n.
Knott, D. 168 n.
Kymlicka, W. 8, 9, 183 n.

labour:
　division of 160
　mobility of 173–4, 177
Lane, R. 97, 97–8
Larmore, C. 126 n., 168 n.
liberal tolerance:
　and enforcement of ethics
　　205–6
　and integration 206, 207–23
　and majority rule 205, 206
　and paternalism 206, 209–10
　and self-interest 206
liberalism 7–8, 11, 13–14, 98
　criticized by communitarianism
　　120–36
　and individual 151–64
　and metaphysics 125–7
　see also liberal tolerance
libertarianism 20, 21, 46–7
Locke, J. 30, 31, 41, 42, 59, 60,
　141, 190
Lomasky, L. 176 n., 181 n.

Machiavelli, N. 59
MacIntyre, A. 3–5, 10, 121,
　127–36
　After Virtue 5, 103, 106, 109–10,
　120
MacIntyre, A., and Taylor, C.
　12 n.
MacKay, J. H. 148 n.
MacPherson 31 n.
majority rule, and liberal tolerance
　205, 206
markets, and community 85
Marshall, T. H. 94 n.
Marx, K. 61–2, 97–8, 120, 160
membership:
　admissions policies 70–84
　advantages of 65–6
　of clubs 75–7
　of families 71, 77–8
　and justice 83–4
　of neighbourhoods 70–5
　political 70
　and territory 78–83
Milgram, S. 115 n.
Mill, J. S. 15, 21, 82 n., 167 n.
Miller, D. 8, 10
minimal state 137, 147 n.
minority groups 179–85
mobility, and membership of
　groups 73–4, 77
Montefiore, A. 6 n.
moral law, rationality of 152–3
　see also ethics; justice
moral relativism 4, 5–6
moral tradition:
　and justice 60–1
　and modern politics 62–4
Morris, W. 99
mutual aid 67–9, 81–3
　see also co-operation

nationalism, *see* nationality;
　patriotism
nationality 77–84
　and citizenship 93–100
　and community 24–8, 85–93,
　109
　and distributive justice 81

and ethnic groups 90
  as identity 86–7, 92–3
  and private culture 93–6
  and socialism 86–93
neighbourhoods:
  membership of 70–5
  in urban areas 115
Nelson, R. H. 71 n.
neutrality:
  and autonomy 169–73
  consequential 166–9
  and cultural structure 173–7,
    178
  definition of 165–9
  and individualism 165–85
  justificatory 166–9
  liberal 165–85
  and perfectionism 171–3, 174–5,
    178–82
  and pluralist culture 170–3
  and welfare provision 167–9
New Deal social programme (US)
    25, 26
Nietzsche, F., *On the Genealogy of
    Morals* 163–4
Nisbet, R. 86 n.
non-voluntary community 118–19
Nozick, R. 9, 29, 38, 55–60, 120
  Anarchy, State and Utopia 31,
    45 n., 46–7, 54, 55–60,
    168 n.
  'Commentary on "Art as a
    Public Good"' 171 n.

objectivity 5–6
Oldenquist, A. 89 n.
original acquisition 55–6, 60

Pareto-optimality 149–50 n.
Parker, J. 94 n.
participation 213
  and justice 151–3
Pateman, C. 101 n.
paternalism 95, 206
  and liberal tolerance 206,
    209–10
patriotism 63, 72, 98 n., 121
  and community 24–8

patterning of distribution 143–50
perfectionism and neutrality 171–3,
    174–5, 178–82
person, conception of 196–7, 203
Pettit, P. 89 n.
Plant, R. 85 n.
Plato, *The Republic* 161–2, 221
pluralism 188
  cultural 179–85
  and neutrality 170–3
political philosophy, role of 24–8
Popper, K. 9 n.
population control 69–70
Powell, Mr Justice 62
practice view of integration
    210–11, 212–13
primacy of right theories 30–50
primary goods 167–8, 187 n.
procedural republic 24–8
property, right to 40–1, 52–64, 148
Protestantism, and moral tradition
    61
Pullman, George 95

racial segregation 71–2, 183
rationality 162
  and justice 202
  of liberal individual 152–4
Rawls, J. 5, 11, 13, 20–1, 54–60,
    120, 123–7, 130, 134, 165–75,
    183, 184 n., 209
  'The Basic Structure as Subject'
    17–18
  'Kantian Constructivism in
    Moral Theory' 20 n.
  'The Priority of Right and Ideas
    of the Good' 5 n.
  A Theory of Justice 1, 2, 3, 13 n.,
    15, 21 n., 67, 95 n., 186–7,
    201 n., 202 n., 204 n.
Raymond, J. 114 n.
Raz, J. 9, 165–6, 170 n.
responsibility 168
  and free affectivity 156–7
Rich, Adrienne 111–12, 117
right, relationship to good 13–20
rights, assertion of 36–41
  belief in 127–9

rights, assertion of (*cont.*)
  and citizenship 94–5
  primacy of 30–50
  to freedom 35, 40–1, 43, 125,
    190
  to life 38–9
Rosenblum, N. 182 n.
Rousseau, Jean-Jacques 1, 160,
  190

Sandel, M. 3, 4, 7–8, 9, 121–7,
  129, 130–6
  Liberalism and the Limits of Justice
    103, 109–10, 111, 112,
    120 n., 129, 185, 204
Sartre, Jean-Paul 131
Scanlon, T. 128 n., 176 n.
Scheman, N. 101 n.
self-consciousness of individual 157
self-determination, *see* autonomy;
  freedom
self-esteem 97
self-fulfillment 173–4
self-identity, *see* identity
self-interest 206, 219–23
  and liberal tolerance 206
self-sufficiency (*autarkeia*) 32, 35,
  39–40, 48
Sennett, R. 115 n.
Sidgwick, Henry 72–3, 74, 82
slavery 192
Smith, Anthony 90
'social self' 102, 104–6
social-contract theory 1, 29, 30–1
socialism:
  and community 85–6
  and inequality 147–50
  and nationality 86–93
socialization process 157–61
society:
  distinguished from state 177–9
  as system of co-operation 193–6,
    199–204
Squier, S. M. 116
state:
  compared to free association
    175–6
  development of 188

distinguished from civil society
  172, 177–9
minimal 137, 147 n.
and moral values 3–4
and nation 87
use of short-term intervention
  181–2 n.
state perfectionism 171–3, 174–5,
  178–82
Stimpson, C. *et al.* 116 n.
subcultures 179–85
Sullivan, W. 173–4, 185 n.
Supreme Court (US) 62

Talmon, J. 9 n.
taxation 52–3
Taylor, Charles 4, 7, 120–1,
  171 n.
  'Language and Human Nature'
    4 n.
teleological conceptions 13–14
territory, and membership 78–83
toleration 192
  and development of modern state
    188
Tonnies, F. 100
transcendental idealism 16–18
Tube, L. 27 n.

Unger, R. M. 120 n., 121, 131,
  135
United States 60, 62, 75–6, 77,
  213, 215
urban communities 104, 113,
  114–17
utilitarianism 1, 13, 15, 20–1, 29,
  73, 141, 188, 189

van Dyke, V. 184 n.
'veil of ignorance' and justice
  (Rawls) 54–5, 57, 200, 201 n.,
  202, 203–4

Waldron, J. 171 n., 181 n.
Walzer, M. 4, 7, 8, 10, 95, 97,
  120 n., 135 n.
Webber, M. 116

'weighing' moral claims 53–4
welfare provision 1, 25, 28, 74, 199
  and neutrality 167–9
White, Justice 205

Winthrop, John 68, 77 n., 81–2
women, *see* feminism; gender differentiation

Young, I. 106 n., 109 n.